JUDICIAL RECUSAL

The doctrine of judicial recusal enables—and may require—a judge who is lawfully appointed to hear and determine a case to stand down from that case, leaving its disposition to another colleague or colleagues. The subject is one of considerable import and moment, not only to 'insiders' in the judiciary, but also to litigants and their lawyers. Understanding the principles which guide recusal is also to understand the fundamentals of judging in the common law tradition. The subject is therefore of considerable interest both at practical and theoretical levels, for it tells us most of what we need to know about what it means 'to be a judge' and what the discharge of that constitutional duty entails. Unsurprisingly therefore, the subject has attracted controversy, and some of the most savage criticisms ever directed at particular judges.

The book commences with an introduction which is followed by an analysis of the essential features of the law, the legal principles (common law origins, the law today in the USA, UK and Commonwealth), and the difficulties which currently arise in the cases and by operation of statute. The third part looks at process, including waiver, necessity, appellate review, and final appeals. The final section addresses three problem areas and the book ends with the author's reflections on likely developments.

Judicial Recusal

Principles, Process and Problems

Grant Hammond

·HART·
PUBLISHING
OXFORD AND PORTLAND, OREGON
2009

Published in North America (US and Canada) by
Hart Publishing
c/o International Specialized Book Services
920 NE 58th Avenue, Suite 300
Portland, OR 97213-3786
USA
Tel: +1 503 287 3093 or toll-free: (1) 800 944 6190
Fax: +1 503 280 8832
E-mail: orders@isbs.com
Website: http://www.isbs.com

Hart Publishing Ltd, 16C Worcester Place, Oxford, OX1 2JW
Telephone: +44 (0)1865 517530 Fax: +44 (0)1865 510710
E-mail: mail@hartpub.co.uk
Website: http://www.hartpub.co.uk

British Library Cataloguing in Publication Data
Data Available

ISBN: 978-1-84113-260-0

Typeset by Compuscript Ltd, Shannon
Printed and bound in Great Britain by
TJ International Ltd, Padstow, Cornwall

To Nanette, Catherine and Caroline

About the Author

Grant Hammond was appointed to the High Court of New Zealand in 1992, and then to the Court of Appeal of New Zealand in 2004.

The Judge is a graduate of the University of Auckland and the University of Illinois. He was a senior litigation partner in a New Zealand law firm for some years before he turned to the academy. After a period as a Professor of Law in Canada, and terms as Director of the Alberta Law Reform Institute and as a Uniformity Commissioner on the Uniform Law Conference of Canada, he returned to New Zealand. He took up a chair there as Professor of Commercial Law in the Faculty of Law at the University of Auckland. He also served as Dean of Law in that institution.

In addition to his recent election as a Robert S Campbell Fellow in Law at Magdalen College, Oxford University, Justice Hammond has been a Visiting Professor at Cornell University and the Law Foundation Professor at the University of Saskatchewan in Canada. He is the author of *Personal Property: Cases and Materials* (Auckland, OUP, 1990), more than 50 published articles around the common law world, and various government and law reform reports.

Foreword

Judges are repeatedly excoriated for not living in the real world (the place where newspaper editors and public moralists live). But when, as is desirably and increasingly the case, links exist between a judge and the world outside the courtroom, problems can arise.

Many of them are problems of perception. That does not make them any less real or relevant, but it does make them a lot harder to evaluate. Others are problems of pecuniary or analogous interest, which may be less difficult to identify but can be more intractable in their consequences. All of them reflect the tension between the desirability of having judges with their feet on the ground and the undesirability of letting a case be tried by a judge who may have a private agenda.

The judicial oath in England and Wales, widely echoed in the common law world, is to do justice 'without fear or favour, affection or ill-will'. Fear and favour are the enemies of independence, which is a state of being. Affection and ill-will undermine impartiality, which is a state of mind. But independence and impartiality are the twin pillars without which justice cannot stand, and the purpose of recusal is to underpin them. That makes the law relating to recusal a serious business.

If this is so, one would expect the principles and procedures governing recusal to be known, established and time-hallowed. One would also hope that if they are not it is because they are so rarely called into play. But neither is the case. Remarkably, as Grant Hammond's monograph demonstrates, neither the circumstances in which judges should stand down nor the procedures for identifying these are clear.

This may be in the nature of the beast. The conventional separation of powers provides no independent adjudicative forum on unacceptable judicial interests. Disciplinary measures for bad behaviour, yes; but not for deciding whether a judge who behaves perfectly well ought nevertheless to be sitting. That has to be (or at least currently is) a matter for the judges themselves, and no less so when, as in the United States, statutes lay down the criteria for recusal. So it comes about that, in order to give effect to a principle which forbids a judge to sit in his own cause, a judge may have to sit in his own cause.

Recusal—an odd word, signifying withdrawal, originating in the religious concept of a recusant—is both an assurance of the impartiality of justice and a field of opportunity for manipulation. If not only every litigant who thinks the judge is going to be against him but every party who has waited for judgment and lost can scout for objections and with luck secure a new court, the already massive cost of litigation will become uncontrollable, legal certainty will become a chimera and the principle that litigants cannot handpick their court will be shot through with exceptions.

Thus there is a risk that a doctrine designed to assure the quality of justice may be used to the opposite effect. But few laws and procedures are not capable of being abused, and the risk of abuse is a price that has to be paid for ensuring, so far as can be done, that judges are independent and impartial.

The public and the legal profession will not, of course, know of the occasions when judges, without even entering court, ask to be taken off a case because some connection they have with it makes them uncomfortable about adjudicating on it.

Equally often, however, a judge who feels no such discomfort will disclose a connection (shares in a particular company; knowing someone; belonging to a particular club: the reasons are endless) simply so that it is in the open. Usually no-one objects; but occasionally one party or the other does, and it's then that the problems start to arise which this book, for practically the first time in our legal literature, sets out to address: when should a judge withdraw, who decides and how do they decide?

The short answer is that, save in a handful of plain cases, there is no short answer. What there is is a modest body of principle, some of it conflicting, and a very substantial body of case-law, not all of it reconcilable.

But readers will be agreeably surprised at how interesting it is. Grant Hammond has the advantage of being both a distinguished academic and a distinguished judge, as well as having been a successful practitioner. His learning is broad and deep, his analysis shrewd, his exposition lucid and his prose enjoyable. It's hard to ask more of a law book.

Stephen Sedley
Royal Courts of Justice, London

Preface

The law relating to judicial recusal deals with when a judge should stand down from a case, he or she having been allocated to sit on it. It rests on the fundamental proposition that a court should be fair and impartial, and that sometimes a judge's personal or prior 'connection' with that case should lead to him or her not sitting on it, notwithstanding the initial lawful allocation. But guaranteeing those axiomatic standards to litigants has unfortunately proven to be a persistent, and to some extent intractable, problem. This is largely because the rules which have been invoked around the common law world which are intended to advance the objective of impartiality in judges, such as the modern approach to bias, have had the downside of rendering recusal law vulnerable to manipulation by litigants and their counsel. And as the number of recusal applications have grown, judicial sensitivity over perceived aspersions to judicial professionalism has become more marked.

Surprisingly, for whatever reason, there is presently no monograph on judicial recusal in the British Commonwealth. There are valuable articles on particular points, and excellent chapters on bias in the standard public law treatises, but one of the problems of such texts is that they are addressed to a wider sphere of adjudication and do not deal directly with the distinct problem of judges in orthodox litigation. Indeed, public lawyers often presume the answer to one of the fundamental issues: whether judges and other public decision makers in tribunals, or arbitrators, should be governed by precisely the same recusal 'rules'.

The lack of a stand-alone monograph as to the position of judges means that there is no 'big picture' work for judges and counsel who, in this subject area, are often acting in conditions of some urgency in fraught trial or appellate situations. Such conditions mean that there is rarely the ability, in considering recusal issues, to have regard to what is done elsewhere around the common law world. This is complicated further by the fact that much of what might be considered recusal law depends upon informal practices and case-management strategies as much as formal law, such as distinct common law rules or statutes. These practices can be somewhat hard to ascertain.

Further, the number of high profile recusal cases seems to be on the rise. A number of these cases have, regrettably, tarnished the image of the judiciary. Law is not immune from the blight of fashion, but one gets the impression that the proliferation of recusal cases is not an instance of 'flavour of the month' litigation, and that we will continue to see far more cases in this subject area than was once the case.

Hence, when Magdalen College at Oxford University was kind enough to elect me as the Robert S Campbell Visiting Fellow in Law in 2008, I thought that I would endeavour to put together a monograph in this subject area. What I had in mind were issues such as: where the idea of judicial recusal came from; how the essential concepts have developed; where the doctrine of judicial recusal presently rests in the common law world; and what if anything can be done to improve this doctrine.

This task was always going to be a daunting and difficult one. In the first place, it has never been my intention to write a textbook in the conventional sense of the term. To accurately describe the precise law in each jurisdiction by adequately ordering all of the case law would be a monumental undertaking, and quite beyond my learning. There is also the time such a task would take. My predominant concern has been rather to articulate as best I can the central concepts that courts have seen fit to employ around the common law world, and offer some commentary on them. This has meant that in many areas, I have chosen cases as illustrations of a general problem, rather than offering a linear exposition of all the law on a particular point. And because not everyone will have access to a good research library for comparative material, I have in places included more particulars on some cases than would be the norm.

Secondly, given the lack of a textbook or monograph of an over-arching kind in this field (other than Mr Flamm's text on disqualification in the United States), there was the problem of having to 'clear the undergrowth', as it is sometimes put. Normally, in undertaking a legal text, there is something against which one can write, or at least something which forms a structure for ordering of the law. Because of this, some issues are assumed to be straightforward which others may think are highly contestable, while others may be elaborated in a way which others may think merited little discussion.

Thirdly, there is not a lot of 'black-letter' law as such in the area of judicial recusal. Much rests on the practices which have been adopted. This poses distinct problems for a commentator even in an area of domestic law. Those problems are further exacerbated in a comparative exercise of this kind. Further, because judges are decidedly cautious about issues which may be seen to go to judicial propriety, ascertaining what 'really happens' behind judicial doors is not altogether easy.

Fourthly, I was aware from my academic background in the United States of the existence of the recusal statutes in the federal jurisdiction in that country. It seemed to me that an issue which warrants commentary is whether 'regulation' of recusal processes is better done by judges themselves, or by legislators through statutes. This issue has not attracted appropriate academic attention.

Fifthly, this is a distinctly difficult and controversial area of the law. There is room for a great deal of debate about many of the issues, and

I have no confidence that I have definitively resolved them. In many instances, I have only been able to raise questions on issues which are hotly contested, and on which reasonable people may, and will continue to, differ. In particular, one of the central arguments of this work—that the impugned judge should no longer determine a recusal application—is relatively radical, but needs full, proper and timeous consideration.

Sixthly, that said, there is great force in Edmund Burke's observation that 'publik [*sic*] life is a situation of power and energy, he trespasses against his duty who sleeps upon his watch, as well as he that goes over to the enemy.' Thus, if the judges can improve the state of recusal law, they should. This subject area is quintessentially their bailiwick. But that requires the formulation of some relatively specific proposals, for consideration of them by others.

Seventhly, in this work I espouse some personal views which are contrary to some judicial pronouncements to which I have lent my name. However, as an English Lord Justice of Appeal, Baron Bramwell, once famously said: 'the matter does not appear to me now, as it appears to have appeared to me then'. This may be thought to demonstrate the benefits (or disadvantages, depending on one's viewpoint) of sabbatical leave for judges. With the benefits of time and appropriate research facilities, it would be surprising if one's views did not alter on some things.

Finally, I have had to bring the work to rest where it lies. Professional life as a judge of the Court of Appeal of New Zealand has meant that I have had to turn my attention back to pressing public business. If what has been done thus far stimulates further research and close discussion on a subject matter of importance not just to judges but to the administration of justice, and hence the public at large, I will be content enough.

After I completed this manuscript in December 2008, some cases of constitutional importance began to unfold in the common law world. I have briefly noted those developments in Appendix F, without endeavouring to accommodate them in the text. They are yet to be finally determined, but readers may wish to follow their ultimate disposition and significance.

Acknowledgements

I would not have been able to undertake this endeavour without the very considerable assistance of Magdalen College, Oxford University. The college provided me with all the physical facilities I required, in a magical setting that I will long treasure.

I am indebted to the librarians at the New Library and the Denning Law Library, both of which I worked in at Magdalen College, and to the librarians at the Bodleian Law Library at Oxford. They were efficient and knowledgeable. They always seemed to know just where to find what it was that I was looking for.

The Fellows of the College, and particularly the Law Fellows, were at all times very supportive and collegial. I also benefited from discussions with other members of the Faculty of Law at Oxford.

I am deeply indebted to my Associate, Mrs Lynne McMenamin, who typed the manuscript whilst I was still at Oxford. The difficulties of working at a distance are not entirely displaced by modern technology. I am grateful to Lynne for all her careful work.

My Judge's Clerk, Matthew Windsor, assisted greatly with the research exercise. He was properly rigorous in his criticisms and was uncomplaining about the many burdensome editorial finishing tasks which were inflicted upon him.

Richard Hart and his team at Hart Publishing were supportive, and highly efficient throughout. I am most grateful to them.

Stephen Sedley kindly contributed a Foreword, and has been very generous in his comments.

Finally, my wife Nanette's professional commitments in New Zealand, and the educational needs of our two children, Catherine and Caroline, meant that they were not able to accompany me to Oxford, at least until the latter part of my Visiting Fellowship. This meant a respectable absence from home life in New Zealand. The whole enterprise would not have been possible without their love, encouragement and support. I am deeply grateful to them.

Hon Grant Hammond
Judges' Chambers
Court of Appeal
Wellington
New Zealand

Contents

Table of Cases

AUSTRALIA

CANADA

EUROPEAN

NEW ZEALAND

SOUTH AFRICA

UK

UNITED STATES OF AMERICA

Part A
Introduction

1

The Essential Questions

THE DOCTRINE OF judicial recusal enables, and may require, a judge who has been appointed to hear and determine a case to stand down from that case and leave the disposition of it to another colleague or colleagues. The subject area might be thought to induce a soporific effect in all but 'insiders' in the law or avid watchers of the judiciary, and be seen as yet another area of arid technicality in that discipline. Nothing could be further from the truth. An understanding of judicial recusal helps clarify both what the adjudication of legal disputes is all about, and the essential nature of judging within the common law tradition. In short, to understand this doctrine is to better appreciate the judicial function and the role of the judge in society. Therefore, it is unsurprising that recusal decisions have often generated considerable controversy, leading to some of the most savage criticisms ever directed at particular judges.

In January 1999, the late Hugo Young, an Oxford law graduate and for many years a highly regarded political columnist for *The Guardian*, published a scathing indictment of Lord Hoffmann, a distinguished Law Lord. The context was that a differently constituted panel of judges had just held that Lord Hoffmann's failure to disclose his links with Amnesty International necessarily aborted an earlier ground-breaking decision in relation to General Pinochet, which had been made by a panel of which Lord Hoffmann was a member.[1] In Hugo Young's view:[2]

> the circumstances of that abortion leave a stain on the British judiciary ... Hoffmann has done damage that can't be undone. His recklessness is solely responsible for what is now unfolding in *Re Pinochet*. His own credibility as a judge—impeccable repository of detachment, sagacity and an unseducible engagement with justice—is shot to pieces. He should break another precedent, and go back to advocacy.

Over the Atlantic, in March 2004, Justice Scalia of the United States Supreme Court issued a Memorandum declining to recuse himself from

[1] *R v Bow Street Metropolitan Stipendiary Magistrate and Ors, ex p Pinochet Ugarte (No 2)* [2000] 1 AC 119 (HL). The earlier decision in which Lord Hoffman participated is at [2000] 1 AC 61 (HL). See generally D Woodhouse (ed), *The Pinochet Case: A Legal and Constitutional Analysis* (Oxford, Hart Publishing, 2000).

[2] H Young, 'The compromising of Lord Hoffman' in *Supping with the Devils: Political Writing from Thatcher to Blair* (London, Atlantic Books, 2003) 212–14.

a pending case, *Cheney v United States District Court for the District of Columbia*.[3] That was a case which arose out of certain actions by the National Energy Policy Development Group, an advisory committee on energy policy chaired by Vice President Cheney. The Sierra Club, a respectable organisation with a long history of environmental concerns in the United States, was one of the parties seeking disclosure of the Development Group's materials. Vice President Cheney responded by arguing that, among other things, such disclosure would amount to an unconstitutional interference with the functioning of the Executive branch of government.

The Sierra Club filed a recusal motion, arguing that Justice Scalia had created at least the appearance of impropriety by going on a duck hunting trip with Vice President Cheney after the United States Supreme Court had accepted review of the case, and on that basis should not sit on the case. This was in the context of a federal statute, to which reference will be made later in this work, which provides that a justice 'shall disqualify himself in any proceeding in which his impartiality might reasonably be questioned'.[4]

In accordance with the accepted practice of the United States Supreme Court, Justice Scalia himself decided whether he ought to recuse and elected to sit. He could hardly have been surprised that the climate for a determination of this nature was likely to be contested, given that a great many Americans had expressed the view that he and other members of the Supreme Court had improperly acted out of a concern for political consequences in *Bush v Gore*.[5] In a Memorandum setting out his reasons for declining to recuse, Justice Scalia asserted that he could impartially adjudicate the issues of statutory interpretation and separation of powers that the *Cheney* case raised. Therefore, the judge concluded:[6]

> The question, simply put, is whether someone who thought I could decide this case impartially despite my friendship with the Vice President would reasonably believe that I *cannot* decide it impartially because I went hunting with that friend

[3] (2004) 542 US 367. Justice Scalia's Memorandum is at (2003) 541 US 913. For academic commentary, see CL Roberts, 'The Fox Guarding the Henhouse?: Recusal and the Procedural Void in the Court of Last Resort' (2004) 57 *Rutgers Law Review* 107; MH Freedman, 'Duck-Blind Justice: Justice Scalia's Memorandum in the Cheney Case' (2004–05) 18 *Georgetown Journal of Legal Ethics* 229; TJ Goodson, 'Duck, Duck, Goose: Hunting for Better Recusal Practices in the United States Supreme Court in light of *Cheney v United States District Court*' (2005–06) 84 *North Carolina Law Review* 181; and LA Foertsch, 'Scalia's Duck Hunt Leads to Ruffled Feathers: How the US Supreme Court and other Federal Judiciaries Should Change Their Recusal Approach' (2006–07) 43 *Houston Law Review* 457.

[4] 28 USC § 455(a). See app C.

[5] (2000) 531 US 98. For academic discussion, see SA Ifill, 'Do Appearances Matter: Judicial Impartiality and the Supreme Court in *Bush v Gore*' (2002) 61 *Maryland Law Review* 606; RK Neumann Jr, 'Conflicts of Interest in *Bush v Gore*: Did Some Justices Vote Illegally?' (2002–03) 16 *Georgetown Journal of Legal Ethics* 375; and GL Priest, 'Reanalysing *Bush v Gore*: Democratic Accountability and Judicial Overreaching' (2001) 72 *University of Colorado Law Review* 953.

[6] (2003) 541 US 913, 928–29.

> and accepted an invitation to fly there with him on a Government plane. If it is reasonable to think that a Supreme Court Justice can be bought so cheap, the Nation is in deeper trouble than I had imagined.

Earlier in the Memorandum, without the slightest hint of apology, Justice Scalia had said that '[m]any Justices have reached this court *precisely* because they were friends of the incumbent President or other senior officials'.[7]

Michael C Dorf, a senior law professor at Columbia University, put things as sharply as Hugo Young had done in the case of Lord Hoffmann:[8]

> The not-so-subtle subtext of the opinion goes something like this: 'We Supreme Court Justices are part of the ruling elite and we're entitled to live like it. How dare you commoners question our integrity!'

For introductory purposes, it is not necessary to consider whether Lord Hoffman and Justice Scalia were right or wrong in the respective positions they had taken. However, what these incidents do illustrate is that the question of judicial recusal is of very significant concern for individual litigants, the particular judges involved, the public at large, and the administration of justice.

From the point of view of individual litigants, it is almost impossible to persuade a losing party that a judge's prior involvement with the subject matter of the litigation or somebody involved in it did not have at least something to do with his or her decision.

For the individual judge, the allegation being levelled is that he or she has not acted fairly or appropriately, in judicial terms. For a judge, this is the unkindest cut of all. The decision as to whether to sit if challenged, or sometimes even if not, can be an agonising one for a judge. Judges readily accept that they will make mistakes of fact or law. But an accusation of a want of probity is quite another matter. No half-competent judge will lightly entertain being 'forced' off a case, not least because he or she has taken a judicial oath to consider all cases even if, on their own merits, they give rise to the deepest kinds of difficulties for that particular judge.

Society rightly looks to the courts as bastions of the Rule of Law. If the public cannot look with confidence to judges (who after all have terms of appointment which are carefully constructed to secure their singular and utmost independence and impartiality with respect to the cases they are called upon to address), the very notion of a 'legal system' as a fundamental pillar of western society would collapse.[9] Further, the existence of a legal

[7] ibid 916 (emphasis added).

[8] MC Dorf, 'Justice Scalia's Persuasive But Elitist Response to the Duck Hunting Controversy' *FindLaw's Writ*, 24 March 2004 <http://writ.news.findlaw.com/dorf/20040324.html> accessed 20 April 2009.

[9] See AM Gleeson, *The Rule of Law and the Constitution* (Sydney, ABC Books, 2000) 82; and S Kenny, 'Maintaining Public Confidence in the Judiciary: A Precarious Equilibrium' (1999) 25 *Monash University Law Review* 209.

system depends heavily on voluntary compliance. Citizens may well not comply with that which they do not trust.

It follows that the stakes are very high indeed with respect to the issues surrounding whether a judge should decline to sit. Yet, given the importance of the issues, less systematic attention than might have been anticipated has been devoted to this subject area. It is almost as if the topic is in the 'too hard basket' for all concerned. We do in fact want unbiased judges or perhaps, more accurately, only those with 'good' biases. It is a perfectly natural tendency to recoil from contemplation of the harm which can be inflicted to individuals and society at large from improperly biased judges. But the issues must be faced.

In the British Commonwealth, the law in this subject area is essentially all judge-made law. In the United States, where recusal applications play a large part in a wide range of litigation, there are two important statutory provisions in the federal jurisdiction, and many states have also legislated in this subject area.

However, there is consensus around the common law world as to the central issues that need to be addressed. For present purposes, these issues can be reduced to three critical questions. When should a judge withdraw from a given case to which he or she has been allocated? Who decides when that judge should withdraw? What process or procedures should be utilised by the decision maker?

The precise answers to these questions may vary from jurisdiction to jurisdiction, but there is much to be said for considering them at the level of broad principle. As a matter of legal technique, it is far preferable to have sound general principles rather than ad hoc rules, or even worse, a 'myriad of single instances'.[10]

Well respected commentators have suggested that the idea of judicial impartiality is subject to a deep 'crisis of confidence' in the common law world.[11] Even if there is only the possibility that may be so (and it must be said that there is at least that possibility), the issues arising in this subject area are worthy of distinct and systematic attention at the level of general principle.

We need to be clear what this monograph does not address and why. 'Adjudication' is today carried out in courts, through consensual arbitral arrangements, and by a vast array of administrative tribunals, many of which have very wide ranging powers including the ability to make significant enforcement orders. These alternative dispensers of administrative justice are of the greatest importance today and 'hear' many more cases than civil courts do.

[10] Lord Mackay, *The Times* (London 3 December 1987), quoted in W Twining and D Miers, *How to Do Things with Rules*, 4th edn (Cambridge, CUP, 1999) 321.

[11] J Leubsdorf, 'Theories of Judging and Judge Disqualification' (1987) 62 *New York University Law Review* 237, 245.

There may be good and sufficient reasons why the person dispensing 'justice' in these bodies, though lawfully appointed, should also stand down. In many respects, the problems and principles to be applied mirror those that confront judges in regular courts of law. But they attract their own considerations in their particular contexts, which include detailed terms of appointment, and often quite complex statutory schemes applying to tribunal members. To cover all these areas of adjudication would require a multi-volume treatise rather than a modest monograph. Nevertheless, the insights to be gained from the struggle to evolve a more defensible and workable scheme for judicial recusal in the general courts will likely be of interest in other areas of modern inquisitorial, administrative, and adjudicative justice.

This work is entitled 'Judicial Recusal'. It could possibly have been entitled 'Judicial Recusal and Disqualification' because in at least some respects it intrudes into the area of 'disqualification'. If a judge is stood aside for actual bias, then in a very real sense he or she is disqualified. However, this work is overwhelmingly concerned with judicial recusal in the sense that it involves a decision to voluntarily stand down by the judge, or a challenge to his or her refusal to do so.

Reference is made throughout the work to the body of law in the 'British Commonwealth', in contrast with the position in the federal jurisdiction in the United States. This may cause some confusion for readers from outside the common law tradition. Australia, Canada and New Zealand, which are sometimes still referred to as the 'Old Dominions', enjoy a legal heritage which until comparatively recent times was essentially derived from that of Great Britain. Each of those jurisdictions now has the fullest legal autonomy and are developing their own laws in a way that has been seen to best accord with the needs and aspirations of those jurisdictions. But we are still close enough in time to the respective points of 'separation' from Great Britain that, for analytical and comparative law purposes, it is convenient, and in some instances illuminating, to observe what the rule was observed to be in Great Britain and how, if at all, it has diverged in those jurisdictions.[12] As we will see, from a very early stage, recusal law in the United States, particularly at the federal level, was given a statutory base. From a comparative perspective, it is particularly useful to contrast the critical mass of British Commonwealth law, which is predominantly common law based, with the prospective advantages and disadvantages of a statutory approach.

[12] In the Foreword to the very first issue of the Oxford Journal of Legal Studies in 1981, the late Patrick Atiyah spoke of 'the continuing unity of much of the common law around the world'. In the most recent House of Lords recusal decision—*Helow v Secretary of State for the Home Department* [2008] 1 WLR 2416—their Lordships utilised a comparative approach and referred to Australian and Canadian authority.

Finally, to clear away a small problem of nomenclature, when reference is made to a decision in the intermediate appellate court in the United Kingdom, the term which will be used is 'the English Court of Appeal'. While the formal name of the court has now changed, it is simpler for present purposes to use a generic term without the problem of tracking changing court names, and citations. No disrespect is intended.

Part B
Principles

2

The Evolution of the Present Law in the Common Law World

HOW DID THE notion of judicial recusal come about? In this chapter, we examine the beginnings of the doctrine.[1] In the next chapter, we summarise the central features of the existing legal regimes in the common law world. In later chapters, we will examine how well this intellectual structure has worked out in practice.

The term 'central features' needs to be emphasised. Patently, it is impossible to collate and critically examine all of the law on this topic in several countries. What we seek to elucidate are the concepts on which recusal law has been made to turn.

ENGLAND

The central feature of the early English common law on recusal was both simple and highly constrained: a judge could only be disqualified for a direct pecuniary interest. What would today be termed 'bias', which is easily the most controversial ground for disqualification, was entirely rejected as a ground for recusal of judges, although it was not completely dismissed in relation to jurors.

This was in marked contrast to the relatively sophisticated canon law, which provided for recusal if a judge was suspected of partiality because of consanguinity, affinity, friendship or enmity with a party, or because of his subordinate status towards a party or because he was or had been a party's advocate.[2]

[1] I am indebted to JP Frank, 'Disqualification of Judges' (1947) 56 *Yale Law Journal* 605, 609–12; H Woolf, J Jowell and A Le Sueur, *De Smith's Judicial Review*, 6th edn (London, Sweet & Maxwell, 2007) 501–04; and RE Flamm, *Judicial Disqualification: Recusal and Disqualification of Judges*, 2nd edn (California, Banks and Jordan Law Publishing Co, 2007) 5–10 for most of the material in this section.

[2] H de Bracton, Twiss (ed), *De Legibus et Consuetudinibus Angliae: Volume 6* (London, Longman & Co, 1883) 249. Quite who to credit *De Legibus* with is still controversial. William de Ralegh was the Chief Justice of the King's Bench from 1234–39 and Bracton was his law clerk. In his translator's introduction, Thorne considers Ralegh was the 'prime mover' of Bracton's work. See H de Bracton, Woodbine (ed), *Bracton on the Laws and Customs of England: Volume 3* (Massachusetts, Belknap Press of Harvard University Press, 1977) xxxvi.

Canon law principles were applied in English ecclesiastical courts[3] and in medieval Scottish courts.[4]

Bracton seems to have suggested that these canon law principles were actually part of the early common law, presumably by incorporation. The better view is that this was not so.[5] It is true that there were scattered features of the common law which might have supported such a proposition, and it is certainly disingenuous to suggest that the canon law would have had no influence. For instance, the grounds of exception to the competency of witnesses for interest and bias had long been extended to jurors of the grand assize.[6] Further, by the early 14th century, common law judges were held to be incompetent to preside over cases in which they were themselves parties.[7] However, a contrary view to Bracton's common law–canon law convergence theory was taken in *Brookes v Rivers,*[8] where it was held that favour was not to be presumed in a judge. In that case, the Chamberlain of Chester was not disqualified from hearing an action in which his brother-in-law was a party.

Blackstone considered that, as a matter of public policy, the common law rule that judges could not be disqualified for relationships or bias but only for a direct pecuniary interest was absolutely correct:[9]

> For the law will not suppose a possibility of bias or favour in a judge, who is already sworn to administer impartial justice, and whose authority greatly depends upon that presumption and idea.

The clear reluctance to see judges challenged was tempered by only two rules, which were tolerably well established. First, there was the rule already adverted to: that the common law simply did not permit a judge to determine a matter in which he had a direct pecuniary or proprietary interest. Perhaps the best known authorities for that proposition are *Sir Nicholas Bacon's Case*[10] and the *Earl of Derby's Case*.[11] The second proposition was

[3] FW Maitland, *Roman Canon Law in the Church of England: Six Essays* (London, Methuen & Co, 1898) 114.

[4] TM Cooper (ed), *Regiam Majestatem and Quoniam Attachiamenta* (Edinburgh, Stair Society, 1947) 324–25.

[5] RE Flamm, above n 1, 5–6; and H Woolf, J Jowell and A Le Sueur, above n 1, 502. See also *Aetna Life Insurance Co v Lavoie* (1986) 475 US 813, 820.

[6] R Glanvill, *De legibus et Consuetudinibus Regni Angliae* Bk II ch 11 in R Pound and TFT Plucknett (eds), *Readings on the History and System of the Common Law*, 3rd edn (Rochester, Lawyers Co-Operative Publishing Co, 1927) 143. For the canon law rules themselves, see JH Wigmore, *Evidence in Trials at Common Law: Volume II*, 3rd edn (Boston, Little, Brown and Co, 1940) 678, n 14.

[7] The early yearbook cases are collected in SE Thorne (ed), *A Discourse Upon The Exposicion & Understandings of Statutes with Sir Thomas Egerton's Advantages* (San Marino, Huntington Library, 1942) 73.

[8] (1668) 1 Hard, 503; 145 ER 569.

[9] W Blackstone, *Commentaries on the Laws of England (1768)* (Buffalo, William S Hein & Co, 1992) 361.

[10] (1563) 2 Dyer 220b; 73 ER 487 (KB).

[11] (1614) 12 Co Rep 114; 77 ER 1390 (KB).

confirmed by Sir Edward Coke CJ in *Dr Bonham's Case*:[12] that a judge could not be a judge in his or her own cause.

Even these limited principles caused their own share of difficulties. A judge might be disqualified, as happened in *Dr Bonham's Case*, because he received the fine which he had the power to inflict. In another well-known case, the Mayor of Hereford was 'layed by the heels' for sitting as a judge in an ejectment case in which he was the lessor of the plaintiff.[13]

The principles could however be pushed too far. For instance, in a case involving a pauper, a judge was disqualified for interest because the decision affected his own taxes.[14] But if judges were to be disqualified as taxpayers, some suits would not be able to be decided. Therefore, in 1743, the English Parliament provided that taxpaying Justices of the Peace might sit in these local government taxation cases.[15] The significance of these kinds of cases is that they are the forerunner of the modern rule of necessity: that judges should not decline to sit where no substitute is readily available.[16]

Relationship issues were treated in a somewhat peculiar way. Early English courts held that a judge was not disqualified by his relationships, but that in some respects a juror could be. This gave rise to a number of cases in which courts had to decide what *degree* of relationship necessitated the disqualification of a juror. In a 1572 case, the line was drawn at the 9th degree. It was said:[17]

> All the inhabitants of the earth are descended from Adam and Eve, and so are cousins of one another [but] the further removed blood is, the more cool it is.

UNITED STATES OF AMERICA

In contrast to the situation in England, judicial recusal in the United States became subject to a federal statutory regime at an early stage. This is important when looking at the broad development of recusal jurisprudence, because one question which must be squarely confronted is whether common law judges have done better in developing their own jurisprudence (a form of self-regulation) as opposed to a statutory regime effectively 'imposed' from without (external regulation).

[12] (1610) 8 Co Rep 114a; 77 ER 638 (CP). See also SE Thorne, 'Dr Bonham's case' (1938) 54 *Law Quarterly Review* 543 and TFT Plucknett, 'Bonham's case and Judicial Review' (1926) 40 *Harvard Law Review* 30.

[13] *Anon* (1698) 1 Salk 396; 91 ER 343 (KB).

[14] *Between the Parishes of Great Charte and Kennington* (1726) 2 Str 1173; 93 ER 1107 (KB).

[15] 16 Geo II, c 18, § 1 (1743).

[16] See ch 12.

[17] *Vernon v Manners* (1572) 2 Plowden 425; 75 ER 639 (KB).

The pre-Revolution American colonies adopted the English common law practice as at the time of the formation of their court systems. It is not entirely clear why Congress intruded into this area as early as it did, but the first federal judicial disqualification statute in America was passed as early as 1792.[18] However, that statute largely reflected the English common law: there was to be disqualification when a judge had a pecuniary interest in a proceeding over which he or she was to preside, had 'acted in' the proceeding, or had been 'of counsel' for a party.[19] This original 1792 statute was amended in 1821 to include relationship to a party as an additional ground for judicial disqualification.[20]

The difficulties that recusal has caused in the United States are reflected in the fact that, on many occasions after 1821, Congress has progressively enlarged the enumerated grounds for seeking disqualification. There was a significant overhaul of the federal disqualification scheme in 1911. According to the United States Supreme Court in *Liteky v US*, it was '[n]ot [however until 1911] that a provision [was] enacted requiring district-judge recusal for bias *in general*.'[21]

CONCLUSION

It will be observed that the historical development of the law relating to judicial recusal has involved substantial enlargements to the initial very narrow, particularised, grounds for recusal. The enlargement of greatest moment has been the inclusion of 'bias', whatever is meant by that. Indeed, as we shall see in later chapters, there is room for distinct argument that the grounds for recusal may now be somewhat at large, with the relevant determination to be made in a context specific manner. Whether that is entirely desirable is a matter for further consideration.

[18] Act of May 8 1792, c 36 § 11, 1 Stat 278.

[19] For a more detailed outline of the history, see *Liteky v US* (1994) 510 US 540. See also PB Lewis, 'Systemic Due Process: Procedural Concepts and the Problem of Recusal' (1990) 38 *University of Kansas Law Review* 381, 387.

[20] Act of 3 March 1821, c 51, 3 Stat 643. This amendment was discussed in *Liteky v US*, above n 19.

[21] *Liteky v US*, above n 19, 544. *Berger v US* (1921) 255 US 22 was a case where the statute disqualifying federal judges in certain circumstances for personal bias or prejudice was enforced. Further reference will be made to the reach of the 1911 federal judicial recusal statute in ch 6.

3

The Classification of the Present Day Recusal Principles in the British Commonwealth

AS WITH ANY other discipline, lawyers and judges have to order their knowledge. Within the area of judge-made law there are very large categories, such as contracts, tort and equity. There are then particular subsets of those categories, such as negligence in the law of torts, to which the principles relating to that particular cause of action relate, and further subsidiary rules.

Whilst the classification of the law is not immutably fixed, it is nowadays well enough established. So much so that very real difficulties can be occasioned when established classifications start to become fractured. There are then often heated, and practically important, debates about just how things are to be rearranged. Indeed it has been argued by a distinguished legal historian that this kind of fracturing and altering of classifications is precisely how the common law has advanced over the centuries.[1]

At one time, it was widely accepted that the classification of the law relating to judicial recusal was divisible into two simple categories of 'bias': actual bias and apparent bias. Actual bias, as the name implies, dealt with the situation where there was something which did indeed give rise to bias in the sense of a court having regard to something other than the true merits of the dispute; apparent bias, again as the name implies, dealt with the situation when it looked as if there might be room for bias of that kind, even if there was not. At any rate, this rather simple division proved to be sufficient for a long time, and indeed most of the textbooks and legal encyclopaedias use just that arrangement.

[1] See SFC Milsom, *Historical Foundations of the Common Law*, 2nd edn (London, Butterworths, 1981), 6: 'The life of the common law has been in the abuse of its elementary ideas. If the rules of property give what now seems an unjust answer, try obligation; and equity has proved that from the materials of obligation you can counterfeit the phenomena of property. If the rules of contract give what now seems an unjust answer, try tort. Your counterfeit will look odd to one brought up on categories of Roman origin; but it will work. If the rules of one tort, say deceit, give what now seems an unjust answer, try another, try negligence. And so the legal world goes round.'

In more recent years the classification picture has changed somewhat. In the *Pinochet* litigation, to which reference has already been made, the House of Lords referred to the notion of 'automatic disqualification' which as we will see clearly covers prohibited relevant financial interests. But it also favours treating some instances of commitment to a cause as giving rise to automatic disqualification. It may well have been possible to treat those latter problems as being instances of apparent bias. But their Lordships were clearly minded to treat some things at least, beyond financial interests, as being of sufficient moment to give rise to what was characterised as 'automatic disqualification'. Just where that line is to be crossed in given fact patterns is still a very live issue.

To further cloud the difficult classification issues, as we will see, the Australian High Court has adopted a relatively radical new classificatory approach, by adopting 'one test for all cases' of bias which has effectively done away with the old category of actual bias.

This would not matter too much if one was writing only about one jurisdiction. One would just use the classification that has been adopted in that particular jurisdiction. But it makes the task of the comparativist very difficult, because one is referring to jurisdictions which do not necessarily see 'eye to eye'.

Classification debates can cause real confusion and be very misleading. They are sometimes very arid debates, and even unproductive.[2] At the same time, the orderliness of the law is very important for its assimilation, understanding, and application.

In what follows, as to the law in the British Commonwealth, the law is ordered into two parts as a matter of convenience: automatic disqualification and bias. This classification would not be entirely correct for Australia, given the state of the law in that jurisdiction. It is rather a classification which enables the tangled skein of judicial recusal law to be presented in an orderly way, for present purposes. It does not presuppose that such a classification is necessarily the only possible one, or indeed the correct one for all jurisdictions.

This approach is adopted for these reasons. First, it is true that, under some circumstances, a judge is automatically disqualified from presiding over a case even if the judge did in fact act in an exemplary manner. This bears some intellectual affinity to the *per se* rule adopted in antitrust law

[2] This is not the place for an extended discussion about the very difficult and important theoretical issues over 'classification' in law. The essential problem is what NN Taleb has rightly called 'the manifestation of Platonicity, the desire to cut reality into crisp shapes': *The Black Swan* (London, Penguin Books, 2007) 15. This is a form of reductionism which is very dangerous, insofar as categorising always produces a reduction in true complexity. Fortunately, in the recusal situation, judges have routinely been less concerned about tight categories, and more with a sense that in some situations—for often overlapping reasons—a judge should simply not be permitted to sit.

in the United States of America. *Per se* rules contemplate that some behaviour is simply 'off limits'. No argument or defence is tolerated. A *per se* rule can be contrasted with a 'rule of reason' approach, which requires an articulated exposition as to why something ought to be proscribed in a particular case.[3]

The rationale usually given for an automatic disqualification approach goes back to the central notion of *Dr Bonham's Case*: that no judge should be a judge in his or her own cause.[4] It is extremely difficult—and certainly undesirable—to try and justify the 'bad look' for the justice system if a judge does decide something patently affecting his or her own interests.

The second part is concerned with 'bias'. For analytical purposes, there is still real benefit in dividing bias itself into two subsets: actual bias and apparent bias.

Cases of actual bias are very rare. They usually involve something quite apparent on the face of the record, or what might colloquially be termed a 'smoking gun'. An affirmative finding of actual bias requires direct evidence or a very strong inference that the judge was so predisposed against a party that he or she had an entirely closed mind and was demonstrably going to decide the case in a particular way, regardless of the arguments and evidence proffered by one or other of the parties. It will be apparent that actual bias is therefore tested in a subjective manner.

The essential concern under the apparent bias limb is not with the actuality of bias, but whether there is an outward appearance of bias. The test is whether a belief may reasonably be entertained by a well-informed external observer that the judge may not bring or have brought to the decision a fair and unprejudiced mind. This is an objective test, looking to how things would be perceived 'from the outside'. As such, it is a test which is much more easily satisfied than the very stiff test applied to claims of actual bias.

Within this broad analytical structure, which suffices to advance the material to be referred to in this work, there is room for a good deal of debate as to the closer features of the principles under each head, to which we now turn.

[3] For a discussion of the per se approach to antitrust liability, see *Broadcast Music Inc v Columbia Broadcasting System Inc* (1979) 441 US 1. What is to be regarded as a per se wrong is not static and may be reconsidered from time to time. See, for example, *Leegin Creative Leather Products Inc v PSKS Inc* (2007) 127 S Ct 2705. For a more theoretical discussion, see O Black, *Conceptual Foundations of Antitrust* (New York, CUP, 2005) 62–93.

[4] (1610) 8 Co Rep 114a; 77 ER 638 (CP).

4

Automatic Disqualification in the British Commonwealth

DISQUALIFICATION FOR PECUNIARY INTEREST

THE STARTING POINT for the modern law is the still highly influential case of *Dimes v Proprietors of Grand Junction Canal* (1852).[1] There, the then Lord Chancellor, Lord Cottenham, owned shares in the Grand Junction Canal Company in whose favour he subsequently made an order. Ultimately it was held that he should not have sat on the case. It is difficult to convey in brief form the ardour of the litigation, though the whole *cause celebre* repays study as a prime example of what can go wrong in the law in general, and for the problems associated with recusal issues.

Mr Dimes came to be the 'owner' of copyhold land, a notoriously arcane form of feudal tenure, across which the Grand Junction Canal Company had built its canal. It seems Mr Dimes was quite an entrepreneurial solicitor, and, in contemporary terms, was something of an 'asset-stripper'. Atlay, Lord Cottenham's biographer, was more pejorative, describing Mr Dimes as a 'crazy attorney'.[2] In any event, Mr Dimes thought that the canal company should pay him something for its use of the land. He also had a problem with a bridge, and may have been attempting to extract repair contributions from other 'users'. The whole question of who had what rights was a frightful mess, reflective of the quagmire of legal and equitable rights that existed prior to the Judicature Acts of the 1870s.

When Mr Dimes got under way with his litigation there was simply no stopping him. Over the next 16 years, there were 24 hearings, 11 of which led to reported judgments.[3] Sharman has commented:[4]

> Dimes was certainly a solicitor and may be thought to have gone fairly mad later on, as his later actions seem unreasonable. Every lawyer has come across the

[1] (1852) 10 ER 301. For the background to this celebrated case, see JB Atlay, *The Victorian Chancellors: Volume 1* (London, Smith Elder, 1906) 384–415; FA Sharman, 'Feudal Copyholder and Industrial Shareholder: the *Dimes* Case' (1989) 10 *Journal of Legal History* 71; and JT Noonan Jr and KI Winston (eds), *The Responsible Judge: Readings in Judicial Ethics* (Westport, Praeger, 1993) 285–86.

[2] JB Atlay, above n 1, 415.

[3] Listed in FA Sharman, above n 1, 71.

[4] ibid 74.

> man who becomes obsessed with some imagined injustice and pursues the matter through both the courts and thick and thin against all advice; and Dimes had himself for a client.

This may well have been an overly scathing assessment of Mr Dimes. He knew a great deal about copyhold land, and it is routinely overlooked that the litigation came to an end with the canal company buying out the requisite interest for £700. So in fact Dimes toppled the Lord Chancellor, and in the end, the canal company also paid him out.

What we are presently interested in is what went wrong for Lord Cottenham. It is appropriate to pick up the legal proceedings at the point where the Vice-Chancellor made an order in favour of the canal company. In 1848, Lord Cottenham affirmed that order on appeal. The following year, after discovering Lord Cottenham's shareholding, Mr Dimes petitioned the Queen of England for her intervention. He then filed a motion in Chancery, asking for Lord Cottenham's decision to be struck out on the basis of his interest in the case. At Lord Cottenham's request, this motion was heard by the Master of the Rolls, Lord Langdale. Lord Langdale advised that the decision should be upheld on the ground of necessity.[5] This was because, as it transpired, there was no other judge of coordinate jurisdiction who could hear the case in the place of the Lord Chancellor.

It was after that decision that Mr Dimes chose to treat all the Chancery decisions as void. He then began some of his extraordinary collateral activities, such as placing a chain across the canal, digging a trench across the towpath, and throwing bricks in the canal.

Mr Dimes did not appeal the advice of Lord Langdale until 1851. In the meantime, Lord Cottenham had again become involved in the case. He issued a warrant for Mr Dimes to be committed for contempt, leading to his imprisonment for several months. Mr Dimes then sought to set aside the order for his committal. He faced the hurdle of the earlier advice of Lord Langdale that there was no ground for setting aside the earlier orders of Lord Cottenham. However, Lord Cottenham 'confirmed' this advice, under the then applicable Chancery procedure and later acceded to a request by Mr Dimes for a writ of *habeas corpus*.

It was in this context that the litigation reached the House of Lords. The Lords made it plain that the reversal of the order of the Lord Chancellor left the order of the Vice-Chancellor, which Lord Cottenham had affirmed, quite unaffected. Their Lordships dismissed Mr Dimes' appeal so far as it related to the merits of the property issue which had been decided by the Vice-Chancellor. But Mr Dimes did win on the point of principle, as to disqualification for pecuniary interest: their Lordships unequivocally held that the Lord Chancellor should not have sat, by reason of his ownership of shares in Grand Junction Canal Company. Nevertheless, in the course of

[5] For a more extensive discussion of the necessity principle, see ch 12.

his judgment, Lord Campbell famously observed that 'no one can suppose that Lord Cottenham could be, in the remotest degree, influenced by the interest that he had in this concern.'[6]

It is not easy to ascertain the exact nature of Lord Cottenham's interests, despite earnest attention by legal historians. We know Lord Cottenham had 92 shares in the company, but they were £100 shares, which would have been very valuable at that time. 17 were held in his own right and 75 in a representative capacity. There is hard evidence that his Lordship received £276 in dividends for the year 1848. That is an interest which it would be difficult to describe as *de minimis*.

Throughout this whole affair, Lord Cottenham had been seriously ill, leading to his resignation from the position of Lord Chancellor, a recuperation period in Malta and his death in Italy in April 1851, on his 70th birthday.[7] Atlay has suggested that it was the stress of this wretched litigation which led to the Lord Chancellor's relatively early death.[8]

The 'no pecuniary interest' principle as expressed in *Dimes* requires a judge to be automatically disqualified when there is neither actual bias nor even an apprehension of bias on the part of that judge. The fundamental philosophical underpinning of *Dimes* is therefore predicated on a conflict of interest approach.

Dimes also expressed a view that has rolled down the years in English jurisprudence, and which has had the significant implication that *all* public law cases should fall under the same rules:[9]

> [Our decision] will have a most salutary influence on these [various] tribunals when it is known that this high court of last resort, in a case in which the Lord Chancellor of England had an interest, considered that his decree was on that account a decree not according to law, and was set aside. This will be a lesson *to all inferior tribunals* to take care not only that in their decrees they are not influenced by their personal interest, but to avoid the appearance of labouring under such an influence.

THE NATURE AND QUANTUM OF THE PECUNIARY INTEREST

The basic proposition in *Dimes*, that a judge who has a pecuniary interest cannot sit, was always going to require considerable qualification in practice. As such, it is too blunt a principle, though it set an important tone for the future.

[6] Above n 1, 315.

[7] FA Sharman, above n 1, 86.

[8] JB Atlay, above n 1, 415. Atlay also says that, at Harrow, Lord Cottenham merely added 'ballast to the ship' and that when he resigned his office, he got an Earldom 'for his resignation rather than his rank'. Who needs an enemy, when one can have a biographer?

[9] Above n 1, 315 (emphasis added).

A pecuniary interest in law has always been understood to be a monetary interest, or something sounding in money. On a strict application, *Dimes* would have it that one share out of a thousand in a company is disqualifying. Indeed, that was precisely how judges approached the pecuniary interest principle in the period after *Dimes*. For instance, in *R v Hammond*, Blackburn J said that *any* direct pecuniary interest in a case is disqualifying: 'The interest to each shareholder may be less than [a farthing], but it is still an interest.'[10] In that case, convictions for travelling without a rail ticket were set aside, on the basis that the judge involved was a shareholder in a rail company. And in *R v Rand*, Blackburn J also said that the rule requiring disqualification was directed to 'any direct pecuniary interest, however small.'[11]

A 'bright line' approach to disqualification such as this has distinct practical advantages.[12] However, in the late 20th century, significant reservations began to emerge under several heads.

One concern was that some kinds of financial interests should be considered too remote or speculative to form the basis for disqualification. For instance, in *Energy Probe v Canada (Atomic Energy Control Board)*,[13] the Federal Court of Appeal of Canada rejected an argument that a member of the Atomic Energy Control Board should be disqualified from hearing Ontario Hydro's application for renewal of its operating licence for a nuclear power plant. He was the president of a company that supplied cables to companies running nuclear power plants, including Ontario Hydro. The majority of that court came to this conclusion on the basis that the particular board member had no direct financial interest in the outcome of the renewal application. Marceau JA dissented in part, rejecting a categorical distinction between direct and indirect financial interests. He would have found that the board member should have been disqualified if there was a reasonable expectation that his company would benefit financially from the outcome of the decision. On the facts of the case however, Marceau JA came to the same conclusion as the majority: that the prospect of financial gain was too contingent and remote to constitute the type of pecuniary interest that gave rise to automatic disqualification.

In *R v Bristol Betting and Gaming Licensing Committee, ex p O'Callaghan*, one of the companion cases to *Locabail (UK) Ltd v Bayfield Properties Ltd*,[14] the hearing judge was a director of a family company that had as one of its

10 *R v Hammond* (1863) 9 LT 423, 423.

11 *R v Rand* (1866) LR 1 QB 230, 232.

12 For a survey of reasons for adhering to an automatic disqualification principle for pecuniary interests, see *Ebner v Official Trustee in Bankruptcy* (2001) 205 CLR 337, [141]–[163] (Kirby J).

13 *Energy Probe v Canada (Atomic Energy Control Board)* (1984) 15 DLR (4th) 48 (FCA). See DJ Mullan, *Administrative Law: Cases, Text, and Materials*, 5th edn (Toronto, Emond Montgomery, 2003) 575–79.

14 *Locabail (UK) Ltd v Bayfield Properties Ltd* [2000] 2 WLR 870 (CA).

commercial tenants the respondent to the particular judicial review application which was before that judge. The English Court of Appeal held that the amount at stake in the judicial review proceedings could have had no impact on the ability of the respondent to pay its rent. Hence the financial impact of the proceedings on the family company was too indirect to give rise to a basis for judicial disqualification.

Even if the general pecuniary interest rule is to remain one of automatic disqualification, assuming that there is a sufficiently 'direct' connection, there remains debate in the British Commonwealth as to whether there ought nevertheless to be a *de minimis* exception to disqualification for financial interests. And, does it matter whether the 'tribunal' being impugned is a regular court of law, or an administrative tribunal?

In New Zealand, in *Auckland Casino Ltd v Casino Control Authority*,[15] there was a combined shareholding between the particular tribunal decision maker and his wife of some 18,000 shares, which were worth more than $1 each. Although this shareholding represented less than 3 per cent of their total portfolio of investments, it was not dismissed as insignificant. However, it was accepted by the Court of Appeal that there may be *de minimis* cases, at least in tribunal situations. The Court of Appeal described the 'however small' test as an exaggeration in the New Zealand context:[16]

> A firm and realistic rule of pecuniary disqualification is necessary to assist public confidence in the administration of justice and the impartiality of licensing bodies. The existence of an irrebuttable presumption in cases of direct pecuniary interest was assumed in argument. As already mentioned, we think that it may be subject to the *de minimis* rule.

An appellate division in South Africa in *BTR Industries South Africa (Pty) Ltd v Metal and Allied Workers' Union* has also taken the view that there should be a *de minimis* exception.[17]

However, in *Locabail* the English Court of Appeal has said that the *de minimis* exception should be limited to situations where:[18]

> the potential effect of any decision on the judge's personal interest is so small as to be incapable of affecting his decision one way or the other; but it is important, bearing in mind the rationale of the rule, that any doubt should be resolved in favour of disqualification.

In the result, there is clearly senior appellate support in the British Commonwealth for the proposition that an exception of a narrow variety is warranted, and probably extends to both regular courts and tribunals.

[15] *Auckland Casino Ltd v Casino Control Authority* [1995] 1 NZLR 142 (CA).
[16] ibid 148.
[17] *BTR Industries South Africa (Pty) Ltd v Metal and Allied Workers' Union* 1992 (3) SA 673, 694.
[18] Above n 14, [10].

The divergence of opinion between Kirby J and his colleagues on the High Court of Australia in *Ebner v Official Trustee in Bankruptcy* is also instructive.[19] In that case, the majority took the view that there is a distinction between a pecuniary interest *in the company* and a direct pecuniary interest *in the outcome* of the litigation. Kirby J, on the other hand, saw the relevant point as being whether or not the judge had a financial interest in the form of a shareholding in a company that was a *party* to the proceedings before him or her.

The courts have to date shown considerable reluctance to allow the financial interests of a judge's family members to amount to a disqualifying pecuniary interest. In *Bank of New South Wales v The Commonwealth*, the High Court of Australia ruled that Starke J was not disqualified by reason of his wife's shareholding in a bank.[20] In another Australian case, the wife of the President of the Industrial Court of Queensland held shares in a mining company which was a party to proceedings before the Queensland Supreme Court. The President himself had never owned shares in the company and had no pecuniary interest in his wife's shares. Relying on *Dimes*, the court held that the President had no direct pecuniary interest. The court then proceeded to apply the alternative test of whether the shareholding generated a reasonable likelihood of bias, and concluded it did not.[21]

A novel attempt by counsel to extend the financial disqualification rule was made in *Muir v Commissioner of Inland Revenue*.[22] Dr Muir was a tax lawyer and the originator of a scheme based on forestry investment which would have attracted millions of dollars in tax relief. In earlier litigation, the Court of Appeal held that this scheme amounted to tax avoidance.[23] Dr Muir then sought to challenge the involvement of Venning J, the High Court judge, who had impugned the scheme on a variety of grounds. One was that the judge had an interest as an investor in another forestry block in Southland, New Zealand. The judge had initially held about one sixth of the shares in the relevant company, which subsequently increased to a 25 per cent shareholding. Counsel for Dr Muir suggested that it was likely that the High Court judge's investment would involve similar tax issues to those considered by him in Dr Muir's case. These considerations would be relevant to the value of his investment. The Court of Appeal held that the similarities between the judge's private investment and that which was before him in the present case had not been appropriately made out.

[19] Above n 12.

[20] (1948) 76 CLR 1 (Latham CJ).

[21] *R v The Industrial Court and The Honourable Mostyn Hanger President of the Industrial Court and Mount Isa Mines Ltd* (1966) Queensland Law Reporter 245.

[22] *Muir v Commissioner of Inland Revenue* [2007] 3 NZLR 495 (CA). The judgment of the court was delivered by the present author. There was no appeal against this decision.

[23] The decision of the Court of Appeal has been upheld by the Supreme Court of New Zealand in *Ben Nevis Forestry Ventures Ltd v Commissioner of Inland Revenue* [2008] NZSC 115.

It had also been suggested that what the judge would 'learn' from his involvement in the *Muir* case would ultimately be beneficial to him. The Court of Appeal rejected that proposition, in these terms:[24]

> The suggestion that a Judge should not 'learn' from things he or she hears in the course of a case is also startling. It must be the experience of all judicial officers (and counsel) that in the course of a case they have to inform, or better inform themselves, on an extraordinary range of matters, some of a highly technical character. Some of this 'sticks' and (mercifully) much of it can be, and is, discarded. The suggestion that the Judge was getting a 'learning benefit', as it were, out of this case, which he could then enhance or apply in his own forestry investment, is fanciful. The learning experience of this case was, and is, that some schemes are hopelessly beyond the pale.

Real problems are likely to continue to arise in the field. Judges own insurance policies, have bank accounts, use credit cards, and own shares in corporations, perhaps directly or through devices like mutual funds. Both practically, and because it is important that judges live 'normal' lives for a deeper personal understanding of the society in which they adjudicate cases, they cannot be expected to put such things aside. Increasingly, the inquiry is likely to become more fact specific: can it fairly be said that the outcome of the proceedings before the particular judge will really affect the judge's interest?[25]

CONNECTION WITH THE CAUSE OF A PARTY TO THE LITIGATION

The law in this area was reviewed by the House of Lords in *R v Bow Street Metropolitan Stipendiary Magistrate and Ors, Ex parte Pinochet Ugarte (No 2)*,[26] to which reference has been made in Chapter 1.

In the first round of that extraordinary litigation, their Lordships held that Mr Pinochet, the former Chilean dictator, was not immune from the arrest and extradition proceedings brought in respect of his conduct during his time in office.[27] Amnesty International, a charitable organisation concerned to educate the public about, and to promote, human rights, had been given leave to appear as an intervenor.

[24] ibid [87].

[25] See also *Clenae Pty Ltd v ANZ Banking Group Ltd* [1999] 2 VR 573, 591, where the Victoria Court of Appeal suggested that 'automatic disqualification should not follow merely because a judge has a shareholding in a party to litigation, but that *something more* is required, an interest in the outcome, or the cause itself, or the subject matter of the proceedings' (Charles JA) (emphasis added).

[26] *R v Bow Street Metropolitan Stipendiary Magistrate and Ors, ex p Pinochet Ugarte (No 2)* [2000] 1 AC 119 (HL).

[27] *R v Bow Street Metropolitan Stipendiary Magistrate and Ors, ex p Ugarte* [2000] 1 AC 61 (HL).

After that decision was delivered, it came to light that Lord Hoffman, a member of the panel in that case, was both a director and chairman of Amnesty International Charity Limited, which was closely linked to the parent body, Amnesty International. There was no suggestion that Lord Hoffman himself received any pecuniary benefit from the litigation, nor was there any suggestion that he was actually biased.

Lord Hoffman's interest was not drawn to the attention of the parties during the hearing. After the result adverse to Mr Pinochet was handed down, an application was made to the House of Lords to have the merits decision set aside on the ground of bias on the part of Lord Hoffman.

Lord Browne-Wilkinson, the senior Law Lord, suggested that there are two ways in which a person could be conceived of as a judge in their 'own cause':[28]

> First [the principle] may be applied literally: if a judge is in fact a party to the litigation or has a financial or proprietary interest in its outcome then he is indeed sitting as a judge in his own cause. In that case, the mere fact that he is a party to the action or has a financial or proprietary interest in its outcome is sufficient to cause his automatic disqualification. The second application of the principle is where a judge is not a party to the suit and does not have a financial interest in its outcome, but in some other way his conduct or behaviour may give rise to a suspicion that he is not impartial, for example because of his friendship with a party. This second type of case is not strictly speaking an application of the principle that a man must not be a judge in his own cause, since the judge will not normally be himself benefiting, but providing a benefit for another by failing to be impartial.

The justification for 'extending' the automatic disqualification rule to the promotion of a cause was put this way by his Lordship:[29]

> If the absolute impartiality of the judiciary is to be maintained, there must be a rule which automatically disqualifies a judge who is involved, whether personally or as a director of a company, in promoting the same causes in the same organisation as is a party to the suit. There is no room for fine distinctions.

Pinochet (No 2) has been the subject of adverse academic commentary, some of it severe. The fundamental concern appears to be that their Lordships had skilfully resorted to a per se rule, resolving a 'real' problem in a formalistic way and avoiding any inquiry into whether Lord Hoffman could be said to have been likely to be biased.[30] There was also concern that

[28] Above n 26, 132–33.

[29] ibid 135.

[30] See D Robertson, 'The House of Lords as a Political and Constitutional Court: Lessons from the Pinochet Case' in D Woodhouse (ed), *The Pinochet Case: A Legal and Constitutional Analysis* (Oxford, Hart Publishing, 2000) 17, 25; and E Grant, '*Pinochet* 2: The Questions of Jurisdiction and Bias' in D Woodhouse (ed), *The Pinochet Case: A Legal and Constitutional Analysis* (Oxford, Hart Publishing, 2000) 41, 51–55.

this expansion of automatic disqualification would cause uncertainty, given the recent restatement of the principles in *Locabail*.[31]

Nevertheless, in the United Kingdom, the boundaries of *Pinochet (No 2)* have been further pressed. In *AWG Group Ltd v Morrison*,[32] the trial judge had informed the parties that one of the proposed witnesses for the claimants was a long-standing family acquaintance. The defendants sought to have the judge stand down. The judge then accepted a suggestion from the claimants that they would call other witnesses instead. This was because there was a grave concern to see that a long and complex trial was not postponed.

On appeal to the Court of Appeal, Mummery LJ was at pains to indicate that 'efficiency and convenience are not the determinative legal values' in this sort of situation.[33] The court took the view that because of the depth of the connection between the judge and the witness, and in light of the fact that the withdrawal of the witness would not for all practical purposes remove him from the events, the judge ought to have recused himself under the automatic disqualification rule.[34]

Other appellate decisions have shown some degree of circumspection as to the full-blooded extension of the doctrine of automatic disqualification to the promotion of a cause. In *Locabail*,[35] a particularly strong English Court of Appeal constituted by the Lord Chief Justice, the Master of the Rolls and the Vice-Chancellor, heard five cases together on the subject of judicial bias. In one of them, a deputy judge had become aware that the law firm in which he was a senior partner was acting against one of the parties to the litigation before him on another matter. The automatic disqualification rule was not applied in that instance since the connection between the firm's success in the case and its profits was said to be tenuous at best. The case is also an important one on waiver, to which we will come in due course,[36] because it was held that the complaining party had effectively waived her right to challenge an adverse decision.

In another of the joined appeals, after a newspaper revelation, there was a challenge to a judge who was a director of certain family property companies whose tenants included the defendant in the case. The Court of Appeal

[31] Above n 14.

[32] *AWG Group Ltd v Morrison* [2006] 1 WLR 1163 (CA). The first-instance decision was that of Evans-Lombe J: [2005] EWHC 2786 (Ch).

[33] ibid [29].

[34] Courts or tribunals may even be collectively tainted. See *Re P (A Barrister)* [2005] 1 WLR 3019, where a member of the disciplinary tribunal of the Council of the Inns of Courts had also been a member of the professional committee of the Bar Council, the body responsible for the decision to prosecute the member of the bar in the first place. It was held that, under the particular procedures appropriate to the case, a member of the complaints committee had a common interest in the prosecution, and was therefore acting as a judge in his or her own cause.

[35] Above n 14.

[36] See ch 11 below.

held that the judge's 'nominal and indirect interest' did not establish a bar to the judge sitting on the case.[37]

What these decisions demonstrate is a reluctance on the part of contemporary appellate courts to see a judge automatically disqualified where the interest involved is minimal, or where the connection with the judge is tenuous or quite unlikely to have had any bearing on the resolution of the case itself. This amounts to a kind of screening process, with the reviewing court asking whether a particular interest 'mattered', in a rather pragmatic way.

WHERE TO WITH AUTOMATIC DISQUALIFICATION?

As indicated, the reception of *Pinochet (No 2)* was somewhat mixed in the United Kingdom. In *Locabail*, the English Court of Appeal was clear that there should not be extensions of the automatic disqualification category 'unless such extension were plainly required to give effect to the important underlying principles on which the rule is based'.[38]

Even in cases where doubt has been cast upon the automatic disqualification approach (such as in the majority decision of the High Court of Australia in *Ebner*[39]), the concern has been less with the principle that disqualification for some types of financial interests is essentially automatic than with the idea that the amount of the interest in question is of little or no consequence in determining when a judge should be disqualified. The majority in *Ebner* said:[40]

> [W]e accept that, in the practical application of the general test to be applied in cases of apprehended bias, economic conflicts of interest are likely to be of particular significance, and that, allowing for the imprecision of the concept, the circumstance that a judge has a not insubstantial, direct, pecuniary or proprietary interest in the outcome of litigation will ordinarily result in disqualification.

Some English commentators have seen the *Pinochet* litigation as extending the 'pecuniary interest' category from situations where the judge's interest in the outcome of a case was financial to much broader situations where other personal interests may be implicated.[41] Other commentators have said that automatic disqualification is merely mechanical jurisprudence that is 'draconian, disproportionate and unnecessary'.[42] Still others have thought that real uncertainty has been caused in the law by the decision.

[37] Above n 14, 906.
[38] ibid 883.
[39] Above n 12.
[40] ibid [58].
[41] Above n 30.
[42] AA Olowofoyeku, 'The *Nemo Judex* Rule: The Case Against Automatic Disqualification' [2000] *Public Law* 456, 475. See also B Rayment, 'Bias: Recent Developments' [2001] 6 *Judicial Review* 93; P Havers and O Thomas, 'Bias Post-*Pinochet* and Under the ECHR'

As to the issue of uncertainty, Lord Bingham of Cornhill has suggested some factors in *Locabail* which would engage a presumptive automatic disqualification rule. Factors which will likely give rise to a real danger of bias include personal friendship or animosity; close acquaintance with a party; and any other reason for 'doubting the ability of the judge to ignore extraneous considerations, prejudices and predilections and bring an objective judgment to bear on the issues before him'.[43] Other factors which would not ordinarily give rise to a real danger of bias include such things as 'religion, ethnic or national origin, gender, age, class, means or sexual orientation of the judge'.[44]

The most serious challenge to the automatic disqualification rule has come from the High Court of Australia judgment in *Ebner*.[45] There, the High Court of Australia went so far as to hold that there is no separate and free-standing rule of automatic disqualification on the basis of a pecuniary interest. The majority in that case preferred to rely exclusively on a unitary 'apprehension of bias' test.[46] The general test posed by the majority was whether a fair-minded lay observer might reasonably apprehend that the judge might not bring an impartial mind to the resolution of the case.[47]

In dissent, Kirby J supported the continuation of an automatic disqualification for financial interest test, at least where it is direct and not saved by the *de minimis* principle. His extensive reasons for this stance include the benefits of a 'bright line' rule; the firmness of various international covenants, including Article 14 of the ICCPR; the 'commonality' of the rule around the common law world; the compatibility of such a rule with other areas of the law, such as fiduciaries; and perhaps, most importantly, that a bright line rule promotes 'manifest integrity in the judicial institution'.[48]

It is worth interpolating here that in the United States of America, Judge Posner has offered an 'economic' rationale for the orthodox bifurcation: occasional 'silly results may be an acceptable price for a rule ... that is straightforward in application and spares the judge from having to make decisions under an uncertain standard apt to be misunderstood'.[49]

In *Muir*, the New Zealand Court of Appeal noted the decision in *Ebner*, but was not required to decide this issue, not least because it had not been

[1999] 4 *Judicial Review* 111. A Zuckerman has argued that the distinction between disqualification for bias and automatic disqualification is now redundant: *Zuckerman on Civil Procedure: Principles of Practice*, 2nd edn (London, Sweet & Maxwell, 2006) 84–86.

43 Above n 14, [25].
44 ibid.
45 Above n 12.
46 ibid [54]–[55].
47 ibid [6].
48 ibid [161].
49 *Union Carbide Corp v US Cutting Service Inc* (1986) 782 F 2d 710, 714.

raised and the court had not heard argument on the point. However, the court did say:[50]

> We do, however, note that there are powerful arguments for simplicity and straightforwardness in this area of law, which has been somewhat bedevilled by contradictory approaches. If a Judge has a direct pecuniary interest of anything more than the most minimal character, it is hard to see how the reasonable observer would not consider that to be 'bias'. Hence no harm, and a great deal of good, in terms of the understandability of the law, would be done by a unitary principle. However, there are policy arguments the other way too, and they are quite complicated in a small jurisdiction such as New Zealand.

Whether to follow the lead of the majority of the High Court of Australia in *Ebner* in dispensing with a stand-alone automatic disqualification test for interest will doubtless depend upon the particular context in a given jurisdiction. Those circumstances will be quite complex but, apart from the considerations already noted, will likely include the following.

First, it may well have to be accepted that in small jurisdictions, size should or will make a difference. The new Supreme Court of New Zealand, which as originally constituted had only five judges, encountered some initial difficulties with voluntary recusals by judges, including the Chief Justice, which posed difficulties for the workings of that Court.[51] These have apparently been largely overcome with an increase in the membership of the court and the ability to resort to acting judges.

Secondly, an important contextual factor will be the extent to which the intellectual approach to law is changing within a given jurisdiction. While some jurisdictions prefer, for better or worse, a 'rules-oriented' approach, there is a growing awareness that scarcely any important question is today ever capable of complete resolution by recourse to a rule. Given that a key tenet of modernity is a reasonable plurality on a plethora of fundamental issues, it is unsurprising that a more contextual and reasoned approach to a particular situation is often preferred.

Thirdly, the practical realities of litigation in a given jurisdiction are also extremely important. It seems plain enough that the Australian jurisprudence on recusal was partly in response to some unhappy tendencies in

[50] Above n 22, [42].

[51] The most prominent example was Elias CJ's recusal from sitting on *Cropp v A Judicial Committee* [2007] NZSC 95, on the grounds that she part-owned a horse that jockey Lisa Cropp rode. See also *Taunoa v A-G* [2006] NZSC 94; *Sestan v The Director of Area Mental Health Services Waitemata District Health Board* [2007] NZSC 10, [2]. In the Court of Appeal, controversy ensued when Wilson J (now a member of the Supreme Court) declined to recuse himself in *Wool Board Disestablishment Co Ltd v Saxmere Co Ltd* [2007] NZCA 349: N Hager, 'Appeal Court Judge faces a question of judgement' *Sunday Star-Times* (Auckland, 24 August 2008). The Supreme Court has granted leave to appeal on the ground of whether the Court of Appeal decision should be set aside because of a reasonable apprehension of bias resulting from Wilson J's business relationship with one of the counsel in that case: *Saxmere Co Ltd v Wool Board Disestablishment Co Ltd* [2008] NZSC 94.

litigation in that country, including a rather belligerent approach towards 'judge shopping', and the growth of rather shrill post-judgment complaints by litigants dissatisfied with the outcome of a case. Judges have even been 'investigated' with a view to identifying some aspect of their personal life that might somehow activate the automatic disqualification rule, at a post-hearing stage.

Fourthly, an overly aggressive bar—if one exists—may not be the worst source of the problems. The rise in the number of 'litigants in person' throughout the common law world is an acknowledged phenomenon. Some 'litigants in person' can be able, and mount arguments that would put many members of the bar to shame. Others fall into the wretched category of merely vexatious litigants, or querulents. Merian-Websters Medical Dictionary defines querulents as being 'abnormally given to suspicion and accusation'.

This 'querulent' epithet is increasingly used to designate humans who are easily susceptible to perceived injustice from a negligible cause and whose behaviour stands in no appropriate relation to the situation to which it is addressed. It is almost a form of desperation where a person, with many battles already lost, nevertheless continues to struggle to advance 'their cause' whatever the personal cost. There is at least some professional literature which sees querulent paranoia as a distinct form of behaviour disorder.[52]

The problems attaching to unrepresented litigants should not be underestimated. As Drewry, Blom-Cooper and Blake said recently in relation to the United Kingdom:[53]

> Litigants in person are characteristically ill-equipped to handle legal material and court procedures (however much the litigant might find assistance from a user-friendly judge). They are often blinded (or, at the very most, blinkered) in appreciation and understanding of the litigation which they have embarked upon, frequently against advice from friends and legal acquaintances. They exhibit an unremitting commitment to the rightness, even self-righteousness, of their cause, often displaying an obsessive attention to peripheral, even irrelevant, detail. The result is that the litigant in person finds it impossible to apply objectivity to legal and factual reality. These personal attributes, when translated into oral advocacy, lead to rambling, unintelligible, even gibberish submissions—what Jeremy Bentham once described as 'grimgribber nonsense'. On occasions, the court is subjected to abuse or even belligerence which, were they displayed by the professional advocate, would lead

[52] Dr Joachim Hellmer, the Professor of Criminal Law and Criminology at Kiel University in Germany, has suggested that otherwise highly intelligent and well-regarded persons such as Martin Luther, Voltaire, and Galileo Galilei were also querulents. <http://www.economy-point.org/q/querulanz.html> accessed 15 April 2009. For a discussion of querulous paranoia from a legal perspective, see I Freckelton, 'Querulent Paranoia and the Vexatious Complainant' (1988) 11 *International Journal of Law and Psychiatry* 127; and G Lester and S Smith, 'Inventor, Entrepreneur, Rascal, Crank or Querulent?: Australia's Vexatious Litigant Sanction 75 Years On' (2006) 13(1) *Psychiatry, Psychology and Law* 1, 13–17.

[53] G Drewry, L Blom-Cooper and C Blake, *The Court of Appeal* (Oxford, Hart Publishing, 2007) 133–34.

> to disciplinary action or even constitute contempt of court. To avoid complaints of justice not being done (or having been seen to be done) litigants are licensed to wander well beyond the limits of the orderly forensic process, to the detriment of a just and fair process, with no discernible advantage to the litigants themselves.

The actual litigation structure and civil procedure rules in a given jurisdiction are important here. In principle, increased case management ought to 'filter out' entirely unmeritorious claims at an early stage; regrettably, in reality it is not unheard of for the particular litigant to then begin to sequentially challenge every judicial officer who is involved in the litigation.

Perhaps the most disturbing phenomenon of all from the standpoint of a fair and efficient litigation system is the practise of litigants 'lying in wait'; that is, storing up ammunition which can then be aimed at the judge after judgment has been handed down in a significant and expensive piece of litigation. How the legal system copes with this phenomenon is further addressed in a later chapter on waiver.[54]

Fifthly, there is a significant public law structural issue: if one rule for bias is to be applied to judges, is that also to be the rule for all public law cases, despite the contextual complexity of many administrative law decision-making processes, where many tribunal members will be appointed precisely because of distinctly held views?

In England, there has been a steady line of authority from *Dimes* to *R v Gough*[55] holding that the automatic disqualification rule applies both to courts, in the strict sense, and to tribunals. In *Gough*, Lord Goff put it this way:[56]

> [T]he same test should be applicable in all cases of apparent bias, whether concerned with justices or members of other inferior tribunals, or with jurors, or with arbitrators.

Doubtless, that approach will be reinforced to a distinct extent by the fact that under the radical over-haul of the tribunals service that took effect from 3 November 2008 in England and Wales, most legally qualified tribunal chairmen (who deal with areas as diverse as tax and child support) are now required to swear a judicial oath and become 'judges'. This will create perhaps 2,700 new 'judges'.[57]

However, there will be jurisdictions where particular statutory schemes explicitly or implicitly recognise that the full force of *Dimes*-type reasoning is not appropriate in some tribunal settings.

[54] See ch 11 below.
[55] [1993] AC 646 (HL).
[56] ibid 670.
[57] F Gibb, 'Tribunal service reform to create 2,700 new judges' *The Times*, 3 November 2008, 12. This terminological shift has occurred under the Tribunals, Courts and Enforcement Act 2007. For commentary, see R Carnwath, 'Tribunal Justice—a New Start' (2009) *Public Law* 48.

5

Apparent Bias in the British Commonwealth

THE IDEA OF IMPARTIALITY

WHAT IS MEANT by impartiality for legal purposes? We at once encounter very real difficulties, which judges everywhere have had to struggle with.

One point should be made at the outset. One view of the judge—and a false one at that—is that this personage is, or should be, rather like the ideal figure of neoclassical economic theory: that is, absolutely and perfectly rational. In fact, judges are prone to human fallibility and everyday heuristic biases, or skewed modes of thinking. These include, but are not limited to, such cognitive errors as hindsight bias (attaching higher probabilities to events after they have happened); availability bias (which causes us to base decisions on information that is more readily available in our memories, rather than the data we 'really' need); confirmation bias (which inclines us to look for confirming evidence of an initial hypothesis, rather than falsifying evidence that would disprove it); and apathetic bias (which inclines us to abdicate individual responsibility when in a crowd). It is not these sort of cognitive reasoning errors with which we are concerned here. They are part of the stuff of 'regular' appeals and go to showing that a judge or a court's actual reasoning process was wrong.

What we seem to be looking for is something that inappropriately affects the reasoning process in that it has nothing, or very little, to do with the actual merits of the case, but is somehow brought into play in the determination of it, whether consciously or unconsciously. A failure to avoid this sort of error is said by the law to amount to a want of impartiality.

The much respected American jurist, Judge Learned Hand, said extra-judicially:[1]

> You must have impartiality. What do I mean by impartiality? I mean you mustn't introduce yourself, your own preconceived notions about what is right. You must try, as far as you can, it is impossible for human beings to do so absolutely, but

[1] Learned Hand, *The Spirit of Liberty: Papers and Addresses of Learned Hand*, 2nd edn (New York, Alfred A Knopf, 1953) 309–10.

> just so far as you can, not to interject your own personal interests, even your own preconceived assumptions and beliefs.

However, Judge Learned Hand's distinguished realist colleague on the powerful Second Circuit Court of Appeals of that time was sceptical that a mechanical separation was possible, or even desirable. In *Re JP Linahan Inc*, Judge Jerome Frank said:[2]

> Democracy must, indeed, fail unless our courts try cases fairly, and there can be no fair trial before a judge lacking in impartiality and disinterestedness. If, however, 'bias' and 'partiality' be defined to mean the total absence of preconceptions in the mind of the judge, then no one has ever had a fair trial and no one ever will ... [W]ere those pre-judgments which we call habits absent in any person, were he obliged to treat every event as an unprecedented crisis presenting a wholly new problem he would go mad. Interests, points of view, preferences, are the essence of living.

It seems that Judge Learned Hand had a 'clean slate' model not only as his ideal, but as a distinct working principle. What he appears to have wanted was as nearly as possible an absolutely blank slate on to which the parties' competing assertions would be written and then clinically assessed. Judge Jerome Frank may be thought to go too far in the other direction: given the 'prior writings' on the judge's slate which emanate from his own being and experience, a judge cannot help *imposing* himself or herself on others.

In *R v Gough*, Lord Goff appears to have thought that the real concern is with a bad attitude, really an impermissible sort of public law *mens rea*:[3]

> [H]aving ascertained the relevant circumstances, the court should ask itself whether, having regard to those circumstances, there was a real danger of bias on the part of the relevant member of the tribunal in question, in the sense that he might unfairly regard (or have unfairly regarded) with favour, or disfavour, the case of a party to the issue under consideration by him.

Put another way, this approach focuses on an inappropriate inclination on the part of a judge to decide an issue influenced by some consideration other than its merits.

Contemporary insights brought to the judging process by some insightful women law professors provide a further perspective. For instance, Professor Cain has suggested that:[4]

> the act of judging [is] an act which seems to require at least momentary separation. A judge should transcend self to listen, and then a judge should decide with

[2] *Re JP Linahan Inc* (1943) 138 F 2d 650, 651. See also S Cravens, 'Impartiality: Balancing Personal and Professional Integrity in Judicial Decisionmaking' <http://works.bepress.com/cgi/viewcontent.cgi?article=1001&context=sarah_cravens> accessed 18 April 2009.

[3] *R v Gough* [1993] AC 646, 670 (HL).

[4] PA Cain, 'Good and Bad Bias: A Comment on Feminist Theory and Judging' (1988) 61 *Southern California Law Review* 1945, 1955 commenting on an excellent paper by J Resnik, 'On the Bias: Feminist Reconsiderations of the Aspirations for Our Judges' (1988) 61 *Southern California Law Review* 1877. See also AH Young, 'Feminism, Pluralism and Administrative Law' in M Taggart (ed), *The Province of Administrative Law* (Oxford, Hart Publishing, 1997) 344–49.

> empathy and understanding—as a new self, if you will, for having experienced the story of the other.

That sort of mediating insight has considerable attractions.

Later in this work, it will be suggested that the term 'objectivity' may be a more important and useful concept. But for now, the conventional term 'impartiality' is employed.

THE JUDICIAL OATH

In all common law jurisdictions, a judge takes a judicial oath on appointment. A relatively common form is an oath to 'do right to all manner of people after the laws and usages of [this country] without fear or favour, affection or ill will'.[5]

Lord Bingham of Cornhill has said of such an oath:[6]

> If one were to attempt a modern paraphrase, it might perhaps be that a judge must free himself of prejudice and partiality and so conduct himself, in court and out of it, as to give no ground for doubting his ability and willingness to decide cases coming before him solely on their legal and factual merits as they appear to him in the exercise of an objective, independent, and impartial judgment.

In the view of another distinguished jurist, Lord Devlin, the essential function of a judge is to remove any sense of injustice. This is something that would be more easily aroused by an apprehension of unequal treatment than by anything else. As his Lordship put it in the fourth Chorley Lecture:[7]

> The social service which the judge renders to the community is the removal of a sense of injustice. To perform this service the essential quality which he needs is impartiality and next after that the appearance of impartiality. I put impartiality before the appearance of it simply because without the reality the appearance would not endure. In truth, within the context of service to the community the appearance is the more important of the two. The judge who gives the right judgment while appearing not to do so may be thrice blessed in heaven, but on earth he is no use at all.

The existence of the judicial oath, apart from requiring impartiality, is often used to support the notion of a 'duty to sit'. As to such a 'duty', the New Zealand Court of Appeal emphasised in *Muir* that:[8]

> [t]he requirement of independence and impartiality of a Judge is counterbalanced by the Judge's duty to sit, at least where grounds for disqualification do not exist

[5] In New Zealand, see Oaths and Declarations Act 1957 s 18. The oath for each federal justice or judge in the United States is set out at 28 USC § 453.

[6] TH Bingham, 'Judicial Ethics' in *The Business of Judging: Selected Essays and Speeches* (Oxford, OUP, 2000) 69, 74.

[7] P Devlin, 'The Judge as Lawmaker' in *The Judge* (Oxford, OUP, 1981) 3.

[8] *Muir v Commissioner of Inland Revenue* [2007] 3 NZLR 495, [35] (CA).

in fact or in law. This duty in itself helps protect judicial independence against manoeuvring by parties hoping to improve their chances of having a given matter determined by a particular Judge or to gain forensic or strategic advantages through delay or interruption to the proceeding. As Mason J emphasised in *Re JRL; ex p CJL* (1986) 161 CLR 342 at 352:

> [I]t is equally important that judicial officers discharge their duty to sit and do not, by acceding too readily to suggestions of appearance of bias, encourage parties to believe that by seeking the disqualification of a judge, they will have their case tried by someone thought to be more likely to decide the case in their favour.

THE EVOLUTION OF THE TEST FOR APPARENT BIAS

Although the law around the Commonwealth is now in a broadly agreed state as to the relevant test under this head, the evolution of the law was not entirely straightforward. Indeed it caused considerable confusion. For that reason, the older cases, including those which are of the highest authority, have to be approached with real caution, and it is worth noting the course which the law has taken.

In 19th-century England, the cases held that if there was no pecuniary interest, the court inquired whether there was a real likelihood of bias.[9] However, in the *Suffex Justices* case in 1924, Lord Hewart CJ said that a reasonable suspicion of bias was sufficient to quash a judicial determination.[10] Some confusion was then caused by cases which appeared to be moving back to the real likelihood of bias formulation, and seemingly disapproved of Lord Hewart's formulation.[11] Then, in *Metropolitan Properties Co (FGC) Ltd v Lannon*, Lord Denning MR appeared to espouse Lord Hewart's formulation.[12] However, Lord Denning's language may have also been a little loose, and it left some room for doubt as to just what the test was.

The House of Lords endeavoured to clarify the state of the law in *R v Gough*.[13] As has been noted, their Lordships held that the same test should be applied across the board in *all* cases of apparent bias, whether they concerned judges, tribunals, jurors, arbitrators or coroners. Their Lordships held that in terms of the degree of bias, the test should be whether there was a real danger of bias on the part of the relevant member of the tribunal. As to the perspective from which that degree of bias should be viewed,

[9] See, for example, *R v Rand* (1866) LR 1 QB 230; and *R v Justices of Sunderland* [1901] 2 KB 357 (CA).

[10] *R v Sussex Justices, ex p McCarthy* [1924] 1 KB 256, 259.

[11] See, for example, *R v Camborne Justices, ex p Pearce* [1955] 1 QB 41.

[12] [1969] 1 QB 577, 598–600 (CA).

[13] Above n 3.

it was not necessary to formulate a test in terms of the reasonable man. The court itself personified the reasonable man, ascertaining the relevant circumstances from that evidence which was before it and which might not be available to the ordinary observer.

This approach to matters did not find favour in other Commonwealth jurisdictions, notably Australia. The basic concern was that Lord Goff's approach in *Gough* tended to emphasise the court's view of the facts. Inadequate attention was given to the public perception of the incident being challenged.[14]

Then, the House of Lords indicated in *Pinochet (No 2)* that it might be necessary to review the test that it had laid down in *Gough*.[15] In fact, the English Court of Appeal undertook such a review in *Re Medicaments and Related Classes of Goods (No 2)*.[16] It was able, and arguably required, to do so because the picture had been further refined, at least in the United Kingdom, by virtue of the emerging European human rights jurisprudence as interpreted by the Strasbourg court. That court had taken the view that the relevant test is whether there was an objective risk of bias in light of the circumstances identified by the court.[17]

Eventually, the issue reached the House of Lords again in *Porter v Magill*.[18] Their Lordships adopted a reformulated test, which owed something to *Re Medicaments*. The question was said to be whether the fair-minded and informed observer, having considered the facts, would conclude that there was a real possibility that the judge was biased. Their Lordships said that they were making a 'modest adjustment'[19] to the law, rather than changing it.

In the result, there was still a difference between the House of Lords and the High Court of Australia. The Australian test was one of a 'reasonable apprehension' of bias, as opposed to the United Kingdom 'real possibility' of bias test.

More recently, the English Court of Appeal has summarised the current English principles, as it apprehends them to be, in *AWG Group Ltd v Morrison*:[20]

> Inconvenience, costs and delay do not ... count in a case where the principle of judicial impartiality is properly invoked. This is because it is *the* fundamental principle of justice, both at common law and under article 6 of the Convention for the Protection of Human Rights. If, on an assessment of all the relevant circumstances,

14 See *Webb v R* (1994) 181 CLR 41.

15 [2000] 1 AC 119, 136 (HL).

16 *Re Medicaments and Related Classes of Goods (No 2)* [2001] 1 WLR 700 (CA).

17 *Pullar v UK* (1996) 22 EHRR 391, 402.

18 [2002] 2 AC 357. That formulation has been unanimously endorsed by the House of Lords in *Lawal v Northern Spirit Ltd* [2004] 1 All ER 187 and *Gillies v Secretary of State for Work and Pensions* [2006] 1 WLR 781.

19 ibid [103].

20 *AWG Group Ltd v Morrison* [2006] 1 WLR 1163, [6], [7] and [9] (CA).

> the conclusion is that the principle either has been, or will be, breached, the judge is automatically disqualified from hearing the case. It is not a discretionary case management decision reached by weighing various relevant factors in the balance.
>
> The test for apparent bias now settled by a line of recent decisions of this court and of the House of Lords is that, having ascertained all the circumstances bearing on the suggestion that the judge was (or would be) biased, the court must ask 'whether those circumstances would lead a fair-minded and informed observer to conclude that there was a real possibility ... that the tribunal was biased' ...
>
> Most of the leading authorities were appeals arising from hearings that had already taken place or were under way and an objection to the judge was based on facts discovered during the course of, or only after the end of, the hearing. Although this is a different case, as the hearing has not yet started, the same principle applies. Where the hearing has not yet begun, there is also scope for the sensible application of the precautionary principle. If, as here, the court has to predict what might happen if the hearing goes ahead before the judge to whom objection is taken and to assess the real possibility of apparent bias arising, prudence naturally leans on the side of being safe rather than sorry.

The UK position has thus become something of a hybrid one. There must be a 'real possibility of bias' but from the perspective of a fair-minded and informed observer.

From time to time, there have been observations both by judges and commentators that these formulations are not really critical. With respect, that is to underestimate the importance of the 'stance' or 'viewpoint' which has been properly recognised by both the High Court of Australia and the House of Lords. That stance is overtly predicated on how an informed and fair-minded member of the public would see things, rather than how the reviewing court or judge might happen to see it.

As to the standpoint of such an observer, the most recent House of Lords decision, *Helow v Secretary of State for the Home Department*,[21] is instructive. The appellant was a Palestinian by birth whose sympathies apparently rested with the Palestinian Liberation Organisation. She sought asylum in the United Kingdom. As a Palestinian refugee living in Lebanon, she said she was 'at risk' from several sources, including Lebanese, Syrian and Israeli agents. Her application was refused by the Home Secretary, and by an adjudicator on appeal. She was refused leave to appeal by the Immigration Appeal Tribunal, and then sought a review of that refusal under the Nationality, Immigration and Asylum Act 2002.

That petition was considered and dismissed by Lady Cosgrove, who is Jewish. On appeal, it was not suggested that Lady Cosgrove could not be impartial simply because she was Jewish. Rather, the argument ran that, by virtue of her membership of the International Association of Jewish

[21] [2008] 1 WLR 2416. See SC Styles, 'Judicial Impartiality: Involvement, Opinion and the Judicial Oath' (2009) 13(2) *Edinburgh Law Review* 312.

Lawyers and Jurists, she 'gave the appearance of being the kind of supporter of Israel who could not be expected to take an impartial view of a petition for review concerning a claim for asylum based on the petitioner's support for the Palestinian Liberation Organisation'.[22] It might be said, in passing, that Association has included Justices of the Supreme Court of the United States, and Lord Woolf of the House of Lords is an Honorary Deputy President.

Counsel for the appellant pointed to the fact that Lady Cosgrove had received various articles in the Association's journal, and had not disassociated herself from the views expressed in them. Hence, or so the argument ran, the fair-minded external observer would identify Lady Cosgrove's views 'from the company that she kept in an association whose President expressed extreme pro-Israeli sentiments.'[23]

Their Lordships were not satisfied that there was any 'connection' between the articles and Lady Cosgrove's own unknown views. Nor would the fair-minded and informed observer make any such imputation. In these respects, the claims of 'association' were very like those rejected by the New Zealand Court of Appeal in *Muir*.[24]

Helow is helpful on the issue of how the fair-minded and informed observer should be conceived. Lord Hope of Craighead, in a passage which is worth repeating in full, said:[25]

> The fair-minded and informed observer is a relative newcomer among the select group of personalities who inhabit our legal village and are available to be called upon when a problem arises that needs to be solved objectively. Like the reasonable man whose attributes have been explored so often in the context of the law of negligence, the fair-minded observer is a creature of fiction. Gender-neutral (as this is a case where the complainer and the person complained about are both women, I shall avoid using the word 'he'), she has attributes which many of us might struggle to attain to.
>
> The observer who is fair-minded is the sort of person who always reserves judgment on every point until she has seen and fully understood both sides of the argument. She is not unduly sensitive or suspicious, as Kirby J observed in *Johnson v Johnson* (2000) 201 CLR 488, 509, para 53. Her approach must not be confused with that of the person who has brought the complaint. The 'real possibility' test ensures that there is this measure of detachment. The assumptions that the complainer makes are not to be attributed to the observer unless they can be justified objectively. But she is not complacent either. She knows that fairness requires that a judge must be, and must be seen to be, unbiased. She knows that judges, like anybody else, have their weaknesses. She will not shrink from the conclusion, if it can be justified objectively, that things that they have said or done

[22] ibid [13] (Lord Rodger of Earlsferry).
[23] ibid [16].
[24] Above n 8, [96].
[25] Above n 21, [1]–[3].

> or associations that they have formed may make it difficult for them to judge the case before them impartially.
>
> Then there is the attribute that the observer is 'informed'. It makes the point that, before she takes a balanced approach to any information she is given, she will take the trouble to inform herself on all matters that are relevant. She is the sort of person who takes the trouble to read the text of an article as well as the headlines. She is able to put whatever she has read or seen into its overall social, political or geographical context. She is fair-minded, so she will appreciate that the context forms an important part of the material which she must consider before passing judgment.

THE POSITION OUTSIDE THE UK IN THE BRITISH COMMONWEALTH

Reference has already been made to *Webb v R*, the Australian authority which has been authoritative in realigning the test for apparent bias in that jurisdiction.[26]

Recently, in *Muir*, the New Zealand Court of Appeal expressly adopted *Webb* and rejected *Gough*, holding that the court should make a two stage inquiry.[27] First, it is necessary, by rigorous inquiry, to establish the actual circumstances that have a direct bearing on the suggestion that the judge was, or may be seen to be, biased. The second inquiry is to ask whether those circumstances, as established, might lead a fair-minded lay observer to reasonably apprehend that the judge might not bring an impartial mind to the resolution of the case.

In Canada, a 'reasonable apprehension of bias' test has been well established since at least 1978.[28] More recently, in *R v S (RD)*, the majority of the Supreme Court of Canada restated the relevant considerations in these terms:[29]

> Impartiality can be described as a state of mind in which the adjudicator is disinterested in the outcome and is open to persuasion by the evidence and submissions. In contrast, bias denotes a state of mind that is in some way predisposed to a particular result or that is closed with regard to particular issues. Whether a decision-maker is impartial depends on whether the impugned conduct gives rise to a reasonable apprehension of bias. Actual bias need not be established because it is usually impossible to determine whether the decision-maker approached the matter with a truly biased state of mind.

26 Above n 14.

27 Above n 8, [62].

28 See *Committee for Justice & Liberty v Canada (National Energy Board)* [1978] 1 SCR 369; and P Bryden, 'Legal Principles Concerning the Disqualification of Judges' (2003) 82 *Canadian Bar Review* 555.

29 [1997] 3 SCR 484. For convenience, the headnote, which appears accurate and which summarises lengthy judgments, is adopted.

> The apprehension of bias must be a reasonable one held by reasonable and right-minded persons, applying themselves to the question and obtaining thereon the required information. The test is what would an informed person, viewing the matter realistically and practically—and having thought the matter through—conclude. This test contains a two-fold objective element: the person considering the alleged bias must be reasonable and the apprehension of bias itself must also be reasonable in the circumstances of the case. Further the reasonable person must be an informed person, with knowledge of all the relevant circumstances, including the traditions of integrity and impartiality that form a part of the background and apprised also of the fact that impartiality is one of the duties the judges swear to uphold. The reasonable person should also be taken to be aware of the social reality that forms the background to a particular case, such as societal awareness and acknowledgement of the prevalence of racism or gender bias in a particular community. The jurisprudence indicates that a real likelihood or probability of bias must be demonstrated and that a mere suspicion is not enough. The existence of a reasonable apprehension of bias depends entirely on the facts. The threshold for such a finding is high and the onus of demonstrating bias lies with the person who is alleging its existence. The test applies equally to all judges, regardless of their background, gender, race, ethnic origin, or any other characteristic.
>
> The requirement for neutrality does not require judges to discount their life experiences. Whether the use of references to social context is appropriate in the circumstances and whether a reasonable apprehension of bias arises from particular statements depends on the facts. A very significant difference exists between cases in which social context is used to ensure that the law evolves in keeping with changes in social reality and cases, such as this one, where social context is apparently being used to assist in determining an issue of credibility.

The test for bias in South African law was set as a 'reasonable suspicion' of bias in *BTR Industries South Africa (Pty) Ltd v Metal and Allied Workers' Union*.[30] This was confirmed by the Constitutional Court in a judicial recusal case, *S v Basson*.[31]

THE POSSIBLE CATEGORIES OF APPARENT BIAS

British Commonwealth courts have not seen it as appropriate to lay down precise categories as to when bias might be said to arise. Rather, courts have tended to mark out areas which potentially give rise to concern in a more broad-based way.

[30] *BTR Industries South Africa (Pty) Ltd v Metal and Allied Workers' Union* 1992 (3) SA 673.

[31] *S v Basson* 2005 (12) BCLR 1192.

For instance, four overlapping categories of cases of appearance of bias were identified by Deane J in *Webb v R*:[32]

(a) disqualification by interest, where some direct or indirect interest in the proceedings, whether pecuniary or otherwise, gives rise to a reasonable apprehension of prejudice, partiality or prejudgement;
(b) disqualification by conduct, including published statements, either in the course of, or outside, the proceedings;
(c) disqualification by association, where the apprehension of prejudgment or other bias results from some direct or indirect relationship, experience or contact with a person or persons interested in, or otherwise involved in, the proceedings;
(d) disqualification by extraneous information, where knowledge of some prejudicial but inadmissible fact or circumstance gives rise to the apprehension of bias.

More recently, the New Zealand Court of Appeal has suggested in *Muir*:[33]

> It is not possible or desirable to create a catalogue of disqualifiers for Judges in which a reasonable apprehension of bias may arise, but some broad principles can be stated. First, a Judge should not decide a case on purely personal considerations. Secondly, there should not reasonably be room for a perception that the Judge will decide the case on anything but the evidence in front of him or her. Thirdly, a Judge must be in a position to consider all potentially relevant arguments. Fourthly, there may conceivably be a series of events or rulings which reasonably warrant an inference that the challenged Judge's perception is warped in some way.

It is unlikely and, in the view of appellate courts, undesirable that a tight series of categories should be developed. Rather, it is a question of applying the general principles evolved by the courts to the circumstances of a particular case. Here again, context is all.

WHO DECIDES?

A matter of the greatest significance is who applies these principles as evolved. Is it to be the impugned judge, or a substituted judge, or what? More will be said on this issue later in this work, but it is important to appreciate at this point what the working position is in the common law world.

Without any real discussion in the cases in the British Commonwealth, the practice has been that it is the judge who is sought to be recused who determines this issue.

[32] Above n 14, 74.
[33] Above n 8, [64].

That present practice is reflected in the suggested disqualification procedure evolved by the Australasian Chief Justices[34] which plainly rests on the proposition that the application should be directed to the impugned judge, and it is that judge who should determine it.

However, given the experience of *Pinochet (No 2)*, the then Lord Chancellor, Lord Irvine, was moved to suggest that future decisions on potential bias in the House of Lords should be collectively taken, with the panel of judges addressing the issue of bias before the hearing, with the Law Lord in the chair making the final decision.[35]

As we will see in later chapters, the same idea—that the impugned judge should not decide—has been raised in other contexts.

THE APPLICATION OF THE REFORMULATED TEST

How well have judges done in the field with the test which has been formulated around the British Commonwealth, broadly in the same direction, in recent years? It is of course relatively early days yet. It takes a certain amount of time for a sufficient number of cases to emerge, let alone go on appeal, with the benefit of such further observations as fall at that level. Some observations can however be made.

In England, Atrill has suggested:[36]

> The English courts have embraced the observer test enthusiastically. The cases have focused on considering the appropriate level of knowledge to be imputed to the 'informed' observer. In particular, his knowledge of law and legal customs has been considered to be detailed.

As an illustration, Atrill refers in particular to *Taylor v Williamson*,[37] in which a trial judge had issued a preliminary judgment to the parties, expressed to be subject to alteration, before hearing final submissions from counsel. In the English Court of Appeal, Clarke LJ objected to the suggestion that the judge's mind might have appeared to have been made up, and was prepared to impute to the relevant observer knowledge of a recently reformed and highly technical procedural rule, as well as the cases interpreting that provision and its predecessor. Quite apart from knowledge of the substantive law as such, in *Sengupta v Holmes*, the observer was taken to be aware of the mechanics of courtroom procedure

[34] See app A.

[35] See K Malleson, 'Judicial Bias and Disqualification after *Pinochet (No 2)*' (2000) 63 *Modern Law Review* 119, 126. The open letter which Lord Irvine sent to Lord Browne-Wilkinson was released to the press: see *The Guardian* (London 29 December 1998) 2.

[36] S Atrill, 'Who is the "Fair-minded and informed Observer"? Bias after *Magill*' (2003) 62 *Cambridge Law Journal* 279, 280.

[37] *Taylor v Williamson* [2002] EWCA Civ 1380 (CA).

and the way in which judges 'test' their views by sometimes stating an opinion at the outset.[38]

In Atrill's view:[39]

> The observer test adopted in *Magill* has proved to be difficult to apply. Although capable of flexibility, the formulation of the test has tempted courts to apply the test literally and detached from the competing policy objectives, producing a confusing and conflicting jurisprudence. A re-affirmation that a more sophisticated balancing approach is inherent in the test would accord better with related concepts in English public law and in the [European Court of Human Rights], and improve the coherence of this fundamental and highly visible form of protection.

The Supreme Court of Canada has recently had to deal with several difficult cases in relation to the apparent bias test and the perspective of the relevant observer.

In *R v S (RD)*,[40] the appellant R was a young person charged with assault on a police officer. At the trial, the appellant gave evidence in his own defence and the only Crown evidence was from the police officer who was allegedly assaulted. The trial judge gave judgment immediately after closing arguments, acquitting the appellant. In the course of her judgment, the trial judge said:[41]

> The Crown says, well, why would the officer say that events occurred the way in which he has relayed them to the Court this morning. I am not saying that the Constable has misled the court, although police officers have been known to do that in the past. I am not saying that the officer overreacted, but certainly police officers do overreact, particularly when they are dealing with non-white groups. That to me indicates a state of mind right there that is questionable. I believe that probably the situation in this particular case is the case of a young police officer who overreacted. I do accept the evidence of [R.D.S.] that he was told to shut up or he would be under arrest. It seems to be in keeping with the prevalent attitude of the day. At any rate, based upon my comments and based upon all the evidence before the court I have no other choice but to acquit.

It should be said that the context of the case did involve an unfortunate history of anti-African racism in Nova Scotia, Canada which had been documented in a very high profile and recent Royal Commission into the prosecution of Mr Donald Marshall.[42]

One of the grounds raised on the appeal was whether the judge's comments could cause a reasonable observer to apprehend bias on her part.

[38] *Sengupta v Holmes* [2002] EWCA Civ 1104 (CA).

[39] Above n 36, 289.

[40] Above n 29.

[41] In relation to the conduct of the trial, see RF Devlin, 'We Can't Go On Together With Suspicious Minds; Judicial Bias and Racialized Perspective in *R v RDS*' (1995) 18 *Dalhousie Law Journal* 408.

[42] Nova Scotia Royal Commission, *Royal Commission on the Donald Marshall Jr Prosecution* (Halifax, The Commission, 1989).

There were distinct differences of opinion on the nine judge Supreme Court of Canada, but in the result the judgment of the Nova Scotia Court of Appeal was set aside and the decision of the trial judge dismissing the charges was restored. The facts of the case, and the kind of remarks the judge made, point to a very troubling issue, which could be approached in a variety of ways. However, in the view of the majority of the Supreme Court, they did not amount to bias in this instance. Perhaps more disturbing were the rather obvious 'fair trial' issues, which did not attract comment.

In 2003, the Supreme Court of Canada faced another difficult case in *Wewaykum Indian Band v Canada*.[43] The context there was that in 1985 and 1989 respectively two Indian bands instituted legal proceedings against each other and the Crown. Each band claimed exclusive entitlement to two reserves on Vancouver Island. The actions were dismissed at trial and that result was upheld in the Federal Court of Appeal of Canada. In December 2002, in reasons written by Binnie J with the concurrence of other members of the Supreme Court, that Court dismissed the bands' appeals.

Thereafter, one band made an access to information request to the federal Department of Justice. It sought copies of all records to, from or which made reference to Binnie J concerning the bands' claims against the Crown. This was because Binnie J had been a (federal) Associate Deputy Minister of Justice from 1982 to 1986. As such he had been responsible for all litigation involving the government of Canada, except tax matters and cases in Quebec. He had supervisory authority over thousands of cases.

The Department of Justice located a number of internal memoranda which indicated that at least in late 1985 and early 1986, Mr Binnie (as he then was) had received some information concerning the Campbell River band's claim and that indeed he had attended a meeting where the claim was discussed. At that point, the Crown filed a motion in the Supreme Court seeking directions as to any steps which should properly be taken. Binnie J recused himself from any further proceedings in the matter. He filed a statement setting out that he had no recollection of personal involvement in the case.

The bands jointly sought an order setting aside the court's judgment. It was accepted by all the litigants that actual bias was not an issue. They also accepted, without reservation, Binnie J's statement that he had no recollection of personal involvement in the case. The point at issue was simply whether his involvements in 1985 and 1986 could have given rise to a reasonable apprehension of bias under the Canadian test.

The Supreme Court of Canada explicitly held that neither Binnie J's past status as Associate Deputy Minister nor his long-standing interest in matters involving First Nations was by itself sufficient to justify his disqualification. The court examined the documentary records closely. The factors that appear

[43] *Wewaykum Indian Band v Canada* [2003] 2 SCR 259.

to have weighed most heavily with the court were that the case was historic, and that Binnie J's involvement in the dispute was 'confined to a limited supervisory and administrative role'.[44] The judge was never counsel of record and played no active role after the claim was filed, neither did he plan litigation strategy. The views attributed to Binnie J earlier on had been made in the context of the wider implications of the negotiation process, and not in the context of this litigation. The issue involved in this case was not unique to it, but was an issue of general application to existing reserves in British Columbia. The court gave significant weight to the (accepted) statement by Binnie J that he had no recollection of his involvement in the case ('because it is a factor that the reasonable person would properly consider'[45] and it therefore makes bias or its apprehension improbable). Further, 'the reasonable person, viewing the matter realistically would not come to the conclusion that the ... role played by Binnie J in this file, over 15 years ago, affected his ability, even unconsciously, to remain impartial in these appeals.'[46]

In a third recent Canadian Supreme Court case, *Mugesera v Canada (Minister of Citizenship and Immigration)*,[47] the context was a deportation order for Mr Mugesera and members of his family. The complaints advanced by the appellants to the Supreme Court of Canada were extraordinary and extreme.

The unfortunate allegation was that, strongly influenced by Jewish individuals and organisations, the relevant Ministers of the Crown had decided to appeal a judgment of the Federal Court of Appeal of Canada, and have Mr Mugesera deported 'at all costs'. To this end it was said that the current Minister of Justice had allegedly plotted to have one of the two newly appointed members of the Supreme Court of Canada appointed. That judge voluntarily recused, but then it was said that the mere presence on the court of a judge whose spouse chaired the Law Crimes Committee of the Canadian Jewish Congress, which was an intervenor in the case at bar, would necessarily impair or be seen to impair the ability of the balance of the members of the court to remain impartial.

The application was, with respect, appropriately described by the court as 'unprofessional and unacceptable'.[48] It constituted a systematic and abusive attack on the integrity of the judges of the Supreme Court. But on the particular point of the position of the court collectively, it was said:[49]

> if there is a duty on the part of one member of our Court to recuse him or herself, it is an astounding proposition to suggest that the same duty automatically attaches to the rest of the Court or compromises the integrity of the whole Court.

[44] ibid [3].
[45] ibid [89].
[46] ibid [90].
[47] *Mugesera v Canada (Minister of Citizenship and Immigration)* [2005] 2 SCR 91.
[48] ibid [16].
[49] ibid [15].

In the New Zealand case of *Muir*,[50] yet another post-judgment attack was made on a High Court judge's conduct after judgment had been delivered in very complex tax litigation in that jurisdiction. Apparent bias in that case was said to have arisen out of the fact that the judge had an interest in another New Zealand forestry venture and his 'association' with certain professional advisors about forestry interests.

The court noted that the suggestion being advanced was that these professional advisors (known to the judge) 'must have voiced (or will possibly voice) their antipathy towards the appellant Dr Muir' arising out of certain matters the judge had canvassed with them. The court noted that the allegation was no more nor less than that the judge did 'listen to scuttlebutt' out of court or that, even if he did not, that is how it would look to a reasonable member of the public. As to those propositions, the court said:[51]

> We reject [them]. Judges and members of the public alike are bombarded with scuttlebutt, but Judges and juries are formally required to abjure from having any regard to it in their professional role, and do so. It is probably necessary to experience professionally the weight with which this duty falls on a judicial officer to appreciate fully its force. The reply, 'well, that is what it might look like' fails to give proper weight to the requirement that something must 'reasonably' appear to be so to the informed observer. We agree with Kirby J in *Johnson v Johnson* (2000) 201 CLR 488 at [53] that 'a reasonable member of the public is neither complacent nor unduly sensitive or suspicious'. That statement was approved of by Lord Steyn (for their Lordships) in *Lawal v Northern Spirit Ltd* [2004] 1 All ER 187 at 193. The informed observer will not, for instance, lightly accept that a Judge has put aside his or her professional oath, or indeed his or her professional training (for as everybody knows, a vast amount of time in litigation is taken up with sifting and weighing 'facts' in evidence).

These sorts of cases are illustrative of the worrying trend around the British Commonwealth in the last several years: once the bar of the apparent bias test was 'lowered', the legal profession has too often endeavoured to impugn a significant judgment after the event, by investigating the judge's private affairs to see whether there might be something which can possibly 'tip up' the judgment. To a real extent such events can be diverted by full disclosure by the judge prior to trial of anything that might conceivably bear on it. But in Dr Muir's case, both the judge and the case management system had been carefully structured to try and avoid any such possibility. Yet claims of bias were still advanced on appeal after delivery of the trial court judgment.[52] In short, in the most difficult cases, the problem has been less with identifying who the reasonable observer is, and rather more with

[50] Above n 8.

[51] ibid [96].

[52] See, in Australia, *Johnson v Johnson* (2000) 201 CLR 488; and G Pesce, 'Disqualification for Judges—The 'Reasonable Man' Test Renamed' (1996) 70 *Australian Law Journal* 484.

the practical consequences of the bar's too ready mounting of personal attacks on the judiciary. This is an unattractive feature of contemporary advocacy.

THE EFFECT OF HUMAN RIGHTS LEGISLATION

For the United Kingdom, the Human Rights Act 1998 brought many ECHR rights into domestic law, including Article 6 as to the provision of a fair trial. Article 6(1) provides that:

> In the determination of his civil rights and obligations or of any criminal charge against him, everyone is entitled to a fair and public hearing within a reasonable time by an independent and impartial tribunal established by law. Judgment shall be pronounced publicly but the press and the public may be excluded from all or part of the trial in the interests of morals, public order or national security in a democratic society, where the interests of juveniles or the protection of the private life of the parties so require, or to the extent strictly necessary in the opinion of the court in special circumstances where publicity would prejudice the interests of justice.

Bills of Rights adopted around the British Commonwealth to date also include like provisions. For instance, under section 25(a) of the New Zealand Bill of Rights Act 1990, in matters of criminal law, there is a right to a fair and public hearing by an independent and impartial court; and in section 27—the 'right to justice' provision of that statute—there is a right to the observance of the principles of natural justice in other matters, which undoubtedly also encompasses the proposition that judges must be independent and impartial. There are similar sections in the Canadian Charter of Rights in section 11(d) (the fair and public hearing provision) and, to a lesser extent, section 7 (the fundamental justice provision).[53]

It has been suggested that the common law standards relating to bias and those under Article 6 are the same.[54] The present authors of *De Smith's Judicial Review* suggest that 'there certainly is no significant difference between them and they are likely in any event to converge.'[55]

Nevertheless, there is surely much more to be said in this area. First, there was powerful, and with respect justified, criticism of the failure of the

[53] For a discussion of the distinction between natural justice and fundamental justice provisions in New Zealand and Canada respectively, see G Huscroft, 'The Right to Justice' in P Rishworth, G Huscroft, S Optican and R Mahoney (eds), *The New Zealand Bill of Rights* (Melbourne, OUP, 2003) 753, 755.

[54] In *Lawal v Northern Spirit Ltd* [2004] 1 All ER 187 (HL), Lord Steyn stated that the purpose of the modification of the common law test of bias in *Porter v Magill* was to bring the common law rule into line with the Strasbourg jurisprudence (at [14]).

[55] H Woolf, J Jowell and A Le Sueur, *De Smith's Judicial Review*, 6th edn (London, Sweet & Maxwell, 2007) 536. See also A Zuckerman, *Zuckerman on Civil Procedure: Principles of Practice*, 2nd edn (London, Sweet & Maxwell, 2006) 72.

House of Lords to take on board sufficiently the human rights dimension of recusal law; in the High Court of Australia, there has been a failure (apart from Kirby J) to consider it at all.[56] The House of Lords in *Pinochet (No 2)* was described as having 'missed a great opportunity to provide leadership' due to its dearth of discussion on ECHR jurisprudence.[57] However, in fairness, *Porter v Magill*[58] has since ameliorated differences between English law and ECHR.

Secondly, Bill of Rights provisions do have the capacity to significantly redefine the relevant issues. An example of this sort of possibility can be found in two cases concerning 'racial bias'. In *US v Brown*, in what must be one of the most appalling judicial statements of all time, the judge had openly said (prior to trial) that he was 'going to get that nigger'.[59] One would have thought that to be an extreme example of actual bias. But equally, an observation of that kind must surely offend any fair trial provision in a human rights instrument. And, in the Canadian case of *R v S (RD)*,[60] where a judge referred to the existence of anti-black racism in Nova Scotia Canada as a factor going to whether a judge should recuse, the recusal dimension could more compellingly have been seen as a 'fair trial' issue. For the more direct issue in that case was whether the judge could appropriately even refer to such a factor, and if so on what evidential basis, in deciding whether to accept the evidence of the officer or the accused.

If the prism becomes that of a fair trial rather than bias, or some amalgam of the two, several matters of concern open up. For instance, there are

[56] Despite ratifying all the major international conventions promoting human rights (including the ICCPR), Australia has not enacted a Bill of Rights. H Charlesworth has described Australia's complacency about human rights as its 'greatest weakness': 'The Australian Reluctance About Rights' in P Alston (ed), *Towards an Australian Bill of Rights* (Canberra, ANU Centre for International and Public Law, 1994) 21. Kirby J argued that the provisions of Art 14(1) ICCPR and Art 6(1) ECHR reflect principles of universal application and should be taken into account in developing the Australian common law on recusal in *Johnson v Johnson* above n 52, 665–66. Yet Kirby J has identified the disconnect between his deployment of international law in Australia and the parochialism of the legal community at large in that jurisdiction: '[t]he provincialism of ... Australian lawyers ... is profoundly discouraging. In Australia they still require a boldness of spirit and a determination to escape the bog of provincial jurisdictionalism.' See M Kirby, 'Implications of the Internationalisation of Human Rights Law' in P Alston (ed), *Towards an Australian Bill of Rights* (Canberra, ANU Centre for International and Public Law, 1994) 298.

[57] P Catley and L Claydon, 'Pinochet, Bias and the European Convention on Human Rights' in D Woodhouse (ed), *The Pinochet Case: A Legal and Constitutional Analysis* (Oxford, Hart Publishing, 2000) 77.

[58] *Porter v Magill* [2002] 2 AC 357.

[59] *US v Brown* (1976) 539 F 2d 467, 468 (5th Cir). As one might expect, there was a context. 'Rap' Brown was a fiery civil rights speaker and leader of the Black Power movement in the late 1960s. His statements, such as 'Violence is as american [sic] as cherry pie', attracted national notoriety. He was usually defended by William Kunstler. See D Langum, *William M Kunstler: The Most Hated Lawyer in America* (New York, New York University Press, 1999) 88–96.

[60] Above n 29.

the downstream consequences. Normally, the lack of a fair trial raises a *post-judgment* appeal point. It is a downside from a human rights perspective that the complaint can only be made after trial. The upside is that the consideration of a fair trial is a rather broader matter than merely bias. *R v S (RD)* is a very good illustration of the problem. Just what a judge may refer to by way of his or her knowledge of contemporary events, and how these came into play in her view, is not just a matter of bias. What is at stake is the more difficult fair trial issue of what a judge may appropriately 'know' for judicial purposes.

New Zealand courts and commentators have to date been surprisingly sceptical that the Bill of Rights legislation in that jurisdiction will add anything in this subject-area. The relevant provisions are referred to at the level of first principle in *Muir*, rather than being determinative of outcome. In that case, the court said:[61]

> From at least the time of John Locke in the late seventeenth century, adjudication of legal disputes by impartial and independent Judges has been recognised as an essential underpinning of western society. That proposition—which was undoubtedly espoused by the common law—is today also found in specific instruments. For instance, under s 25 of the New Zealand Bill of Rights Act 1990, in matters of criminal law, there is a right to a fair and public hearing by an independent and impartial Court (reflecting Art 14(1) of the International Covenant on Civil and Political Rights); and in s 27 (the 'Right to Justice') of that statute there is a right to the observance of the principles of natural justice in other matters, which undoubtedly also encompasses the proposition that Judges must be independent and impartial.

Optican and Rishworth have opined that section 25(a) will have no added impact, given the existing common law on bias:[62]

> The requirement that tribunals hearing criminal charges be impartial is independently imposed by the common law rules about bias. Accordingly, s 25(a) will have no added impact ... Because of the unity between the 'impartial' requirement for trials imposed in s 25(a) and the underlying common law about bias, the cases in this field are often argued under the common law and not as Bill of Rights cases. There is overlap in any event with s 27(1)—the right to natural justice, which extends to criminal cases, and includes the right to a tribunal free of bias. Further, it is equally possible to approach the issue of bias through the concept of a 'fair trial', because a trial in which there is real danger of actual bias cannot be fair. But however these cases are approached, the position is the same as if the common law alone applied. *In the field of bias, the Bill of Rights has not added anything.*

[61] Above n 8, [32].

[62] S Optican and P Rishworth, 'Minimum Standards of Criminal Procedure for Trial, Sentencing, and Appeals' in P Rishworth, G Huscroft, S Optican and R Mahoney (eds), *The New Zealand Bill of Rights* (Melbourne, OUP, 2003) 673–74 (emphasis added).

However, Butler and Butler argue that international analogues will be relevant in the interpretation of section 25(a):[63]

> [Section] 25(a) has not been the subject of significant litigation in New Zealand and no comment was made upon it in the commentary to the White Paper equivalent provision, draft art 17(1)(a). It is likely that in this area Canadian Charter jurisprudence under s 11(d) of the Charter and ECHR case law under art 6(1) of the ECHR will prove relevant.

Nevertheless, Butler and Butler maintain that the common law in relation to bias prevails:[64]

> Section 25(a) of BORA does not dictate a different test to that adopted under the common law. It can be anticipated, therefore, that the substantive common law test for bias will continue to govern in this field.

The Bill of Rights made an appearance in a different recusal context in New Zealand in *Collier v Attorney-General*.[65] In that case, the appellant tried to 'poll' the appellate judges by questionnaire directed at any conflict of interest, prior discussion of the case with others, or membership of 'Religion of Islam, Judaism, Church of Scientology, Theosphical Society, Church of Latter Day Saints, Illuminati, Orange Lodge, Druids, Skull and Bones, Ku Klux Klan, or any society or organisation or group which requires oaths to be taken which would conflict with the judicial oath.' The Court of Appeal held that:[66]

> To invoke membership of any association listed in [these] questions as a sufficient basis for disqualifying a Judge from sitting would also be inconsistent with the unlawful discrimination provisions of the Human Rights Act 1993 and the New Zealand Bill of Rights Act 1990.

Thus, human rights can cut both ways when it comes to recusal jurisprudence: provided a Druid judge with a proclivity for freemasonry brings an open mind to adjudication, he is immune from attack; indeed, attack based on a judge's extra-curricular 'interests' might be regarded as tantamount to unlawful discrimination, on the authority of *Collier*.

The greatest significance of human rights provisions relating to a fair trial will surely lie in the area of the presently forbidden garden: that of the claim of judges to preside over their own recusal. Somewhat surprisingly, this area has not yet been pursued by counsel, perhaps because it is such a widespread practice that counsel think judges will not change.

63 A Butler and P Butler, *The New Zealand Bill of Rights Act: A Commentary* (Wellington, LexisNexis, 2005) 884.

64 ibid 898.

65 *Collier v A-G* [2002] NZAR 257 (CA).

66 ibid [24].

CONCLUSION

The present rules relating to actual bias have posed no real difficulties. The standard of proof required is very high, and as with allegations of fraud in the civil law, what is relied on must be strictly pleaded and strictly proved.

Apparent bias has, unsurprisingly, created much more in the way of difficulties. One criticism of the present principles relate in part to their vagueness and difficulty of application.

Secondly, there is a consequential concern. The test which has been predominantly adopted throughout the Commonwealth of a fair-minded and well informed observer is a 'second level' rule. Because it is a much less stiff rule than that of actual bias, the test unfortunately lends itself to forensic manoeuvring. There has been increasing concern as to the strategic deployment of apparent bias appeal grounds after an adverse decision. This is due to an unhappy perception on the part of too many members of the bar which requires a mechanical, 'clean slate' indication of judicial impartiality that fails to give sufficient weight to what appellate courts have steadily held, namely that impartiality does not require a totally empty mind. That said, it must be conceded in fairness that where the line is to be drawn is difficult, and context-specific.

Thirdly, the real sting of the criticism of the present apparent bias test is that it is too concerned with formality and appearance, and less concerned with actualities. Provided a judge overtly adopts the 'right' approach, strongly held beliefs, which may be conscious or unconscious, are not directly addressed.[67] At rock bottom, the argument is that what is involved here is a triumph of form over substance.[68]

Fourthly, against these sorts of concerns, it is appropriate to return to the difficult question as to whether the approach of the High Court of Australia in *Ebner*[69] was on a sounder footing in adopting a single standard for bias. Under that formulation, disqualification is no longer automatic and instead depends on the circumstances of each case. This gives rise to a context sensitive rule against bias. A court is required to 'articulate the connection between the alleged source of bias and the potential departure from impartiality'.[70] This involves assessing and evaluating the effect of the interest in question upon the decision maker. To adopt phraseology utilised earlier, the approach becomes one of a 'rule of reason'. The arguments for and against that approach have already been noted.

[67] For further discussion of unconscious bias, see ch 17.

[68] This criticism, cast more broadly, is at the center of EW Thomas, *The Judicial Process: Realism, Pragmatism, Practical Reasoning and Principles* (Cambridge, CUP, 2005).

[69] *Ebner v Official Trustee in Bankruptcy* (2001) 205 CLR 337.

[70] M Groves, 'The Rule Against Bias' in M Groves and HP Lee (eds), *Australian Administrative Law: Fundamentals, Principles and Doctrines* (Cambridge, CUP, 2007) 316, 320.

The practical problems inherent in standing on a single unitary standard in public law generally can be illustrated from the further High Court of Australia decision in *Minister for Immigration and Multicultural Affairs; ex p Jia*.[71] In that case, a Minister of the Crown spoke on a talk-back radio programme. He explained what it was that might lead him to conclude a person was not of good character for the purposes of migration legislation. Mr Jia had been convicted of several offences, some of which included the sort of behaviour the Minister referred to. Then, as it transpired, Mr Jia's case came before the Minister. The Minister made an adverse determination.

The issue for the High Court was whether the Minister's statement gave rise to a reasonable apprehension of bias. There was also a significant question as to whether the Minister's political activities (which actually required him to provide media interviews and discuss issues falling within his ministerial portfolio) could be taken into account in fashioning the requirements of the rule against bias.

Gleeson CJ and Gummow and Hayne JJ accepted that the principles applicable to judges should be *modified* when applied to the Minister. This is because great care had to be taken with respect to the political responsibilities of the Minister. In their view, there was no reason to conclude that the Australian Parliament intended to impose what might be termed the 'full blast' of standards to be imposed upon a judge, upon the Minister, 'and [indeed] every reason to conclude otherwise'!

This demonstrates the necessarily context sensitive nature of the rule against bias. Perhaps more significantly for administrative law in general, quite what that means for decision makers other than judges has left Australian law in what Groves has described as a 'state of flux',[72] and arguably contributes a further layer of uncertainty.

[71] *Minister for Immigration and Multicultural Affairs; ex p Jia* (2001) 205 CLR 507.
[72] Above n 70, 322.

6

Federal Recusal Law in the United States of America

INTRODUCTION

THERE ARE TWO very important federal recusal provisions in the United States Code—28 USC §§ 144 and 455—which are set out in full at Appendices B and C.[1] There are also statutory disqualification provisions in some states but it is beyond the scope and practicality of this monograph to address them as well.[2] Judicial recusal disputes are a 'growth industry' in the United States of America, and there is extensive case-law in this subject area.

In the United States, there are also far more extensive codes and model codes of judicial conduct than are to be found in the British Commonwealth jurisdictions. The pre-eminent one is the American Bar Association *Code of Judicial Conduct*.[3] It is therefore necessary when considering disqualification and recusal principles in the United States to take into account the way in which those codes are resorted to and the extent to which they affect the determination of cases.

It has been suggested that the current state of recusal law in the United States amounts to a 'vicious cycle'.[4] For instance, Frost suggests:[5]

> The development of the law of judicial disqualification in the United States has followed a recognisable pattern. First, Congress sets the standard governing when

[1] See DL Bassett, 'Judicial Disqualification in the Federal Appellate Courts' (2002) 87 *Iowa Law Review* 1213. A comprehensive report, published by the Federal Judicial Center in 2002, listed 230 reported federal cases as at that date: *Recusal: Analysis of Case Law under 28 USC §§ 455 and 144* (Tennessee, University Press of the Pacific, 2005). The monograph can also be downloaded from the Federal Judicial Center website <http://www.fjc.gov/public/pdf.nsf/lookup/recusal.pdf/$file/recusal.pdf> accessed 18 April 2009.

[2] For a thorough treatment of disqualification provisions and cases at the state level, see RE Flamm, *Judicial Disqualification: Recusal and Disqualification of Judges* (California, Banks and Jordan Law Publishing Co, 2007) 753–906.

[3] There is a very recent reworked American Bar Association *Model Code of Judicial Conduct* (2007).

[4] J Leubsdorf, 'Theories of Judging and Judge Disqualification' (1987) 62 *New York University Law Review* 237, 245.

[5] A Frost, 'Keeping up Appearances: A Process-Oriented Approach to Judicial Recusal' (2005) 53 *University of Kansas Law Review* 531, 538.

judges must remove themselves from sitting on cases in which they are not able, or might not be able, to be impartial. That standard is then narrowly construed by the judges who must apply it to decide whether they themselves should be disqualified from a case. Eventually, a particularly egregious situation arises in which a judge sits on a case when most outside observers think that she should have stepped aside. The situation comes to the attention of the press, the public, and ultimately Congress, which amends the law to provide stiffer standards for recusal. And then the whole process begins anew.

THE RELATIONSHIP BETWEEN THE FEDERAL STATUTES

Section 144 of 28 USC is entitled 'Bias or Prejudice of Judge'. Section 455 of 28 USC is entitled 'Disqualification of Justice, Judge, or Magistrate Judge'. It overlaps and substantially subsumes § 144.

However, although it is not obvious at first blush from a reading of the bare sections, § 144 is aimed exclusively at 'actual bias', in British Commonwealth parlance, while § 455 deals not only with actual bias and conflicts of interest, but also with the appearance of bias.

Section 144 only applies to federal district court judges and is best thought of as a peremptory disqualification mechanism. It enables a party to a proceeding to file an affidavit, which must be 'timely and sufficient', alleging that a judge has a personal bias or prejudice either against him or in favour of any adverse party. The affidavit must state the facts and the reasons for the belief that bias or prejudice exists. In such an event, the federal judge should proceed no further and another judge is to be assigned to hear the proceedings. But as we will see, this has been construed as not literally meaning that the party filing the affidavit has a power of veto.

Section 455 covers '*any* justice, judge, or magistrate judge of the United States' (emphasis added), stipulating that these persons must disqualify themselves of their own motion in any proceedings where their impartiality might reasonably be questioned. While § 455(a) deals exclusively with the appearance of partiality in any circumstance, § 455(b) deals with conflicts of interest in specific instances.

For completeness, there is a third federal recusal statute dating back to 1948 (28 USC § 47) which applies only to appellate judges or trial judges who are sitting by designation on appellate panels. Section 47 provides that '[n]o judge shall hear or determine an appeal from the decision of a case or issue tried by him'.

THE PEREMPTORY CHALLENGE PROCEDURE IN THE DISTRICT COURT

Before the Judicial Code of 1911, a litigant in the federal courts who believed that the assigned judge had demonstrated bias against him or her had no recourse for relief.[6] This was thought to be quite inappropriate. Orfield cites the Congressional debates in 1910 and 1911 as showing 'a surprising unanimity' in favour of a § 144-style peremptory challenge remedy.[7] The sponsor of the statute was a Congressional representative from Indiana who was quite specific as to the intended meaning of the statute. When asked if the judge would have a discretion he replied: 'it provides that the judge shall proceed no further with the case. The filing of the affidavit deprives him of further jurisdiction in the case.'[8]

Notwithstanding what seems to have been the clear intentions of the sponsor of the bill, and the actual language of the statute, a series of decisions quickly eradicated the intent of a peremptory challenge which lay behind the statute. The decision of the United States Supreme Court in *Berger v US* has been particularly influential.[9] In that case, the petitioners, who were accused of espionage, filed an affidavit for the recusal of the trial judge on the grounds that the judge was biased against German Americans. They deposed that the federal judge had stated, among other things, that '[o]ne must have a very judicial mind, indeed, not to be prejudiced against the German Americans in this country. Their hearts are reeking with disloyalty'.[10] The judge, who refused to recuse himself, then presided at a trial where the defendants not only were convicted, but each was sentenced to 20 years in prison!

While the Supreme Court concluded that the trial judge could not himself decide the truth of the allegations of bias, it did permit the judge to review the application for disqualification and the accompanying affidavit to ensure that these were legally 'sufficient' before being required to recuse himself. To be legally 'sufficient' rather than 'frivolous', the Supreme Court held that the affidavit 'must give fair support to the charge of a bent of mind that may prevent or impede impartiality of judgment.'[11]

Hence, despite Congress's clear intention that the affidavit would have a jurisdiction-depriving character, the effect of *Berger* was that trial judges were given a very large measure of discretion in deciding whether to disqualify themselves.

In 1948, Congress recodified § 144 without significant change, but made two distinctive changes to § 455.[12] First, the requirement that a party initiate disqualification proceedings was eliminated, which converted § 455 from a peremptory challenge provision to a 'self-enforcing obligation.'[13]

[6] See JP Frank, 'Disqualification of Judges' (1947) 56 *Yale Law Journal* 605, 609.

[7] LB Orfield, 'Recusation of Federal Judges' (1967) 17 *Buffalo Law Review* 799, 804 citing H Putnam, 'Recusation' (1923) 9 *Cornell Law Quarterly* 1, 10.

[8] DL Bassett, above n 1, 1224.

[9] *Berger v US* (1921) 255 US 22.

[10] ibid 28.

[11] ibid 33–34.

[12] DL Bassett, above n 1, 1225.

[13] RE Flamm, above n 2, 740.

Secondly, the adjective 'substantial' was added before the word 'interest' in articulating the grounds for invoking § 455, thereby reducing the likelihood of recusal. Bassett has noted that 'the impact of these amendments was to grant judges vast discretion to use their own subjective opinions to decide whether recusal was necessary.'[14]

One aspect of American recusal jurisprudence that has received very significant attention in the federal case law is the notion of a duty to sit, already mentioned in relation to British Commonwealth jurisprudence. It is plain that Congress's intention in amending § 455, just as it was to eliminate a 'substantial interest' requirement, was to get rid of the 'duty to sit' idea. But that Congressional intent has been substantially ignored.[15]

THE ETHICAL CODES OF CONDUCT

The American Bar Association's *Code of Judicial Conduct* and the new *Model Code of Judicial Conduct* both stress the importance of the 'appearance' of justice.[16] Canons 3E and 3C of the Codes respectively deal with recusal and disqualification, setting out a general standard of disqualification from any proceeding 'in which the judge's impartiality might reasonably be questioned'. Canon 1 of the 2007 *Model Code* states that a judge should uphold and promote the independence, integrity, and impartiality of the judiciary, and shall avoid impropriety and the appearance of impropriety.

The Codes themselves are relatively detailed documents, but the federal judiciary has made little reference to them in their decisions. Generally speaking, courts are not of course formally bound by these ethical codes, although some states give them the force of law. They could, however, have been expected to carry real weight. Instead, in the view of United States commentators, judges have tended to focus almost exclusively on the statutory provisions in § 144 and § 455.

Part of the difficulty here is that the ABA *Model Code* itself carries no formal force until adopted. 49 of the 50 states adopted some form of the former ABA *Model Code*, although there are differences in the power accorded to the particular rules.[17] Likewise, the Judicial Conference of the United States, which formally adopted the *Code of Judicial Conduct*, holds no statutory grant of authority to enact binding ethical rules, which

[14] DL Bassett, above n 1, 1225.

[15] See RJ Litteneker, 'Disqualification of Federal Judges for Bias or Prejudice' (1978–79) 46 *University of Chicago Law Review* 236, 243.

[16] For an overview of the iterative changes to the *Code of Judicial Conduct*, see MI Harrison, 'The 2007 ABA Model Code of Judicial Conduct: Blueprint for a Generation of Judges' (2007) 28 *Justice System Journal* 257. The author was the chair of the ABA Commission that developed the 2007 *Model Code*, in its first comprehensive revision since 1990.

[17] LW Abramson, 'Appearance of Impropriety: Deciding when a Judge's Impartiality 'Might Reasonably be Questioned'' (2000) 14 *Georgetown Journal of Legal Ethics* 55, 55.

accordingly can be of 'persuasive weight' only.[18] That said, the provisions of Canons 3E and 3F of the former *Model Code* were quite close to the provisions of § 455. Indeed, it seems that Congress in fact intended that § 455 should conform closely to the *Model Code*.[19]

The short point, for present purposes, is that by treating the professional ethical codes as having no more than persuasive weight, courts can create their own interpretation of the statutory proscriptions in § 455, sometimes with bizarre results.[20] For instance, in *Carter v West Publishing Co*,[21] a judge declined to recuse himself from a case where he had previously travelled to resort-style locations at the defendant's expense, allegedly was personal friends with the defendant's top executives, and even appeared before a legislative sub-committee to advocate a product made by one of the defendants. The judge in that case relied on § 455 and referred, it may be thought perversely, to the *Code of Judicial Conduct* which permits judges to participate in 'extra-judicial activities', albeit he did not refer to the appearance of bias standard in Canon 3![22]

THE TERMS OF 28 USC § 455

Section 455(a) is a general mandatory provision: 'any justice, judge or magistrate judge of the United States *shall* disqualify himself in any proceeding in which his impartiality might reasonably be questioned' (emphasis added).

Section 455(b) then particularises certain circumstances under which a judge is impugned: where that judge has a personal bias or prejudice concerning a party, or personal knowledge of disputed evidentiary facts concerning the proceeding; where the judge has served as a lawyer in the matter in controversy; where the judge has come into contact with the matter while in government employment; where his or her spouse or minor child has a financial interest in the matter in controversy or is a party to the proceeding; and a prohibition of relationships, down to the third degree.

It will be observed that a 'financial interest' in § 455(b)(4) means ownership of a legal or equitable interest, however small, or a relationship as director, adviser, or other active participant in the affairs of a party. That prohibition applies 'only if the outcome of the proceeding could substantially

18 See *Re Cargill* (1995) 66 F 3d 1256, 1267 (1st Cir) (Campbell J).
19 DL Bassett, above n 1, 1230.
20 ibid 1232.
21 (1999) No 99–11959-EE, 1999 WL 994997 (11th Cir).
22 In that case, Judge Tjoflat said: 'what a strange creature plaintiffs seek to create—a ... friendless thing, extremely detached from the ordinary circumstances of everyday life, hermited away on some mountaintop where he can be certain that no person could possibly influence his juridicial scribblings' (at 22).

affect the value of the interest', but the proviso extends only to a mutual insurance company or a similar proprietary interest.

Waiver may only be accepted under the general prohibition in § 455(a), where it is preceded by a 'full disclosure on the record of the basis for disqualification'. Disqualification is not required where a judge can divest himself of a financial interest in a party (other than an interest that could be substantially affected by the outcome) prior to judgment.

A judge is required to inform himself about his personal and fiduciary financial interests and make a reasonable effort to inform himself about the personal financial interests of his spouse and minor children residing in his household (§ 455(c)).

THE TEST OF AN APPEARANCE OF BIAS

United States federal judges have faced the same difficulty as British Commonwealth judges under the head of an appearance of bias, as both objects and interpreters of the relevant test.

The standard rationale put forward for the appearance of bias test in the United States is the need for an unimpeachable judicial system in which the public can have confidence.[23]

Although § 455 on its face goes some distance prescriptively beyond the more flexible case law holdings in the British Commonwealth, it has not been as powerful a set of principles as might have been expected. One interpretative difficulty that arises under federal jurisprudence as a result of the structure of § 455 is that where a party resorts to the general prohibition in § 455(a), this seems to constitute a tacit concession that the more particularised grounds for believing a judge to be biased (under §455(b)) cannot be made out. However, this may be more of a drafting issue. A British Commonwealth statute drafter would almost certainly have provided a general prohibition, but then have stated that, without detraction from the generality of that statement, certain instances come within it.

A matter of greater difficulty in the United States, which will be discussed later in this work, is that the alleged bias must arise out of extra-judicial events.[24] This cuts out claims of bias arising from things occurring within the courtroom. The rationale for the distinction between judicial and personal or extra-judicial biases appears to rest upon a view of a judge's obligation to reach judicial conclusions on the proceedings before him or her. Further, a consistent judicial philosophy demands that a judge have certain preconceptions on matters of legal principle, even though that may disadvantage a party. However, as we discuss later in this work,

[23] RE Flamm, above n 2, 108–09.

[24] See ch 16 below.

outright personal animosity towards a party outside the four corners of the courtroom is impermissible.

As to the standpoint for determining an appearance of bias, there has been considerable debate in the United States cases as to whether questions about a judge's impartiality should be answered from the vantage point of the applicant party, the judge, or a 'reasonable person'. There is federal appellate authority for each of these propositions,[25] but the 'vast majority' of federal courts that have considered the question have said that the standard is an objective one: that 'a charge of partiality must be based on facts that would create a reasonable doubt concerning the judge's impartiality not in the mind of the judge or the litigant but in the mind of a reasonable, uninvolved observer.'[26] As in the contemporary British Commonwealth cases, there is an emphasis on the proposition that bias must ordinarily be viewed from the standpoint of not merely a reasonable observer, but a well-informed one.

WHO DECIDES?

The general practice in the United States, both in the federal and state jurisdictions, is that it is the judge to whom the application to recuse is directed who determines that application.[27]

In theory of course, there could be automatic or discretionary transfer of a recusal application but Litteneker has noted that 'the policy against automatic transfer is so firmly imbedded in court practice ... that it is sometimes seen as precluding *any* transfer' (emphasis added).[28] Indeed, the influential Washington DC Circuit has discouraged transfer, calling it 'at most permissive'.[29]

There are however some state statutes that specifically provide for transfer, generally on a discretionary basis. For instance, the State of Illinois has provided that the state or any defendant may move at any time for substitution of a judge for cause, supported by affidavit, in both civil and criminal cases.[30]

A good example of a case arising under that sort of provision is *People v Mercado*.[31] Mr Mercado had been convicted on drug charges (possession of a controlled substance, namely heroin) for which he had been tried, convicted and sentenced to 20 years imprisonment. One of the grounds of appeal to the Illinois appellate court was alleged trial judge prejudice. The

[25] RE Flamm, above n 2, 118–29.

[26] ibid 125–26.

[27] ibid 506. See also F James, GC Hazard Jnr and J Leubsdorf, *Civil Procedure*, 5th edn (Minnesota, West Publishing Co, 2001) 394.

[28] RJ Litteneker, above n 15, citing *US v Bell* (1965) 351 F 2d 868, 878 (6th Cir) *cert denied* (1966) 383 US 947.

[29] *US v Haldeman* (1976) 559 F 2d 31, 131 (DC Cir) (en banc) *cert denied* (1977) 431 US 933.

[30] See 737 ILCS 5/2 1001 (Civil); 735 ILCS 5/114–5 (Criminal).

[31] *People v Mercado* (1993) 614 NE 2d 284.

context of the application was that the trial judge had declined to appoint a Spanish speaking interpreter for the Latino defendant. There was clearly a strong clash between the trial judge and defendant's counsel. The judge had threatened counsel with committal for contempt, and he had even detained counsel in his chambers at one point. By now of course things had got worse: it was being said that the court's hostility with respect to counsel was likely to be visited on Mr Mercado.

An application was made to Judge Kelly to recuse himself. He declined. So an application followed under the Illinois Code. In fact, that application was heard by another judge (Judge Reyna) who ultimately declined it, and returned the case for trial to Judge Kelly. The appeal to the Illinois appellate court was dismissed.[32]

Another illustration of the day-to-day difficulties which can arise is *US v Zagari.*[33] There Mr Zagari faced a four count indictment for tax evasion. The allocated trial judge was Judge Conti, who was apparently known as a 'strong' sentencing judge. He was invited by counsel to recuse because of his reputation in the 'criminal business'. In that particular jurisdiction, there was no statutory substitution provision. So there was a petition for the writ of mandamus to the 9th Circuit Court of Appeals, on the basis that Mr Zagari would not get a fair hearing. The Court of Appeal granted a stay. Judge Conti, not deterred, thereupon asked that the matter of his disqualification be heard by a judge from outside his district. That occurred, and the recusal issue was heard by a senior district court judge, Judge Brewster, who ultimately determined that the allegations which had been raised 'were warped, unreasonable and exaggerated'.[34]

The overall position in the United States appears to be still heavily in favour of the judge who is sought to be impugned determining the application. To the extent that there has been an 'inroad' into that principle, it appears to be mainly under discretionary provisions, such as the Illinois Code, but even then, those exceptions raise their own kind of questions as to who should determine that application. The theoretical basis for this sort of provision rests on fair trial principles.

THE IMPACT OF THE UNITED STATES SUPREME COURT JURISPRUDENCE

Final appellate courts set the 'tone' for critical issues affecting the administration of justice in a given jurisdiction. Apart from pure questions of

[32] For further comment, see PW Tone, 'The Substitution of Judges in Illinois Criminal Cases' (1978) *Illinois Law Forum* 519.

[33] (1976) 419 F Supp 494.

[34] ibid 505.

constitutional law, these are arguably the most important issues that final appellate courts grapple with.

Notwithstanding an ostensibly more flexible test than is to be found in § 455, the House of Lords has, generally speaking, taken a very firm line in relation to recusal matters. On the other hand, federal courts, and particularly the United States Supreme Court, have been less firm than their Congressional mandate would seem to have required. It is appropriate to look further to some leading United States Supreme Court cases for illustrations of the difficulties this has given rise to.

As a matter of procedure, prior to the enactment of § 455, the question of whether a member of the United States Supreme Court should sit was treated as a matter for that judge alone to determine. Before what Professor Frank termed 'the Jewell Ridge incident',[35] disqualification had always been the prerogative of each individual justice and no member of the court had ever pronounced public judgment on the practice of another.

Jewell Ridge Coal Corporation v Local No 6167 United Mine Workers of America[36] raised some real concerns on this point. On a petition for rehearing, Justice Jackson considered that a petition which was addressed to all of the court for the disqualification of Justice Black was misconceived. He took the view that the court was entirely without power to exclude one of its members. He said:[37]

> The petition is addressed to all of the Court and must either be granted or denied in the name of the Court and on the responsibility of all of the Justices. In my opinion the complaint is one which cannot properly be addressed to the Court as a whole and for that reason I concur in denying it.
>
> No statute prescribes grounds upon which a Justice of this Court may be disqualified in any case. The Court itself has never undertaken by rule of Court or decision to formulate any uniform practice on the subject. Because of this lack of authoritative standards it appears always to have been considered the responsibility of each Justice to determine for himself the propriety of withdrawing in any particular circumstances. ...
>
> There is no authority known to me under which a majority of this Court has power under any circumstances to exclude one of its duly commissioned Justices from sitting or voting in any case.

The enactment of § 455 did not alter the 'law' in this respect.[38] Hence it remains the practice that the individual Supreme Court justice determines

[35] JP Frank, above n 6, 612.

[36] *Jewell Ridge Coal Corporation v Local No 6167 United Mine Workers of America* (1945) 325 US 161.

[37] (1945) 325 US 897.

[38] KH Nadelman described the status of the law as 'considered beyond doubt before 1948, and the changes of 1948 were not designed to alter the law on this point.' See 'Disqualification of Constitutional Court Judges for Alleged Bias' (1968) 52 *Judicature* 27, 28.

whether he or she will sit, a decision which is not subject to review.[39] Under current United States Supreme Court practice, when a justice has disqualified himself, there will appear at the end of the reported judgment a sentence saying that 'Justice Z took no part in the consideration or decision of the case'.

The giving of reasons for the course taken in relation to recusal, akin to Justice Scalia's Memorandum in *Cheney*, is a comparative rarity. Reasons were given by Justice Rehnquist (as he then was) in *Laird v Tatum*, because of the 'peculiar circumstances' of the case.[40] A statement was later made by Justice Rehnquist as Chief Justice[41] which was attached to the Supreme Court's Statement of Recusal Policy.[42] In *McGrath v Kristensen*,[43] Justice Jackson withdrew from a case with a brief statement, saying he wished his reasons 'to be a matter of record'.[44]

As to the actual number of recusals, Professor Henry Abraham of the University of Virginia has said:[45]

> The members of today's Supreme Court, unlike most members of Congress, are extremely cautious about even the faintest taint of conflict of interest, be it of a social, economic, personal or political nature. Among the Justices, 'When in doubt, do not sit' is a firmly established custom, called 'recusing', partially reinforced by two federal statues and a canon of the American Bar Association. This was not always so, particularly not in the early days of the Court—witness Marshall's refusal to disqualify himself in *Marbury v Madison* [(1803) 1 Cranch 137] in which he was personally and directly involved.

Recusal has been far from uncommon. For instance, in his first term on the court (1967–68), the then recently appointed Justice Thurgood Marshall frequently recused himself, largely because he had been a prominent civil rights attorney and also the Solicitor General of the United States. However, by the end of the first five months of that term, Justice Marshall had abstained in 31 of 44 formally decided cases. This led two senior Harvard law professors to enter a caveat against excessive recusing, on the basis that a tendency to recuse at the federal level was 'challenging the consistency and balance of our judicial system'.[46]

[39] See *Laird v Tatum* (1972) 409 US 824, n 7.

[40] ibid 824. Justice Rehnquist noted 'while neither the Court nor any Justice individually appears ever to have done so, I have determined that it would be appropriate for me to state the reasons which have led to my decision with respect to the respondent's motion.'

[41] (1993) 114 SCT 54.

[42] See app D.

[43] (1950) 340 US 162.

[44] See also JP Frank, 'Disqualification of Judges: In Support of the Bayh Bill' (1970) 35 *Law and Contemporary Problems* 43, 47–48.

[45] HJ Abraham, *The Judicial Process: An Introductory Analysis of the Courts of the United States, England, and France*, 7th edn (Oxford, OUP, 1998) 219–20.

[46] EN Griswold and E Gellhorn, '200 cases in which justices recused themselves' *The Washington Post* (Washington DC 18 October 1988) PA25.

As to the cause of recusals, it seems plain enough that certain justices of the Supreme Court frequently recuse themselves from cases because they own shares in one of the parties.[47]

That said, as might have been expected, in the United States the principal difficulties have arisen less with 'run of the mill' recusal situations than with politically charged, high profile cases.[48] Some of the particularly controversial situations leading to the amendment of § 455 have included the revelations during Judge Haynsworth's unsuccessful 1969 Supreme Court confirmation hearings that he had sat on five different cases in which he had a small financial interest. Then there was the United States Senate's rejection of Justice Fortas' nomination to the position of Chief Justice, on the basis that he had served as counsellor to the President while serving on the court.[49] During the Senate confirmation hearings, Justice Fortas admitted attending White House conferences concerning terribly sensitive matters facing the administration, such as the escalation of the Vietnam War, and domestic civil disturbances.[50]

The background to Justice Rehnquist's difficulties in *Laird v Tatum*[51] arose out of a constitutional challenge to the Army's surveillance of civilian political activity. While still serving in the Department of Justice, Justice Rehnquist had appeared as an expert witness at Senate hearings on that very subject. He had made a comment on the application of the law to the facts of *Laird v Tatum*, which at that time was progressing through a lower court. After a five–four loss in the Supreme Court, the respondents in *Laird v Tatum* filed an application that Justice Rehnquist recuse himself, and that the case be entirely reheard with eight justices.

It was in those circumstances that Justice Rehnquist issued a Memorandum, explaining his refusal to recuse himself.[52] He asserted that while he had been given some information about the case, he had no 'personal knowledge' of it.[53] He said that he had not been 'of counsel' nor substantially involved in it. Neither did he think his public statements and opinions on the law should lead him to recuse himself under the discretionary component of § 455. Justice Rehnquist's decision in this case is of particular interest because he openly acknowledged his recusal decision as 'a fairly debatable one'.[54] But he placed considerable emphasis on the 'duty to sit', a duty that is particularly compelling

[47] See T Mauro, 'Furor over Scalia-Cheney Trip Casts Light on Murky World of Recusals' (2004) 175 *New Jersey Law Journal* 732.

[48] DL Bassett, 'Recusal and the Supreme Court' (2005) 56 *Hastings Law Journal* 657.

[49] A Frost, above n 5, 545.

[50] JP MacKenzie, *The Appearance of Justice* (New York, Scribner, 1974) 71–76.

[51] Above n 39.

[52] ibid.

[53] ibid 827.

[54] ibid 836–37.

in the Supreme Court, where there is no substitute for a recused justice and where recusal would lead to the real possibility of affirmation by an equally divided Court.[55]

Justice Scalia, in his Memorandum relating to the *Cheney* case, similarly observed that a decision to recuse is 'effectively the same as casting a vote against the petitioner'.[56] What this suggests, as a matter of process, is that there is a world of difference between a final appellate court, such as the United States Supreme Court, in which there is no way of replacing the recused justice, and courts which can call upon a substitute judge in one way or another.

The Supreme Court Justices made an endeavour to clarify some matters in a Statement of Recusal Policy issued in 1993.[57] Seven justices—Justices Rehnquist, Stevens, Scalia, Thomas, O'Connor, Kennedy and Ginsburg—issued the joint press release; Chief Justice Roberts adopted the policy in November 2005, while Justices Blackmun and Souter did not sign.

THE JUDICIAL CONDUCT AND DISABILITY ACT OF 1980 REVIEWED

A judge's conduct of recusal or disqualification related issues can spill over into disciplinary proceedings against a judge. It has increasingly become the case in the common law world that more rigorous measures are being put in place to encourage education about ethical standards, and mechanisms to enforce them where necessary.

The United States federal jurisdiction is a useful illustration of what can happen when perfectly sensible and appropriate ethical measures (such as the United States protocols) are not observed. That is, there is a reactionary tendency to then introduce stronger measures where observance has not occurred.

The Judicial Conduct and Disability Act 1980 established a formal process for dealing with allegations of judicial misconduct, vesting primary responsibility in circuit judicial councils as the locus of judicial governance. Some Senate members had advocated a more radical scheme, whereby a national tribunal would have power to remove judges who had committed serious misconduct.[58]

The 1980 Act was ultimately a product of compromise, and was described in the first empirical study of the legislative regime as one of 'decentralised

[55] A Frost, above n 5, 545.

[56] (2004) 541 US 913, 916.

[57] See app D.

[58] AD Hellman, 'The Regulation of Judicial Ethics in the Federal System: A Peek Behind Closed Doors' (2007) 69 *University of Pittsburgh Law Review* 189, 207.

self regulation'.[59] The Act authorised any person to file a complaint alleging that a federal judge was engaged in conduct 'prejudicial to the effective and expeditious administration of the business of the courts'. It also permitted the filing of a complaint, relating to a judge's inability to perform his or her duties because of 'mental or physical disability'. Congress amended the 1980 Act in 2002, and gave the judicial misconduct provisions their own chapter in the US Code (Chapter 16).

In 2004, Chief Justice Rehnquist was concerned that there had been recent criticism from Congress about the way in which the Judicial Conduct and Disability Act of 1980 had been implemented. He appointed a Committee, chaired by Supreme Court Justice Stephen Breyer, to assess the administration and implementation of the 1980 Act. This Committee comprised three judges who, as former circuit chief judges, had considerable experience administering the Act, two district court judges who had served as chief judges and members of their circuits' judicial councils, and administrative assistants who had experience in judicial branch administration. When Chief Justice Roberts was appointed, he asked the Committee to continue its work.

Some of the observations of the Breyer Committee in its recent Report are worth repeating in full. It said:[60]

> The federal judiciary, like all institutions, will sometimes suffer instances of misconduct. But the design of any system for discovering (and assessing discipline for) the misconduct of federal judges must take account of a special problem. On the one hand, a system that relies for investigation upon persons or bodies other than judges risks undue interference with the Constitution's insistence upon judicial independence, threatening directly or indirectly distortion of the unbiased handling of individual cases that Article III seeks to guarantee. On the other hand, a system that relies for investigation solely upon judges themselves risks a kind of undue 'guild favoritism' through inappropriate sympathy with the judge's point of view or de-emphasis of the misconduct problem.

The Committee made 12 major recommendations which are (very broadly) of an administrative character. In the result, the Judicial Conference then asked the Committee to prepare new rules, which were adopted by the Conference in March 2008.[61]

[59] See JN Barr and TE Willging, 'Decentralised Self Regulation, Accountability and Judicial Independence Under the Federal Judicial Conduct and Disability Act of 1980' (1993) 142 *University of Pennsylvania Law Review* 35.

[60] Judicial Conduct and Disability Act Study Committee, *Implementation of the Judicial Conduct and Disability Act of 1980: A Report to the Chief Justice* (2006) 239 FRD 116, 1.

[61] Judicial Conference of the United States, *Rules for Judicial-Conduct and Judicial-Disability Proceedings* (Adopted March 11 2008). For discussion, see AD Hellman, 'Judges Judging Judges: The Federal Judicial Misconduct Statutes and the Breyer Committee Report' (2007) 28 *Justice System Journal* 426.

Professor Hellman has suggested that under the 2008 Rules:[62]

> [S]elf-regulation continues, but the decentralisation has been cut back to a considerable degree. This development is manifested in three aspects of the new arrangements: the imposition of mandatory national rules, the implementation of an oversight function for the Conduct Committee, and the expansion of the Committee's jurisdiction to review orders of the circuit councils.

The intensive work of the Breyer Committee over a period of years provides a valuable empirical basis as to the nature of the complaints against judges which are made in the United States. For instance, the Committee found that the number of complaints 'terminated', or dealt with, had 'hovered between 600 and 800 per year' in recent years. Almost all these complaints were filed by prisoners or litigants, and all concerned alleged misconduct rather than disability. Almost all the complaints had been dismissed by the relevant chief judge. In the relevant period Table 5 shows that of a total of 5,277 allegations, by far the largest single class of allegation was 'prejudice/bias' (1,497). The second highest was abuse of judicial power (1,236). The other categories of complaints paled by comparison. What many judges might have anticipated as figuring highly—complaints about delay in delivery of decisions—came to only 364 out of 5,277 complaints.

Significantly, the Breyer Committee found that 'a very good overall job' was being done in handling complaints filed under the 1980 Act. However:[63]

> legislative and public confidence in the Act's administration is jeopardised by less-effective handling of the small number of complaints that are in the public eye.

The Committee thought this could well be counter-productive to the whole scheme. Closing out a complaint precisely because it was one that got into the public eye 'could send the message to persons who believe they have a valid complaint that filing it will do no good because it will not be adequately investigated'.[64]

What all this demonstrates is that recusal law skates not just on the edge of disability law, but also disciplinary law. It is when judges are not properly recusing that matters can escalate to the disciplinary end of the scale. That said, although by far the largest number of complaints under this statute are in fact recusal related on the grounds of lack of impartiality, very few of them have come to anything.

[62] AD Hellman, 'When Judges are Accused: An Initial Look at the New Federal Judicial Misconduct Rules' (2008) 22 *Notre Dame Journal of Law, Ethics and Public Policy* 325, 333.

[63] Above n 60, 5.

[64] ibid 108.

Part C
Process

7

The Importance of Process

INTRODUCTION

THE LEAST DEVELOPED, but arguably the most important, aspect of recusal law lies in the processes adopted, if not expressly formulated, by courts. In discussing the processes attendant on recusal and disqualification applications, it is vital to appreciate why it is that process is so important in the law more generally, and what characteristics a sound juridical process for recusal ought to reflect.[1]

THE JUDGE'S VIEWPOINT

At the risk of over-generalisation, lawyers and judges are prone to assess the fairness of court proceedings by reference to the outcome of those proceedings. That is, they ask whether a case was disposed of correctly by considering whether the 'right' party prevailed. In the criminal law context, they consider whether the accused was rightly convicted and an appropriate sentence passed. In the civil law, they reflect on whether the result rested on a sound doctrinal basis, and whether the relief afforded was appropriate and fair.

One of the unhappy consequences of this singular focus on outcome is that judges may too readily come to believe that only half of the litigants who appear before them will ever be satisfied with their decisions. The belief that winners will be happy and losers will be unhappy gives rise to a judicial perception that judges are 'damned-if-they-do, damned-if-they-don't'. If judges think that the preponderance of people who appear before them will leave their courtroom unhappy, as Sir Robert Megarry memorably noted, the most important person in the courtroom becomes the litigant who is about to lose.[2] Sir Robert's statement contains a respectable

[1] I am indebted in this chapter to JM Greacen, 'Social Science Research on 'Procedural Justice': What Are the Implications for Judges and Courts' (2008) 47 *Judges Journal* 41 on which I have drawn freely. See, more generally, SS Nagel, *The Legal Process from a Behavioural Perspective* (Illinois, Dorsey Press, 1969); and GW Adams, *Mediating Justice: Legal Dispute Negotiations* (Ontario, CCH Canadian Ltd, 2003).

[2] R Megarry, 'The Judge' (1983) 13 *Manitoba Law Journal* 189, 193–94.

measure of insight, and shows due sensitivity to the need to convince the losing litigant that their position has been heard and understood. But it is not the whole measure.

Social science research on the issue of 'procedural justice' is of great assistance here.[3] Judges should not lightly shrug their shoulders when that term is mentioned. In summarising this research, Greacen has noted that the public at large including litigants do not, like judges, see fairness as inherently linked to outcome, but rather consider that fairness is inextricably linked to the process that produces those outcomes.

That is not to suggest that litigants do not care about the outcome of their case. The commercial party who has significant financial interests at stake is going to have a burning interest in the outcome. So too are the Albert Haddocks of this world,[4] who may have a strong desire to prove that the removal of the bicycle which they had chained to a fence in High Street, Oxford was in fact an unlawful and dreadful trespass on the inalienable rights of bicycle riders in Oxford. However, litigants understand that everyone cannot win in court and will usually comprehend that there are almost always at least two sides to every argument.

If court proceedings are conducted in accordance with a fair process, judges can achieve distinct levels of satisfaction with what occurred, quite apart from the actual outcomes of decisions. A fair process can yield that most satisfying of all results for a trial judge, whereby a losing litigant acknowledges that at least they had a 'fair crack of the whip'. Conversely, it is extremely disquieting for a judge to hear a litigant bemoan that the court process was appalling and inhuman, regardless of the result the litigant received.

Procedural fairness also has a beneficial impact on a party's compliance with court orders. There is empirical evidence that parties in mediation sessions which they regarded as fair were much more likely to implement a mediated agreement six months after the mediation session than parties who rated the session as less fair.[5] Family law studies have similarly shown that child support was more likely to be paid after a fair mediation, than after the litigation process.[6]

[3] A pioneering work on the topic is J Thibaut and L Walker, *Procedural Justice* (Hillsdale, Lawrence Erlbaum Associates, 1975). A useful recent collation of research is K Burke and S Leben, 'Procedural Fairness: A Key Ingredient in Public Satisfaction' American Judges Association White Paper, 26 September 2007 <http://aja.ncsc.dni.us/htdocs/AJAWhitePaper9–26–07.pdf> accessed 18 April 2009.

[4] Albert Haddock is the alter-ego satirically deployed by AP Herbert, *Misleading Cases in the Common Law* (London, Methuen, 1989).

[5] DG Pruitt, RS Pearce, NB McGillicuddy, GL Welton and LM Castrianno, 'Long-Term Success in Mediation' (1993) 17 *Law and Human Behaviour* 313.

[6] RE Emery, SG Matthews and KM Kitzmann, 'Child Custody Mediation and Litigation: Parents Satisfaction and Functioning One Year After Settlement' (1994) *62 Journal of Consulting and Clinical Psychology* 124.

Trial courts routinely suffer under dreadfully long lists, with resulting time constraints and pressures. This is not a propitious environment for 'kid-glove' handling of litigants. Delay in delivery of some judgments is inevitable. It too becomes a prime factor in litigant dissatisfaction.

As to appellate courts, they all too often live in a harsh and rarefied atmosphere, some of it of their own making. Every appellate judge is all too familiar with the problem of impossible workloads, endless streams of appellants, hopelessly over-loaded briefs, and generalised cries from appellants of a 'dreadful miscarriage of justice' in their particular cases. In such an atmosphere, it is almost inevitable that judges will attempt to cut straight to the chase by identifying the key legal issue early on in proceedings, which can give an impression of undue brusqueness.

There is much to be said on the other side of this kind of issue. Intermediate appellate courts exist primarily for the purpose of error correction; such courts are reviewing what has happened at trial, and historically have never been much in the business of fortifying a perception of the justice system as being gentle.

It is fairly commonplace, at least in the British Commonwealth, that counsel remark on the more relaxed and wide-ranging review which is conducted in a final appellate court. That would suggest that it is the sheer pressure of workload and efficiency concerns which have much to do with the difficulties of intermediate appellate courts. The vast majority of intermediate appellate courts around the British Commonwealth are not 'leave' courts, which means they have to deal with everything that is put in front of them. A court which does not require leave to appeal has no alternative but to continue to hear the Mr Dimes of this world on all their causes of action and the multiplicity of interlocutory skirmishes which accompany them. Final 'leave' courts are better placed to filter out unmeritorious and troublesome litigation in their selection of cases.

It follows that a fair dose of realism is required in assessing the context in which processes are structured and courts run. But that does not mean that we should not try to better understand and implement processes that will improve litigants satisfaction with their day in court.

ENHANCING PROCEDURAL JUSTICE

In a recent study oriented towards a judicial audience, Tyler noted four essential elements that contribute to perceptions of high levels of 'procedural justice' on the part of litigants.[7]

[7] T Tyler, 'What do they Expect/New Findings Confirm the Precepts of Procedural Fairness' (2006) *California Courts Review* 22.

The first is treatment with dignity and respect. The essential issue here is whether the particular party was treated as a person and as a valued member of society. Scurrilous asides by a judge during the hearing, which may not be enough to tip a judgment over on appeal, have the potential to cause vast and lasting offence to the parties concerned.

Secondly, there is the issue of participation. Parties feel very strongly about having the opportunity to participate in the process. Participation can take many forms, but the ability to fully present one's case in court is regarded as critical.

Thirdly, there is trustworthiness. There is a general concern that the judge should actually care about the case, and that the judge should attempt to do what is right for the litigants. A further tenet of trustworthiness as an aspect of procedural fairness is that everything should be done in the open. For example, if at the beginning of a judicial review case involving a telecommunications company, the judge mutters to counsel from the bench that his home telephone number is provided by that company, counsel's acceptance that this connection is of no consequence may not entirely quell the concerns of the litigants themselves. Everybody else involved may want to get on with the case and think that such a relationship is of no moment, save the miserable litigant crouched in the right rear of the courtroom. Obviously that miserable litigant will be even more miserable if the judge removes him or herself to chambers to discuss the matter with counsel, only to resurface and simply announce that she has decided to sit.

Fourthly, there is neutrality. This is not just a question of the judge treating all the parties the same. There is acute sensitivity on the part of litigants to whether the judge was basing a decision on objective factors, such as articulated legal rules, or on the judge's personal values and biases.

It has to be said that a very respectable proportion of recusal cases in the common law world appear to have surfaced from litigants who are not only concerned about having lost their case, but are even more deeply concerned at the officious way in which they have been treated.

Quite apart from the social science research, political scientists and legal theorists have suggested that quality procedure can serve as an important legitimating mechanism for judicial institutions. For the most part around the common law world, judges are appointed rather than elected, have working life tenure and are only removable in extreme circumstances.[8] On the other hand, legislative representatives and the bureaucracy which serves them are more accountable, in the sense of electoral supervision. The adoption of quality procedures are therefore even more important with respect to judicial institutions than other institutions of public life.

[8] For a historical perspective, see WR Lederman, 'The Independence of the Judiciary' (1956) 34 *Canadian Bar Review* 769, 779–88.

THE CENTRAL INGREDIENTS OF LEGAL PROCESS

If the central premise that process is extremely—perhaps critically—important to litigants is accepted, what should we look for in our judicial processes?

One place to begin is with the extremely influential 'Legal Process' school of thought, developed by Professors Hart and Sacks of Harvard University in the 1950s.[9] That school of thought identified a number of elements which are central to an adequate and legitimate procedural system. They suggested that, first, it should be litigants and not courts who initiate disputes and define the parameters of them. Secondly, such disputes should be presented through an adversarial system in which the various parties advance their conflicting views. Thirdly, a rationale must be given for decisions. Fourthly, the decisions must refer to and be restricted by some identifiable body of law. Fifthly, the decision maker must be impartial.

In 1979, Professor Fiss of Yale usefully enlarged on the fifth element, in the following terms:[10]

> The judge is entitled to exercise power only after he has participated in a dialogue ... It is a dialogue with very special qualities: (a) Judges are not in control of their agenda, but are compelled to confront grievances or claims they would otherwise prefer to ignore. (b) Judges do not have full control over whom they must listen to. They are bound by rules requiring them to listen to a broad range of persons or spokesmen. (c) Judges are compelled to speak back, to respond to the grievance or the claim, and to assume individual responsibility for that response. (d) Judges must also justify their decisions ... [T]he judge is required to listen and to speak, and to speak in certain ways. He is also required to be independent. This means, for one thing, that he not identify with or in any way be connected to the particular contestants. He must be impartial, distant, and detached from the contestants, thereby increasing the likelihood that his decision will not be an expression of self interest (or preferences) of the contestants, which is the antithesis of the right or just decision.

PROCESS AND JUDICIAL RECUSAL

It will be apparent that recusal law suffers from significant disabilities in relation to the process criteria just discussed. There is a range of procedural approaches around the common law world as to who initiates a concern over recusal. Sometimes it is the judge who takes the matter up, while

[9] HM Hart and AM Sacks, *The Legal Process: Basic Problems in the Making and Application of Law* (Westbury, Foundation Press, 1994). This text was prepared for publication from the tentative 1958 edition by WN Eskridge Jnr and PP Frickey. See also WN Eskridge Jnr and PP Frickey, 'The Making of *The Legal Process*' (1994) 107 *Harvard Law Review* 2031.

[10] OM Fiss, 'The Forms of Justice' (1979) 93 *Harvard Law Review* 1, 13–14.

sometimes it is the litigants themselves. Those disputes cannot properly be described as always being conducted in an 'adversarial' fashion. The ability to advance conflicting views is often stultified by simple 'yes' or 'no' responses, rather than reasoned decisions on the part of a judge.

The overwhelming deficiency however is the obvious concern that the judge, required to be impartial, must decide whether he or she is sufficiently impartial to decide the case. Of all the offences against the legal process criteria, this last must be a candidate for a condign sentence.

It is readily apparent from the foregoing that it is of the highest importance that there should be well understood methods for dealing with recusal concerns.[11] Whether this should be by the traditional methods of dealing with such matters, or by protocols, or by defined rules of court forms the subject of another chapter.

[11] One of the great difficulties in dealing with this area is that judges thinking about these issues and the processes used in any given court are distinctly obscure. See TB Marvell, *Appellate Courts and Lawyers: Information Gathering in the Adversary System* (Westport, Greenwood Press, 1978) 7–14 referring to: (1) the secrecy surrounding many decision-making activities; and (2) the inaccessible nature of a decision-maker's thinking processes in actual judgments.

8

Prudence: If in Doubt, Out?

INTRODUCTION

FROM THE AGGRIEVED plaintiff's perspective, judicial recusal can be characterised as a 'last-ditch' remedy for something that has gone wrong in the adjudicative process. But the recusal problem really begins with the way cases are assigned, and perhaps with how judges are appointed in the first place.

Ideally, the processes in a given court relating to the actual allocation of cases to judges will have kept judges who should not be involved in a case off the bench. Many trial and appellate courts have case-management systems to minimise the risk of relevant connections being overlooked. In assembling a calendar of cases for a given period, the names of the parties in a case and a brief summary of the case are often circulated to all judges within a registry. Allocation systems may be used within a registry whereby judges can avoid particular cases where those cases are identified by that judge from the outset.[1]

APPOINTING JUDGES

Of some significance to what may happen in actual recusal decisions is the question of appointment of judges, particularly if they are deeply 'cause oriented'. It is therefore worth dealing with these issues in a little more depth.

Leaving to one side judicial elections, a process which raises its own severe kinds of problems, and dealing only with the more traditional appointment process, it is now commonplace to find such positions being advertised, often with lists of criteria as to what that appointment should reflect.[2]

[1] For a discussion of the principle of 'neutral assignment of cases' with recourse to the case allocation procedures in New Zealand, United States and Germany, see P Butler, 'The Assignment of Cases to Judges' (2003) 1 *New Zealand Journal of Public and International Law* 83.

[2] In New Zealand, see N Anderson, 'The Appearance of Justice' (2004) 12 *Waikato Law Review* 1, 2–4. Initial expressions of interest are called for by public advertisement. For the protocol employed by the High Court of New Zealand, see <http://www.justice.govt.nz/

What is missing from these rather bureaucratic lists are two qualities that most members of the profession, and likely most judges, would rate as being far more important.

The first is what is sometimes referred to as 'judicial bones', or a sense of what being a judge is really all about. Sadly, some judges, who have been particularly fine advocates and who have exemplary records of service, are never entirely able to shake the fact that they were once, for instance, a prosecutor or a civil rights lawyer. It is almost as if there is an indelible stamp upon them.[3]

Another quality can be referred to as sound judgment.[4] This much prized virtue can be broken down into at least two subsets, qualities of mind and qualities of character. Qualities of mind include an ability to think about multiple factors at the same time and to order and weigh the considerations; a tendency to consider the 'downstream' consequences of a decision; and in some situations, the ability to come up with creative alternative solutions to seemingly intractable problems. But perhaps the most significant element is a sense of proportion: the ability to see the relationship between the wrong and the remedy being considered.

There is doubtless room for debate about the qualities of character which go to sound judgment, but they arguably include the following: an intuitive instinct for the pattern of things; a relatively self disciplined approach to the task before them; the quality of being able to separate and prefer a reasoned response to one based on emotion; and an acceptance of the necessity to make decisions, which are quite often based on incomplete data.

Perhaps straddling qualities of mind and qualities of character is the characteristic of prudence. Some academics have seen prudence as a quality of character of a judge, while others have seen prudence as overlapping qualities of mind and character. For instance, Professor Kronman of Yale once described Alexander Bickel's 'philosophy of prudence' as both

pubs/other/pamphlets/2003/judicial-appointments/high-court-judge.html> accessed 18 April 2009. In the United Kingdom, as a result of the Constitutional Reform Act 2005, the Judicial Appointments Commission was set up, responsible for the selection of judges and tribunal members in England and Wales. The Commission is required by statute to select solely on merit, select only people of good character, and have regard to the need to encourage diversity in the range of persons available for selection by appointments. See Baroness Prashar, 'Equality in Justice Day', Speech at the Royal Courts of Justice, London, 24 October 2008, 1–2.

[3] See, for example, *R v Fotu* [1995] 3 NZLR 129 (CA), where Cooke P noted that 'if the approach to the conduct of a trial followed by the trial Judge in these cases is intended to suggest that there should be some shift away from the New Zealand tradition of a fair trial, in the direction of more active semi-prosecutorial participation by the Judge, it is a suggestion that this Court is unable to find acceptable' (at 142). That was a case of a distinguished former Crown prosecutor becoming altogether too prosecutorial.

[4] See S Sherry, 'Judges of Character' in C Farrelly and LB Solum (eds), *Virtue Jurisprudence* (Palgrave Macmillan, Basingstoke, 2008) 88–106.

'an intellectual capacity and a temperamental disposition'.[5] As Sherry has said:[6]

> Prudence, or practical wisdom, in turn depends upon what Kronman himself later labelled 'traits of character': those habits of mind and spirit that allow an individual to make judgement *where intellect runs out.*

Probably all judges would like to think that the course they are embarking on does involve strong 'practical wisdom', to use Kronman's phrase.[7] Even so, just what wisdom requires in a given case can remain distinctly debatable. A good example, at the highest level, concerned the United States Supreme Court's intervention in the 2000 Presidential election. The Justices in the majority in that case seem to have been motivated by a sense of obligation towards the nation's constitutional well being.[8] In writing for the majority, Justice O'Connor noted the court's 'unsought responsibility'.[9] Posner defended the majority's willingness to act notwithstanding the risk of endangering its own legitimacy: '[j]udges unwilling to sacrifice some of their prestige for the greater good of the nation might be thought selfish'.[10] But in dissent, Justice Breyer attributed to his colleagues an intent simply 'to bring this agonisingly long election process to a definitive conclusion'.[11] This suggests a 'prudential', rather than strictly legal, approach to the case, predicated on whether a continued deadlock would have brought about a genuine national crisis of considerable moment. Reasonable people *can* differ on an issue of that kind.

It surely comes to this. When the then Attorney-General, Nicholas Katzenbach, spoke to the Senate Judiciary Committee about the nomination of Robert Bork to the United States Supreme Court, he advised them thus:[12]

> Were I in your position ... the central question I would be asking is this. Is Judge Bork a man of judgement? Not intellect, not reasoning, not lawyering skills, not ideology, not philosophy—simply judgment. Is he a wise person?

That is routinely the judges' burden in a recusal situation: where lies the *wise* course?

[5] AT Kronman, 'Alexander Bickel's Philosophy of Prudence' (1985) 94 *Yale Law Journal* 1567, 1569.

[6] Above n 4, 102 referring to AT Kronman, *The Lost Lawyer: Falling Ideals of the Legal Profession* (Harvard, Harvard University Press, 1993) (emphasis added).

[7] See AT Kronman, 'Practical Wisdom and Professional Character' in J Coleman and EF Paul (eds), *Philosophy and Law* (London, Blackwell, 1987) 203.

[8] Above n 4, 94.

[9] *Bush v Gore* (2000) 531 US 98, 111.

[10] RA Posner, *Breaking the Deadlock: the 2000 Election, the Constitution, and the Courts* (Princeton, Princeton University Press, 2001) 161.

[11] Above n 9, 158.

[12] Above n 4, 101 citing A Lewis, 'Abroad at Home; Question of Judgment' *New York Times* (New York 27 September 1987) D23.

PRUDENT RECUSATION

There are a number of statements by courts of high authority around the common law world to the effect that, in matters of recusal, 'if in doubt, out'. Such statements seem to rest on an instrumental concern. If the judge elects to preside, and it is held that he or she should not have done so, then the remedy is almost always going to be that the case will have to be heard again. If the case was primarily factual, it is almost inevitable that it will have to be reheard because the findings of fact which are so critical at the trial level may have been 'influenced' by whatever bias the judge exhibited. If the central point was one of law, then it may be more possible to 'rescue' the case on the familiar theorem that the reviewing court is in as good a position as the trial judge to say what the outcome ought to have been.

It is conceivable that a judge faced with an unpalatable case where there is a possible tinge of bias may use that as an escape route to avoid his or her professional burden. A New Zealand High Court judge once observed in a letter to his son:[13]

> And now it is time for me to go. I am wanted in Courtroom No 7 where a judicial colleague has just announced, in a dramatic speech which might have been delivered from the battlements of Elsinore, that he is disqualified from presiding because his grandmother once was a shareholder in the company by which the plaintiff is currently employed as an apprentice storeman. So I must step into the breach. In our business, we all work together, there is no other way.

That said, good faith should be presumed, and the recusing judge may be left with an awkward feeling that he or she has not picked up the burden when they ought to have done so. What is to be said to such a judge? This is a question which younger judges often ask senior judges, and indeed it is raised around appellate common rooms from time to time.

There is no convincing 'one size fits all' legal or professional answer to such concerns. It does come down to an evaluation of competing practical considerations, and where the balance of the greater prudential wisdom lies. Judges need have no shame about determining such an issue on that basis.

[13] See P Mahon, *Dear Sam ...* (Auckland, William Collins Publishers, 1985) 119.

9

Practice Rules and Protocols

PRACTICE RULES

PROCEDURAL LAW DEALS with the processes by which courts make decisions. This body of law has been described as 'painstaking, ministerial, and ultimately boring',[1] and it has not received a 'good press' around the common law world in recent years. Indeed a leading United States commentator on civil procedure has spoken of the 'failing faith in adjudicatory procedure'.[2] This is most unfortunate, for the subject area matters greatly.

It is difficult to review the procedural law in the recusal area because by and large there is none. By that it is not meant that there is no available procedure to which resort may be had, but rather that there is not a separate, demarcated body of law relating to judicial recusal. The nearest thing to a stand alone procedure which has yet been devised (and which ultimately was not very successful) was 28 USC § 144 in the United States.

The answer to the question of a perplexed litigant as to how a potential recusal issue may be raised procedurally is something like this.

In the first instance, the recusal request may be dealt with entirely informally. In the normal course of events, counsel would communicate with the judge, through the court registry, and it is quite common for counsel to meet with the judge for at least a preliminary discussion in chambers. The whole issue may simply go away at that stage. If the judge's attention is drawn to something of which he or she was simply not aware, he or she may readily accept without any concern at all that it is not an appropriate case on which he or she should sit.

If, at the trial court level, the judge is not minded to recuse and counsel wish to persist in the suggestion that he or she should, counsel will have to make what could be generically termed an originating application under whatever rules of court are appropriate in that particular jurisdiction. This would normally involve some form of application, supported by affidavits, to which a response can be made. There would then be a contested hearing.

[1] J Zekoll, 'Comparative Civil Procedure' in M Reimann and R Zimmermann (eds), *The Oxford Handbook of Comparative Law* (Oxford, OUP, 2006) 1327, 1328.

[2] See J Resnik, 'Failing Faith: Adjudicatory Procedure in Decline' (1986) 53 *University of Chicago Law Review* 494.

To what extent the judge is required, if at all, to deliver a reasoned decision is again problematic. While a judge should ideally give at least short reasons, and in jurisdictions with Bill of Rights-type provisions they are arguably required, a judge will often simply announce an outcome.

The significance of this last point should not be underestimated. Not only is there an intrinsic question of the best way to deal with a contested recusal application but the appeal provisions in a given jurisdiction may also turn on the character of what the trial court judge does at the contested recusal application stage.[3]

The position of intermediate appellate courts, which typically sit in panels, and are collegiate in nature, is more complicated. The nature of the bias alleged at the appellate level is likely to be more limited, arising out of some suggested pre-existing interest on the part of one judge in the subject matter of the action. Alternatively, the appeal may arise out of an association between an appellate judge and the parties or perhaps their legal representatives. Sometimes, persistent litigants will allege that the particular appellate court 'has it in for them'. Objections to a panel member sitting on an intermediate court of appeal are rarely founded on the conduct of that member of the court during the hearing of the appeal, although even that class of case may be on the rise.

In intermediate appellate courts, there is then an issue as to whether it is for all the panel of the court as constituted on the particular case to determine the issue (absent the judge concerned) or whether, as a matter of fundamental principle, that issue can only be decided by the judge against whom objection is raised. The conventional answer is that the matter is for the particular judge, with whatever assistance that judge may derive from his colleagues. But that appears to be simply a matter of 'practice'. If the judge stands down, a substitute can be appointed.

If one turns to final appellate courts, the matter is further complicated by whether the enabling legislation of the court permits a 'substitute' judge to be called on, or whether the court is going to wind up short handed if the judge stands down. But again, with whatever assistance the judge who is faced with recusation can get, the conventional answer is that the issue is for that judge (not the presiding judge or the court as a whole) to determine.

SHOULD THE CHALLENGED JUDGE DECIDE?

It is this vexing question which understandably causes consternation on the part of external observers, given that this issue seems to be a paradigm example of the challenged judge being a judge in his or her own cause.

[3] For an overview of the basic procedural issues, see MA Perry, *Disqualification of Judges: Practice and Procedure–Discussion Paper* (Victoria, Australian Institute of Judicial Administration Inc, 2001).

What is the rationale for this central practice? The answer which is routinely given is that the challenged judge is best apprised of the facts, and is in the best position to determine any such application. The proposition that somebody in the best position to judge should make a decision is both plausible and defensible, at both a moral and professional level. Indeed, that sort of response is routinely made in relation to other kinds of legal decision making.

However, the proposition runs into all sorts of difficulties in the case of bias. First and foremost there is the principle, enunciated by Sir Edward Coke CJ in *Dr Bonham's Case*, that a judge should not be a judge in his or her own cause. It is true that the adoption of an objective test for bias may ameliorate difficulties here somewhat. But in a situation where there are disputed facts, or questionable behaviour during a trial raising contextual issues of degree, the judge is effectively being asked to decide whether he or she 'overstepped the mark', in the eyes of a well-informed external observer.

Leubsdorf has suggested:[4]

> Introspection has obvious advantages and disadvantages as a disqualification procedure. The judge hearing a case knows better than anyone else what she really feels about the parties and issues. She can therefore tell better than others whether she should sit. Yet even honest judges—and disqualification law is not primarily directed at conscious thought—may be swayed by unacknowledged motives. The most biased judges may be the most persuaded that their acts are just. Moreover, judges need guidance to tell them what tendencies to look for. Hence, though judges should be free to withdraw voluntarily, no sensible judicial system would leave disqualification entirely to the discretion of the judge in question.

The rule that the impugned judge should determine the objection in the first instance has other downstream consequences. Counsel should be able to raise whatever objections are appropriate in a fearless manner, without fear of repercussions. Yet this practice puts counsel in an invidious position where they may entertain respectably well-grounded fears that the judge may become alienated against them.[5]

If there is any area of recusal law which may be ripe for challenge under Article 6 of the European Convention of Human Rights, or other rights provisions in the British Commonwealth or due process clauses in the United States, it is this particular feature. The difficulties of constructing a

[4] J Leubsdorf, 'Theories of Judging and Judge Disqualification' (1987) 62 *New York University Law Review* 237, 277. See also MH Redish and L Marshall, 'Adjudicatory Independence and the Values of Procedural Due Process' (1986) 95 *Yale Law Journal* 455.

[5] For a discussion of the fear of judicial retribution, see RE Flamm, *Judicial Disqualification: Recusal and Disqualification of Judges*, 2nd edn (Banks and Jordan Law Publishing Co, California, 2007) 16–21.

more compliant process at the initial trial judge level are real, though not insurmountable. It would be undoubtedly easier to construct such a scheme at the intermediate appellate and final court level, because the views of the impugned judge could be 'fed in' to a judgment made by the particular panel, or the court as a whole.

LOSS OF A JUDGE ON A FINAL COURT

A proper concern, if a judge is 'lost' to a final court by recusal, is that it will end up short-handed, and may have no power to substitute another judge or justice. The only final appellate court in the common law world that appears to have this difficulty is the United States Supreme Court, and it has already been noted that this has caused real difficulties in that court.

Under section 5 of the Appellate Jurisdiction Act 1867, the House of Lords in the United Kingdom is made up of between seven and 12 Lords of Appeal in ordinary. A panel of three judges is required for a given appeal. More normally five or seven Lords have sat, and very occasionally nine.[6] With respect to the new United Kingdom Supreme Court, which is being established under the Constitutional Reform Act 2005, there will be twelve 'Justices', including the President and a Vice-President. A panel of at least three justices will be required to sit, but it is thought unlikely that in this area the practice will change much, if at all, from the practice adopted in the House of Lords.[7]

With respect to the Supreme Court of Canada, which has nine justices who usually sit *en banc* on substantive cases, any five of the judges of that court shall constitute a quorum.[8] It is convenient to note here that under rule 47(1) of the Supreme Court Rules an originating motion shall include, if there is a concern over a judge's previous involvement or connection with the case which would result in it being inappropriate for the judge to sit, a certificate in a prescribed form, setting out the issues giving rise to concern.

In Australia, the High Court of Australia is composed of seven justices. A Full Court may be constituted by any two or more of the justices sitting together.[9] In constitutional cases a Full Court consisting of less than all the justices shall not give a decision on a question affecting the constitutional powers of the Commonwealth, unless at least three justices concur in the decision.[10] However, it is customary for all seven justices of

[6] As in *A v Secretary of State for the Home Department* [2005] 2 WLR 87.
[7] *The Times* (London 20 November 2008).
[8] RS 1985 c S-26.
[9] Judiciary Act 1903 (Cth) s 19.
[10] ibid s 23.

the High Court to be listed when the constitutionality of a federal statute is contested, unless one of their number does decide to recuse. If the remaining six justices are divided, the decision of the lower court stands. In the exercise of the original jurisdiction possessed by the High Court, the opinion of the Chief Justice or the next most senior judge sitting is to tip the balance.

Some notable recusals in Australia have included Menzies J and Mason J in the important copyright case of *UNSW v Angus & Robertson*[11] because both were (unremunerated) Chancellors of major universities (Monash and the Australian National University) that would be affected by the central issue in the case, namely photocopying in universities. Kirby J did not sit in the important constitutional case of *Kruger v Commonwealth* for various proper reasons.[12] Hence the position in Australia is that there could be a split court in significant constitutional cases, as in the United States Supreme Court.

In New Zealand, that potential outcome has been avoided, because the enabling statute of the Supreme Court provides that if one of the five justices recuses, an acting justice can be brought in to constitute the court.[13] That acting justice will be, in general terms, a retired judge of the Supreme Court or the Court of Appeal.

PROTOCOLS

In an endeavour to assist judges, and enhance the administration of justice as a whole, some jurisdictions have implemented protocols which, if observed, might go some distance to meeting the various concerns that have been raised over recusal issues.

An example of such a protocol is the *Guide to Judicial Conduct*, evolved by the Council of Chief Justices of Australia (which includes the Chief Justice of New Zealand). That protocol is annexed as Appendix A.

It will be noted that under that protocol, disqualification still remains a decision for the judge to whom the concern is directed. However, certain other features of the procedure should be emphasised. First, it will be noted that consultation with judicial colleagues is said to be permissible and may be helpful. Secondly, in cases of uncertainty, an 'open court' hearing should be held with submissions. Thirdly, if the judge does decide to sit, the reasons for that decision should be recorded in open court. Fourthly, the consent of

[11] (1975) 133 CLR 2.

[12] (1997) 190 CLR 1.

[13] See Supreme Court Act 2003 s 23. For a discussion of such provisions, see J Varuhas, 'Acting Judges' (2006) *New Zealand Law Journal* 172; M Kirby, 'Acting judges: a non-theoretical danger' (1998) 8 *Journal of Judicial Administration* 69; and M Taggart, 'Acting Judges and the Supreme Court of New Zealand' (2008) 14 *Canterbury Law Review* 217.

the parties is highly relevant, but not determinative in reaching a decision to sit. Fifthly, the obligation to sit is still given some real weight where it is necessary to do so. The New Zealand Court of Appeal in *Muir* drew attention to this protocol as being 'helpful'.[14] As an illustration of that point, in the New Zealand Court of Appeal, there is now a 'convention' that a recusal application is at least 'discussed' with the other members of the hearing panel.[15]

[14] [2007] 3 NZLR 495, [66]–[67]. See also *Ethical Principles for Judges* (Ontario, Canadian Judicial Council, 1998).

[15] See *R v Chatha* [2008] NZCA 466, [16].

10

Disclosure

INTRODUCTION

THERE ARE TWO aspects of disclosure which warrant commentary in this work. The first is what disclosures should be made by a judge at the inception of litigation, or when something comes to his attention during the course of it relating to his or her interests, and the consequences of any non-disclosure. The second is of an institutional character: how far, if at all, should courts as institutions disclose what practices and procedures they follow when dealing with recusal issues?

DISCLOSURE BY A JUDGE

Common sense and prudence would suggest that many recusal cases could be avoided, or the difficulties at least minimised, if there was proper disclosure at the outset by trial or appellate judges. Prophylactic measures are always preferable to after the event ones in the conduct of litigation. Once something potentially concerning has been raised, and drawn to the attention of the parties, a judge will know what their attitude is, and will be in a much better position to determine whether he or she should recuse.

However, there are issues as to what the status of the desirable disclosure principle is, and what non-compliance should lead to. These issues can be usefully illustrated by some recent Australian cases.

The first is *Najjar v Hames*.[1] The context there was a dispute relating to certain construction work for a public school in New South Wales, for the Ministry of Public Works. As is not uncommon in disputes of that kind, which are not entirely suitable for in-court examination, a referee was appointed to report to the court, pursuant to Part 72 of the New South Wales Supreme Court Rules 1970.

Unfortunately, as Kirby JA noted, 'At the very time he was conducting this protracted, hard-fought investigation towards his report, the referee's company was negotiating a large contract with the very department which

[1] *Najjar v Hames* (1991) 25 NSWLR 224 (NSWCA).

was in contest with the appellant'.[2] Indeed, the contract was signed soon after the referee's report was signed.

The case is an important one on several points, including the differential expectations which may exist in relation to judicial officers and referees.[3] In this instance, the referee was held to be a judicial officer with judicial immunity. This had consequences with respect to costs, which we will refer in due course. Given the referee was found to have been fulfilling a judicial function, Kirby JA said:[4]

> If there is any interest or association with the parties which, undisclosed, could give rise to a reasonable apprehension of bias in an impartial observer knowing the relevant facts, that interest must be disclosed ... It is then left to the parties to make submissions as to disqualification or to indicate they raise no objection.

In this case there had been no disclosure of the true situation, either by the referee or through the Minister of Public Works. The appellant knew nothing about the relationship. Further, there was no evidence that this was a trivial, remote or indirect interest.

The Court of Appeal held that the non-disclosure itself gave rise to apprehended bias. Kirby JA said it was 'wholly unthinkable' that a judicial officer would not have revealed such a context, and it was 'most unlikely' that he or she would sit.[5]

The outcome of *Najjar v Hames* was that the court considered that the referee should have disclosed these ongoing and major contracts from the outset. But given the referee was acting as a judicial adjunct, he was entitled to resist being joined as a party to an application for costs against him personally. This may be thought harsh, but not without some diffidence, the court did not award costs to the successful appellant. This was because the referee's resistance to joinder as a party had ultimately been vindicated.

In *Ebner v Official Trustee in Bankruptcy*, it was argued that a trial judge's failure to disclose his acquisition of shares in a bank was either a ground of, or constituted evidence in support of, disqualification. Gleeson CJ, for the majority in that case, drew a distinction between 'considerations of prudence and requirements of law'. It is worth noting his remarks, in full:[6]

> As a matter of prudence and professional practice, judges should disclose interests and associations if there is a serious possibility that they are potentially disqualifying. It is common, and proper, practice for a judge who owns shares in a company which is involved in a case in which the judge is sitting to inform the parties of that fact and to give them an opportunity to raise an objection should

[2] ibid 229.
[3] See also *Tracomin SA v Gibbs Nathaniel (Canada) Ltd* [1985] 1 Lloyds Rep 586.
[4] Above n 1, 228.
[5] ibid 230.
[6] (2001) 205 CLR 337, [69]–[72].

they wish to be heard. In most cases, the outcome is that no objection is raised and, by reason of waiver, any potential problem disappears. One reason for the practice is that it gives the parties an opportunity to bring to the attention of the judge some aspect of the case, or of its possible consequences, not known to, or fully appreciated by, the judge.

It is, however, neither useful nor necessary to describe this practice in terms of rights and duties. At most, any 'duty' to disclose would be a duty of imperfect obligation. A failure to disclose is relevant (if at all) only because it may be said to cast some evidentiary light on the ultimate question of reasonable apprehension of bias. A failure to disclose has no other legal significance. In particular it does not, of itself, give a litigant any right to have the judge desist from further hearing the matter or to have the ultimate decision in the matter set aside for want of procedural fairness.

To describe the practice of making disclosure as a matter of right or duty may distract attention from the fundamental question to be answered which is whether the reasonable apprehension of bias test is established. That question will be litigated on appeal from the substantive decision in the matter or in proceedings for prohibition, certiorari or similar relief. Whatever the process which the person alleging reasonable apprehension of bias may adopt, there will, in those proceedings, be a full opportunity to make whatever case for disqualification of the judge the moving party can. Inquiring whether the moving party was denied some opportunity to make submissions on the question of disqualification to the judge in question is irrelevant. The question of disqualification can and will be litigated fully in the appeal or application for prerogative or like relief and no separate question of denial of procedural fairness could arise. The point can be illustrated by what happened in *Clenae*. The fact that the judge did not disclose his shareholding gives no different or additional right to the present appellants. All that they were denied by the fact that there was no disclosure was an opportunity to put an argument which we consider must fail.

Disclosure of association may raise more difficult questions than are presented by the straightforward case of ownership of shares in a corporation. It is impossible to identify all of the kinds of association which might be thought to reveal a serious possibility of being potentially disqualifying. As we have said earlier, the application of the apprehension of bias principle requires identification of what it is said might lead a judge to decide a case other than on its legal and factual merits, and the articulation of the logical connection between that matter and the feared deviation from the course of deciding the case on its merits.

In a separate judgment, Kirby J (by now sitting in the High Court of Australia) said:[7]

Many authorities emphasise the prudence and desirability of disclosing to the parties any facts or circumstances which could lead to a disqualification for bias. Moreover, in some circumstances, failure to disclose such an interest will not only remove the possibility of an informed waiver but will lead to a sense of disquiet,

[7] ibid [171].

> and perhaps the suggestion that the want of disclosure has an improper or sinister explanation. In Australia, for lack of a public register, a litigant cannot ordinarily be expected to ascertain, in advance, any relevant undeclared pecuniary interest of the judge. Often the litigant will be unaware of the identity of the judge until immediately before the hearing.

Difficulties do not only arise with non-disclosure as such. In too many cases, what is revealed through disclosure is minimalist, or so minimalist as to be misleading. It is easy to see why judges are cautious with respect to their own privacy, and their own personal financial affairs. Many judges will query why they should hand counsel a stick, with which they can then be beaten. But in this context there is a question of judicial ethics, as well as a prudential concern for judicial stewardship of the litigation which is in front of them. Judges have a duty of candour here.

A good illustration of what can go wrong when there is incomplete disclosure was demonstrated by the recent Australian case of *Smits v Roach*.[8] In that complex case, one firm of lawyers sued their clients for recovery of a respectable amount of legal costs relating to a claim against another firm of solicitors for professional negligence. Before the hearing, the judge indicated to counsel for both parties that the second defendant was personally known to him. Counsel were invited to raise any concerns but no objection was raised. After the hearing, the judge prepared a draft judgment which he circulated to counsel. It was at that time that the judge first disclosed that his brother was chairman of the partners of Freehills, the firm that had been sued.

When he was invited to recuse, the judge declined because he was of the view that there was no apparent bias. More importantly for present purposes, he said that the senior counsel for the plaintiff knew of his relationship with the managing partner of the second defendant and that any right to object had been waived. The Supreme Court of New South Wales agreed[9] and the High Court of Australia ultimately affirmed that result. However, several observations can usefully be made here.

First, the initial disclosure was clearly of a relatively non-precise variety.

Secondly, the initial disclosure was belated. The majority of the appellate judges held the delay did not matter because it was accepted on the facts that the relevant counsel actually knew the truth of the matter, notwithstanding the limited initial disclosure by the judge.

Thirdly, the issue of 'imputed knowledge' was of some difficulty here. Kirby J said that 'attributing to the appellants all relevant knowledge in the possession of their senior counsel, although not expressly shared with them or brought to their attention, presents several difficulties'.[10] Obviously attribution of this character is a fiction, especially in circumstances where

[8] (2006) 227 CLR 423.
[9] (2004) 60 NSWLR 911.
[10] Above n 8, [133].

the question to be answered is whether a litigant has waived a disqualifying association. It also sits awkwardly with the general principle of waiver, which as we will see is that waiver by a party must be a free, informed and positive decision.[11]

In dealing with this issue, the New South Wales Court of Appeal had adopted the language of Lord MacNaghten in *Blackburn, Low & Co v Vigors*:[12]

> There is nothing unreasonable in imputing to a litigant all the information with regard to proceedings which the barrister to whom the management of those proceedings is committed, possessed at the time and should in the ordinary course of things have communicated to the litigant.

Although Kirby J was much troubled by the application of this principle to the present context, he said there was 'no escaping reliance on the judgments made by the legal representative'.[13] Ultimately, Kirby J was won over by pragmatism, holding that 'it is hard to see how this system of adversarial trial could operate otherwise'.[14]

These difficulties also raise an issue as to whether there should be a register of judges' interests, akin to senior officials in other spheres of public life. Professors Campbell and Lee have raised this issue as a 'question for the future'.[15] To the best of this author's knowledge, there is presently no register of judges' interests anywhere in the British Commonwealth. Any suggestion that there should be is likely to encounter vehement opposition. From a constitutional standpoint, it would be said that creation of a register would result in an illegitimate intrusion into the affairs of the judicial branch of government.[16] There is also the question of sanctions for disobedience as well as whether failure to register should lead to automatic disqualification, perhaps of an *ex post* variety. Moreover, some interests are hard to define. For instance, Lord Hoffmann could legitimately have been heard to observe in relation to the *Pinochet* litigation that he did not consider that his relatively distant association with a charity was caught. Would it be caught by a register?

In the United States federal jurisdiction, it is now well recognised that, as an ethical obligation and as a statutory obligation under 28 USC § 455, a judge should be sufficiently well informed about his or her affairs and associations that he or she can appropriately make known to counsel and

[11] See ch 11 below.
[12] [1887] 12 AC 531, 542.
[13] Above n 8, [138].
[14] ibid [138].
[15] E Campbell and HP Lee, *The Australian Judiciary* (Cambridge, CUP, 2001) 152.
[16] In New Zealand, the judiciary is a branch of government under Part 4 of the Constitution Act 1986. Gleeson CJ was of the view that the Australian judiciary is also a branch of government. See also Gleeson CJ, 'Some Legal Scenery', Speech to the Judicial Conference of Australia, Sydney, 5 October 2007.

litigants anything which might give rise to concern, so that they can consider their position in a timeous way. While this may well go to apparent bias, and may lead to disciplinary proceedings, it is neither a free standing ground for recusal nor dispositive of a recusal application.

DISCLOSURE OF PROCESS AND POLICIES BY COURTS

One of the very real difficulties with this whole subject area has been that what judges actually do about recusal issues is done behind closed chambers doors. The processes used by judges—if any have been formulated at all—are obscured from the view of those directly affected, namely the bar and litigants. And if particular courts have any policies, whether more or less definitive, is again not readily apparent.

This is unhealthy and out of step with the commonly accepted standards of public administration today. Nobody can legitimately expect judges to disclose the agonising that goes into a recusal decision, just as no one can legitimately expect the details of judges' conferences regarding the resolution of a case to be revealed. There are all sorts of reasons that such matters should be protected, not least of which is the necessity for there to be able to be full and frank discussions within chambers as to the appropriate course to be adopted. But there should be no doubt about what policies there are if such exist and what processes are being distinctively adopted in a given court. Particular courts should be encouraged to evolve and promulgate such matters, whether in the form of protocols, memoranda or practice notes.

There have been at least two welcome initiatives in this respect. The first is the recommended disqualification procedure evolved by the Council of Chief Justices of Australia.[17] While some features of that protocol are questionable, such as the impugned judge being the locus of decision making, the initiative to evolve such a protocol and the promulgation of it is to be greatly commended. Secondly, the Statement of Recusal Policy, evolved by a substantial majority of the United States Supreme Court, is of distinct interest.[18] Given there is no available avenue by which this document might be challenged, the Statement is law in a very real sense.

In short, it is in the public interest to make it as transparent as is practicable what the particular processes and policies being followed in a given court are. In that sense, the Supreme Court Statement of Recusal Policy, as well as the Council of Chief Justices of Australia's disqualification procedure, have to be regarded as welcome steps in the right direction.

[17] See app A.
[18] See app D.

11

Waiver

INTRODUCTION

WAIVER HAS ALWAYS been a difficult term in the law. It crops up in a number of areas. It can have different meanings in different legal contexts.[1] The consequences of waiver can also vary. For example, it may give rise to a relinquishment of some or all of one's rights under a contract, in which instance it looks suspiciously like a variation. Or, in a narrower sense, it may simply be akin to forbearance. The latter meaning is closer to the meaning of the term in recusal law.

It is clear on the recusal law authorities, both in the British Commonwealth and in the United States of America, that a litigant can, either expressly or by their conduct, validly waive an objection that the court is not independent and impartial, or an objection grounded in apparent bias.[2] The principle is most conveniently considered under the heads of express waiver and implied waiver.

EXPRESS WAIVER

The easiest cases are those where a judge who has some connection with the litigants, their counsel or the subject matter of the case, but who does not consider that connection to be an impediment, raises the matter at a very early stage of the case. This is routine in cases where, for example, a judge has a minor shareholding in a large telecommunications company. Indeed, in some jurisdictions, a judge must own shares in order to obtain a service. Normally there would be an express indication of 'no concern' or waiver by counsel. It would be quite wrong if a party could raise an objection thereafter, having got wind of where the judge was likely to go with the case, or after an adverse decision.

[1] In the contract context, see *Mardorf Peach & Co Ltd v Attica Sea Carriers Corporation of Liberia* [1977] AC 850, 871, where Lord Wilberforce considered that 'the word "waiver", like "estoppel", covers a variety of situations different in their legal nature, and tends to be indiscriminately used by the courts as a means of relieving parties from bargains or the consequence of bargains which are thought be harsh or deserving of relief.'

[2] See generally B Toy-Cronin, 'Waiver of the Rule Against Bias' (2000–03) *Auckland University Law Review* 850; and J Goudkamp, 'The Rule Against Bias and the Doctrine of Waiver' (2007) 26 *Civil Justice Quarterly* 310.

A good articulation of the rationale for waiver can be found in the High Court of Australia decision in *Vakauta v Kelly*:[3]

> By standing by, such a party has waived the right subsequently to object. The reason why that is so is obvious. In such a case, if clear objection had been taken to the comments at the time when they were made or the judge had then been asked to refrain from further hearing the matter, the judge may have been able to correct the wrong impression of bias which had been given or alternatively may have refrained from further hearing. It would be unfair and wrong if failure to object until the contents of the final judgment were known were to give the party in default the advantage of an effective choice between acceptance and rejection of the judgment and to subject the other party to a situation in which it was likely that the judgment would be allowed to stand only if it proved to be unfavourable to him or her.

To be effective, any waiver must be free from any reasonable fear that objecting to the judge would have disadvantaged a party in some way, and also free of pressure from the party's own legal representatives to accede to the judge's suggestion.

In *Millar v Dickson*,[4] four accused appealed a decision holding that they had waived their right to a trial before an independent and impartial tribunal because they were unaware that they had a valid objection to being tried by temporary sheriffs. Lord Bingham of Cornhill said that 'in most litigious situations the expression "waiver" is used to describe a voluntary, informed and unequivocal election by a party not to claim a right or raise an objection which it is open to that party to claim or raise'.[5] As Lord Browne-Wilkinson had put it in *Pinochet (No 2)*, waiver can only run on the basis that the person who is said to have so waived 'has acted freely and in full knowledge of the facts'.[6] Applying these principles to *Millar*, it simply could not be said that the accused had voluntarily elected not to raise an objection; they were simply unaware that it was open to them to do so.

In the United States, Flamm puts the principle of express waiver in very much the same way:[7]

> [I]f all of the parties to a proceeding agree, the judge is willing to handle the case, and the disqualifying circumstance does not involve a matter of public policy, the parties may expressly consent to allow a judge who would otherwise be disqualified to continue to sit in a matter; and, thereby, waive a statutorily prescribed ground for disqualification.

[3] *Vakauta v Kelly* (1989) 167 CLR 568, 572 (Brennan, Deane and Gaudron JJ).

[4] *Millar v Dickson* [2002] 1 WLR 1615 (PC).

[5] ibid [31].

[6] *R v Bow Street Metropolitan Stipendiary Magistrate, ex p Pinochet Ugarte (No 2)* [2000] 1 AC 119, 137.

[7] RE Flamm, *Judicial Disqualification: Recusal and Disqualification of Judges*, 2nd edn (California, Banks and Jordan Law Publishing Co, 2007) 583.

In the federal courts, however, an express waiver may not be accepted unless there has been a full disclosure by the judge of the basis for his possible disqualification, and the parties and their counsel have agreed in writing, and independently of the judge's participation, that the judge's relationship is immaterial or that his financial interest is insubstantial.[8]

IMPLIED WAIVER

As a matter of legal doctrine, implied waiver is a particularly difficult area. It most commonly arises late in the proceedings, regularly on appeal, and all too often it stems from a distinct dissatisfaction with the outcome of the given proceedings. The matter which has been of most concern to the courts has been forensic manoeuvring: the employment of the sort of 'cards-up-the-sleeve' tactics to which reference has already been made in attempts to unhorse judgments in trial courts after an adverse result.

Courts do not look favourably on these sorts of activities. As Sedley LJ said recently in *Amjad v Steadman-Byrne*:[9]

> We would ... stress that the time to draw the attention of a tribunal to a clear manifestation of bias on its part is ordinarily when it occurs. There is no reason why a judge to whom it is courteously pointed out that he or she may have overstepped the mark should not accept that it may be so and stand down. Equally, however, it is only in a clear case that an advocate can responsibly take this course and a judge accede to it, both because such applications have been known to be made opportunistically and because of the expense that a recusal will inevitably throw upon one or both parties, neither of whom will ordinarily be to blame for what has happened. The law of waiver is not simple, but appellate and reviewing courts tend not to look favourably on complaints of vitiating bias made only after the complainant has taken his chance on the outcome and found it unwelcome.

The English Court of Appeal has laid down guidelines which are designed to avoid the scope for 'late' objections in a potential waiver situation. It is worth setting these out in full:[10]

> (i) If there is any real as opposed to fanciful chance of objection being taken by that fair-minded spectator, the first step is to ascertain whether or not another judge is available to hear the matter. It is obviously better to transfer the matter than risk a complaint of bias. The judge should make every effort in the time available to clarify what his interest is which gives rise to this conflict so that the full facts can be placed before the parties.

[8] ibid 585. See the United States Notice Concerning Waiver of Judicial Disqualification in MA Perry, *Disqualification of Judges: Practice and Procedure–Discussion Paper* (Victoria, Australian Institute of Judicial Administration Inc, 2001) 86.

[9] *Amjad v Steadman-Byrne* [2007] 1 WLR 2484 (CA).

[10] *Jones v DAS Legal Expenses Insurance Co* [2003] EWCA Civ 1071, [35].

(ii) Some time should be taken to prepare whatever explanation is to be given to the parties and if one is really troubled perhaps even to make a note of what one will say.

(iii) Because thoughts that the court may have been biased can become festering sores for the disappointed litigants, it is vital that the judge's explanation be mechanically recorded or carefully noted where that facility is not available. That will avoid that kind of controversy about what was or was not said which has bedevilled this case.

(iv) A full explanation must be given to the parties. That explanation should detail exactly what matters are within the judge's knowledge which give rise to a possible conflict of interest. The judge must be punctilious in setting out all material matters known to him. Secondly, an explanation should be given as to why the problem had only arisen so late in the day. The parties deserve also to be told whether it would be possible to move the case to another judge that day.

(v) The options open to the parties should be explained in detail. Those options are, of course, to consent to the judge hearing the matter, the consequence being that the parties will thereafter be likely to be held to have lost their right to object. The other option is to apply to the judge to recuse himself. The parties should be told it is their right to object, that the court will not take it amiss if the right is exercised and that the judge will decide having heard the submissions. They should be told what will happen next. If the court decides the case can proceed, it will proceed. If on the other hand the judge decides he will have to stand down, the parties should be told in advance of the likely dates on which the matter may be re-listed.

(vi) The parties should always be told that time will be afforded to reflect before electing. That should be made clear even where both parties are represented. If there is a litigant in person the better practice may be to rise for five minutes. The litigant in person can be directed to the Citizens Advice Bureau if that service is available and if he wishes to avail of it. If the litigant feels he needs more help, he can be directed to the chief clerk and/or the listing officer. Since this is a problem created by the court, the court has to do its best to assist in resolving it.

More recently, in *Smith v Kvaerner Cementation Foundations Ltd*, Lord Phillips CJ emphasised that 'the vital requirements are that the party waiving should be aware of all the material facts, of the consequences of the choice open to them, and given a fair opportunity to reach an unpressured decision.'[11]

This is an area of recusal law where a number of appellate courts have seen judicial economy and administrative convenience to be of real importance. A trial, whether civil or criminal, does not commence the day the judge walks into court. Indeed the whole thrust of contemporary procedural reforms has been to see that the issues to be litigated are carefully

[11] *Smith v Kvaerner Cementation Foundations Ltd* [2007] 1 WLR 370, [29].

delineated; that the run up to the hearing is carefully managed; and that judges appreciate that the efficient dispatch of a case turns at least as much on adequate preparation before a trial as post-trial reflection. If a trial goes off because of a late claim of bias or disqualification, there is routinely a very significant waste of judicial resources, which include the effort that the first judge has already put into the case as well as the 'gearing up' of another judge.

That said, it has to be acknowledged that there are appellate court decisions in the British Commonwealth and the United States in which it has been said that judicial economy and administrative inconvenience are not appropriate factors to take into account at all. For instance, in *People v Walker*, it was said that 'the vindication of such rights often entails inconvenience for some. This is the small price paid for upholding the letter and spirit of our law.'[12] And in a California appeal, it was suggested that the parties' and court's expenditure of time and resources was 'weightless'.[13]

It would however be a brave counsel who assumed that all appellate courts could be persuaded to take that point of view. This is particularly so in those jurisdictions which have rules of court that emphasise the importance of the efficient dispatch of court business. Appellate courts can then quite reasonably point to the legislative imperative, and maintain that waiver arguments are part and parcel of bending the knee to the will of Parliament.

Finally, it should be noted that there are some serious unresolved constitutional issues relating to waiver. One concern is that waiver should not be possible at all where there is bias. Some commentators have suggested that whilst waiver is a personal thing, there is often a larger public interest which is at stake, and which should not be ignored.[14]

[12] *People v Walker* (1988) 519 NE 2d 890, 896.

[13] *United Farm Workers v Super Court* (1985) 170 Cal App 3d 97, 107 where the court held that 'while the waste of eight trial weeks would be unfortunate, the parties' right to a fair trial cannot be compromised by such considerations'.

[14] See B Toy-Cronin above n 2; E Campbell, 'Waiver of judicial disqualification for bias or apprehended bias—a constitutional issue' (1999) 2 *Constitutional Law and Policy Review* 41; and P Craig, *Administrative Law*, 6th edn (London, Sweet & Maxwell, 2008) 425–26.

12

Necessity

THERE HAS LONG been a rule of necessity in the common law which operates as an exception to the bias principle.[1] It is thought that the earliest case concerned the Chancellor of Oxford in 1430. There, although the Chancellor was a party to the case, it was held the Chancellor could sit because there was no provision for the appointment of another judge.[2]

Pollock succinctly stated the rule in these terms:[3]

> [T]he settled rule of law is that, although a judge had better not, if it can be avoided, take part in the decision of a case in which he has any personal interest, yet he not only may, but must do so if the case cannot be heard otherwise.

The essential rationale for the rule is that litigation cannot be a *non sequitur*. In other words, there cannot be a litigation system in which it is impossible to litigate a given case.

Three important points need to be made. First, the operative effect of the rule of necessity is to override the disqualification of an adjudicator which would otherwise arise.

The second point is an important one of demarcation. As it has been colourfully put in the United States, the rule amounts to an 'easement by necessity', which requires that a judge be completely 'land locked' before the doctrine will apply at all.[4] To elaborate on the metaphor, the land lock must be complete. Where a trial judge visits a particular area 'on circuit' and there is not another judge either immediately available or for some time to take over the case, the necessity doctrine is not activated. It is not, in other words, an easement of convenience but rather a true easement of necessity.

Therefore, the circumstances in which the rule of necessity can be pressed into service are distinctly limited. The most likely circumstance in single

[1] See generally RRS Tracey, 'Disqualified Adjudicators: The Doctrine of Necessity in Public Law' [1982] *Public Law* 628.

[2] For a discussion of that case, see MS Horwitz, 'Judges and the Rule of Necessity: *Ignacio* and the Ninth Circuit's Judges' (2007) 28 *Justice System Journal* 241, 241.

[3] F Pollock, *A First Book of Jurisprudence for Students of the Common Law* (London, Macmillan, 1896) 253.

[4] *Re City of Houston* (1984) 745 F 2d 925, 930 (5th Cir).

judge courts will be where all the judges of that court are subject to the same disqualifying characteristic. An obvious example would be where there is litigation about judicial remuneration or benefits and all judges would be affected by the outcome.

The third point is that the circumstances in which the rule of necessity may come into play are not circumscribed. For instance, in an unusual situation involving litigation with Microsoft, an American appellate court found itself obliged to say that '*each* judge on this court uses the Windows 98 operating system ... To the extent that there may be a conflict of interest, we conclude that the rule of necessity requires us to proceed.'[5]

Whether the rule of necessity can be resorted to in final courts depends very much on the structural arrangements of that court, which we have noted in Chapter 9.[6]

[5] *Pomerantz v Microsoft Corp* (2002) 50 P 3d 929, 931 (emphasis added).
[6] See above at 84–85.

13

Appellate Review of Lower Court Decisions

COMMON NOTIONS OF justice are taken to require that there should be at least one appeal from a 'decision' of a lower court. Unfortunately, in the case of a judge who declines to recuse when asked to do so, difficult procedural and substantive questions are raised about rights of appeal. These questions differ according to the particular place of a court in the hierarchy of courts in a given jurisdiction.

It has never been suggested that the refusal of a judge to stand aside may not be advanced as a ground of appeal in an appeal against a substantive judgment.[1] In such a situation, it is not a 'defence' to the claim of bias that the judgment is correct in all other respects. The judgment cannot stand if it is not the outcome of a fair hearing before an independent and impartial court or tribunal and one that appears to be impartial. The requirements of independence and impartiality are core tenets of natural justice in the exercise of judicial power.

In some countries, however, even merit appeals are not now as of right. For instance, in England, the ability to advance a substantive appeal is affected by the far-reaching changes to the English appellate system in 2000.[2] Given that the English reforms may herald the way the law will evolve elsewhere, it is worth saying something more about them, and their impact on recusal appeals.

The current appeal provisions in the English Civil Procedure Rules came out of the Woolf Report[3] and the earlier Review of the Court of Appeal (Civil Division) chaired by Sir Jeffery Bowman (commonly called the Bowman Report).[4] The Bowman Report noted that an appeal process

[1] See *R v Watson; ex p Armstrong* (1976) 136 CLR 248, 266, and *Muir v Commissioner of Inland Revenue* [2007] 3 NZLR 495 (CA), where the challenge to Venning J having sat was raised on the merits appeal.

[2] See generally A Zuckerman, *Zuckerman on Civil Procedure: Principles of Practice*, 2nd edn (London, Sweet & Maxwell, 2006) 831–908.

[3] Lord Woolf MR, *Access to Justice: Final Report to the Lord Chancellor on the Civil Justice System in England and Wales* (1996) ch 14. See also 'Access to Justice Final Report: Overview' in Lord Woolf, *The Pursuit of Justice* (Oxford, OUP, 2008) 311–22.

[4] J Bowman, *Report to the Lord Chancellor by the Review of the Court of Appeal (Civil Division)*, Lord Chancellor's Dept, 6 November 1997.

serves both a private purpose and a public one. The private purpose goes to the interests of the particular parties to the litigation. The public purpose, apart from promoting authoritative interpretations of the law and effective machinery to develop it in response to socio-economic changes, is to maintain high standards of adjudication in order to promote public confidence in the administration of justice.[5] That said, there are also both public and private interests in the finality of litigation and in promoting legal certainty.

In England, under section 54 of the Access to Justice Act 1999, there was a particular concern to reconcile these various interests under the rubric of proportionality. This requires that once parties have had an adequate opportunity to present their case and a judicial decision has been taken, any further judicial investigation by way of appeal should be reserved for those cases that really require it. This of course applies only to civil appeals; criminal appeals in England and elsewhere in the British Commonwealth are governed by their own regimes. At a broad level of generality, those regimes enable an accused to appeal his conviction or his sentence or both.

The minimalist approach with respect to civil appeals in the United Kingdom is not solely based upon a 'resource' philosophy. Rather, it is thought that the concentration should be on getting the decision right at first instance, with lower courts having the onus of responsibility for the outcome of the conduct of litigation. The relationship between the appellate court and the trial court is one of interdependence, and supervision is the primary role of the appellate court.[6]

This sets an entirely different context for an appeal against a recusal decision of a judge after the substantive judgment has been delivered. In contradistinction to the position elsewhere in the British Commonwealth, an appeal cannot now be mounted without court permission in England. This is subject to some very narrow exceptions which are not relevant here. Permission may be given by the court against whose decision an appeal is sought or by the Court of Appeal. This exercise is commonly referred to by the acronym PTA ('permission to appeal'). The principle criterion for PTA is whether the appeal has a real prospect of success, though permission may also be given if there is some other compelling reason for hearing an appeal.

As to appeals from interlocutory recusal decisions, there appears to be little discussion in the English cases. In principle, 'a final decision' is a decision of a court that would finally determine the entire proceedings whichever way the court decides interlocutory or pre-trial issues earlier in the

[5] A Zuckerman, above n 2, 831.

[6] ibid 833, citing R Noble and D Schiff, 'The Right to Appeal and Workable Systems of Justice' (2002) 65 *Modern Law Review* 656.

proceedings (subject of course to any possible appeal).[7] However, appeals are also allowed against case management decisions, which is presumably where recusal appeals would most easily sit. Case-management decisions would include such things as adding parties, disclosure, security for costs and the like. As a general proposition, in an application for PTA in relation to decisions of this kind, the court must consider whether the issue possesses sufficient significance to justify the costs and procedural consequences of an appeal, and whether it would be more convenient to determine the issue before or after trial. In short, as Zuckerman puts it, the court must 'decide whether it would be better to put the issue to rest by permitting an appeal now, or whether it would be more sensible to postpone the matter until judgment.'[8]

Whatever doubts there might have been about the appropriateness of this regime under Article 6 ECHR, pertaining to a fair trial, have long since disappeared. This is because the requirement for PTA is itself an opportunity for reassessment. The point was put this way by Sir Andrew Morritt VC in *Colley v Council for Licensed Conveyancers*:[9]

> There is no substantial restriction—and certainly no intrinsically unjust restriction—on the right of appeal, since there is, in our view, no reason in justice why a person should be entitled to occupy the time of the court, and put opposing parties to expense and trouble, in conducting appeals which have no real prospect of success and where there is no other compelling reason why the appeal should be heard.

The short point is that, subject only to this additional forensic hurdle of PTA in the United Kingdom, there is a right of appeal against the declinature of recusal before or after a substantive judgment has been delivered.

In the United States federal jurisdiction, as in the British Commonwealth, there is also the ability to wait until the completion of proceedings, then appeal from the final or substantive judgment.[10]

The difficulties in waiting until after the delivery of a substantive judgment are obvious. In a lengthy commercial cause, a substantial amount of resources, both public and private, will have been expended on the case. It is not uncommon for those resources to run to millions of dollars in the common law world today. As the United States Supreme Court acknowledged as long ago as 1921, in *Berger v US*,[11] an appeal after the merits are determined can provide a quite inadequate remedy.

[7] ibid 837.

[8] ibid 874.

[9] *Colley v Council for Licensed Conveyancers* [2001] 4 All ER 998, [32] (CA).

[10] RE Flamm, *Judicial Disqualification: Recusal and Disqualification of Judges*, 2nd edn (Banks and Jordan Law Publishing Co, California, 2007) 960. See, for example, *Christo v Padgett* (2000) 223 F 3d 1324, 1333 (11th Cir).

[11] *Berger v US* (1921) 255 US 22, 36: 'to commit to the judge a decision upon the truth of the facts gives chance for the evil against which the section is directed. The remedy by appeal

Delay also generates substantial downstream issues for the reviewing court. As only one illustration, take the question of costs. If it is found that Judge X should have recused, but did not, and the trial went on for a lengthy period, what is the outcome going to be in costs? This may not be so much of an issue in the United States, which generally speaking does not have party and party costs regimes (apart from specific statutes). Normally, in the British Commonwealth, the starting point is that costs follow the event. But the 'event' here is that a judge has refused to do something that he or she ought to have done. Should the party who resisted a recusal order have to pay costs? Perhaps it is more appropriate to regard this sort of thing as an error on the part of the court, with neither party being burdened with the cost of revisiting the litigation. In such a case, it is easy to imagine strong representations being made to Ministers of Justice or the Attorney-General that the state should contribute to the costs thrown away by a wrong recusal decision.[12] In some jurisdictions there have been indications that the court itself could award costs against the state for judicial error.[13]

Quite apart from the appalling waste of public and private monies in court costs and fees, most commercial litigants would also point to the heavy burden in indirect costs, such as the amount of executive time that has to be diverted to this kind of case.

The point need not be further elaborated. Ordinarily, for a court's disqualification decision to be 'practical' in the field, it needs to be one which can be reviewed more or less immediately. Parties need to know whether the particular judge is going to be presiding when the trial is got on.

There are some further points of fundamental principle, which raise real difficulties in practice.

One point of principle is that when a judge announces that he or she will or will not sit, that is *all* that the judge is doing. There is therefore an argument that such a 'decision', as Sir Anthony Mason has put it, 'does not constitute a curial order from which an appeal would lie to a supreme court in the hierarchy'.[14] This is a contentious point in Australia and New Zealand, and perhaps elsewhere. On the one hand, in a real sense a decision has been given which relates to the conduct of proceedings in court.

is inadequate. It comes after the trial and if prejudice exists, it has worked its evil and a judgment of it in a reviewing tribunal is precarious. It goes there fortified by presumptions, and nothing can be more elusive of estimate or decision than a disposition of mind in which there is a personal ingredient.'

[12] It is understood the New Zealand Government contributed costs to the unfortunate case of *Williams v Willems* HC HAM A62/00 21 March 2001, where a case 'went off' because of the actions of the trial judge.

[13] In New Zealand, see *Rawlinson v Rice* [1997] 2 NZLR 651 (CA). In Australia, see E Campbell and HP Lee, *The Australian Judiciary* (Cambridge, CUP, 2001) 97.

[14] A Mason, 'Judicial Disqualification for Bias or Apprehended Bias and the Problem of Appellate Review' (1998) *Constitutional Law and Policy Review* 21, 22.

That in turn triggers another line of argument: the decision may be merely interlocutory and in some jurisdictions not sufficiently 'final' to ground an early appeal. The argument that has sometimes prevailed in the Australian cases is that it is conceptually absurd to regard a decision of this kind as an order by the judge to himself or herself, authorising or forbidding that judge to do something. Even more importantly, there is no means by which the decision can be enforced.[15] At the end of the day, this general issue must turn on the construction of the particular enabling legislation, which varies from jurisdiction to jurisdiction.

There are however two ways out of the appeal dilemma if the recusal decision is not to be regarded as 'final'. The first is to treat the decision as an interlocutory order. Some jurisdictions have treated the kind of 'decisions' or 'orders' which can be appealed under this head very widely. For instance, if the judge makes even a small procedural order, say, that a case be placed in a hearing list—*that* order is said to provide a basis for an appeal against the underlying recusal decision which led to the order.[16]

It would be helpful if a specific statutory exception were to be created for recusal cases, either in the rules of court, or if necessary as an amendment to the court's empowering statute (normally a Judicature Act or its equivalent). In short, the matter is sufficiently important that it would well justify a stand alone statutory amendment, particularly if the definition of an interlocutory appeal is not wide enough in a given jurisdiction to support an appeal.

It is worth noting under this head that difficulties can also arise in the context of a criminal trial. The verdict of a jury is subject to the usual substantive appeal provisions. Any jury misconduct is taken care of, post-trial, under those provisions. But what if it is claimed that the trial judge was 'biased' in relation to pre-trial or trial matters? This issue arose recently in New Zealand in *R v Bain*.[17] *Bain* is arguably the most high-profile criminal jury trial ever in New Zealand. Mr Bain was alleged to have murdered his parents and three siblings in 1994. He was tried in 1995 and found guilty by a jury. Ultimately, the Privy Council set aside those verdicts and directed a new trial,[18] which at the time of writing was yet to come to a hearing because various interlocutory matters were still being determined.

As matters stand, the re-trial has been scheduled before a senior High Court judge, in respect of whom a recusal issue then arose. The nature of that issue cannot be referred to at time of writing, because of certain

[15] See *Barton v Walker* [1979] 2 NSWLR 740, 749 (CA).

[16] See *Gas & Fuel Corporation Superannuation Fund v Saunders* (1994) 123 ALR 323; and EM Campbell, 'Review of Decisions on a Judge's Qualification to Sit' (1999) 15 *Queensland University of Technology Law Journal* 1.

[17] *R v Bain* [2008] NZCA 455.

[18] *Bain v R* [2007] 23 CRNZ 71 (PC).

suppression orders that are in place. However, for present purposes, the case is a very good illustration of the jurisdictional difficulties which can be created by interlocutory appeals in recusal cases, even in criminal cases. New Zealand has a relatively generous pre-trial appeal regime, but section 379A of the Crimes Act 1961, which provides for appeals, with leave, from a relatively extensive range of pre-trial rulings does not extend to decisions on recusal applications. Given that difficulty, Mr Bain's counsel sought to rely on section 66 of the Judicature Act 1908, which gives the Court of Appeal 'jurisdiction and power to hear and determine appeals from any judgment, decree, or order ... of the High Court, subject to the provisions of this Act'. The difficulty for the appellant in this case was that the Supreme Court of New Zealand has held that provision to be applicable only to the exercise of the civil jurisdiction of the High Court.[19] Recognising that hurdle, counsel for the appellant sought to argue that Mr Bain has a 'free-standing right' to a fair trial under the New Zealand Bill of Rights Act 1990 and that rulings bearing on that right should be treated as involving the civil rather than the criminal jurisdiction of the High Court. The Court of Appeal held that if the fair trial right was breached then there was a substantive right of appeal, and matters would be taken care of at that level. It agreed with an English divisional appellate court that an allegation that a trial judge was affected by presumptive bias by reason of an association with a witness can be the subject of investigation and assessment in a conviction appeal.[20]

These sort of contortions over appeal rights are quite inappropriate. The merit issue should be able to be addressed more directly and timeously.

A second alternative with respect to disallowed trial court recusal applications is to apply for one of the prerogative writs of mandamus or prohibition, as may be appropriate. There would seem to be nothing in principle to prohibit the adoption of this course in the British Commonwealth.[21] To take mandamus as an example, the primary historical function of this writ was to compel inferior tribunals to exercise jurisdiction and discretion according to law.[22] Lord Mansfield was of the view that the writ ought to be used upon *all* occasions where the law had established no specific remedy, or where in justice and good government there ought to be one.[23] A plaintiff had to have a personal legal right to performance, and a substantial

[19] *Mafart v Television New Zealand Ltd* [2006] 3 NZLR 18 (SC).

[20] See *R v Mason* [2002] 2 Crim App R 38.

[21] In *Ebner v Official Trustee in Bankruptcy* (2001) 205 CLR 337, the High Court of Australia held that it is for the judge against whom the objection is taken to decide the application, and that can only be reviewed on the merit appeal after the case is heard, or *in proceedings for certiorari, prohibition or similar relief* (emphasis added). See also *Gas & Fuel Corporation Superannuation Fund v Saunders*, above n 16. In *Priestley v Godwin* [2008] HCA 59, French CJ did not question the application of the prerogative writs in this subject area.

[22] See H Woolf, J Jowell and A Le Sueur, *De Smith's Judicial Review*, 6th edn (London, Sweet & Maxwell, 2007) 796.

[23] *R v Barker* (1762) 3 Burr 1265, 1267 (emphasis added).

personal interest in the correct and lawful performance of the particular tribunal. Professor Craig, a leading administrative law scholar, has suggested that the writ is available for an improper consideration of jurisdiction or misuse of power.[24]

In many Commonwealth jurisdictions, resort to mandamus and other prerogative writs now has a statutory basis, with attendant renaming (usually 'judicial review') and altered procedures.[25] But in principle, whether by one of the old prerogative writs (if they are still on foot) or under one of the newer statutory remedies, an erroneous exercise of jurisdiction can be reached. Of course, the remedy, in whatever form it now exists in a given jurisdiction, is discretionary and it may be that a reviewing court will take the view that a party should be left to his or her remedy after trial. This may explain why there does not appear to be a great many cases on the point in the recusal context in the British Commonwealth.

Flamm notes that resort to the mandamus procedure is a standard course in American recusal jurisprudence.[26] A clear illustration of recourse to mandamus to remove a judge comes from a protracted school asbestos case in the United States.[27] Judge Kelly was a judge in the Third Federal Circuit, who had been presiding in a substantial class action suit over school asbestos hazards, for nine years! In 1990, while the litigation was still alive, the judge went to a conference on asbestos, presumably to learn more about it. The problem was that the plaintiffs had funded the conference. The judge 'forgot' that he had granted an *ex parte* request of the plaintiffs to use $50,000 from the proposed settlement fund for that purpose. All this came to light, after extensive discovery. The judge declined to recuse. Ultimately he was removed by a writ of mandamus, but there were very severe downstream consequences for the litigation. In the end, the Third Circuit Court of Appeals left a number of the judge's rulings intact, although, in theoretical terms, the decision should have been voided *ab initio*. The Court of Appeals sensibly recognised that having to repeat nine years of litigation was unduly onerous.

As a general conclusion, after an adverse recusal determination at the trial level, an aggrieved litigant has three alternatives: an interlocutory appeal, if that is possible under the legislation in a given jurisdiction; resort to the prerogative writs or their modern successors, if that is possible in a given jurisdiction; or, a substantive appeal of the decision on the merits, with the recusal issue being included in that appeal.

[24] P Craig, *Administrative Law*, 6th edn (Sweet and Maxwell, United Kingdom, 2008) 840, citing *Padfield v Minister of Agriculture, Fisheries and Food* [1968] AC 997.

[25] For example, in the United Kingdom, the writ of mandamus is now a mandatory order under s 31 of the Supreme Court Act 1981 and governed by the special procedure in pt 54 of the Civil Procedure Rules. In New Zealand, see the Judicature Amendment Act 1972.

[26] RE Flamm, above n 10, 967–75.

[27] *Re School Asbestos Litigation* (1992) 977 F 2d 764 (3rd Cir).

14

Recusal Procedure in Appellate Courts

IN GENERAL, THE law and practice pertaining to recusal applications in relation to trial judges has also been applied to appellate judges both in the British Commonwealth and in the United States. That is, it is for the appellate judge who is the subject of the application who determines whether he or she should or should not sit. In the case of intermediate appellate courts, there is of course the possibility of a further appeal.

There are however particular difficulties when the 'impugned judge decides' principle is applied to final courts.

For one thing, it is difficult to penetrate the curial veil as to how these issues are handled 'behind the scenes'. Furthermore, many final court judges have said the issue of recusal is a 'personal' one, for them alone to make.

The sort of difficulties which can arise are illustrated by two well known cases, one in the United States and one in Australia, which are worth considering in some detail.

The American case is the well known decision in *Jewell Ridge Coal Corporation v Local No 6167 United Mine Workers of America*.[1] The background is that there had been ongoing differences of opinion by the Justices of the Supreme Court over the limits of judicial restraint, particularly in relation to the interpretation of the Fair Labour Standards Act 1938. This was one of President Franklin's prominent New Deal measures during the Depression of the 1930s. The debate continued into World War II where it was further complicated by the working conditions of the miners, the War Labour Board's negotiations with the miners, a national coal strike, and, ultimately, government seizure of the industry. It was in that context that the United States Supreme Court granted certiorari to review in *Jewell Ridge*. As it transpired, the court was split evenly, giving Justice Black a deciding vote.

[1] *Jewell Ridge Coal Corp v Local No 6167 United Mine Workers of America* (1945) 325 US 161. For the background to the case, I have drawn on T Freyer, *Hugo L Black and the Dilemma of American Liberalism*, 2nd edn (London, Prentice Hall, 2008); and T Freyer, 'The Jackson-Black Feud' in KL Hall (ed), *The Oxford Companion to the Supreme Court of the United States*, 2nd edn (New York, OUP, 2005) 514.

The recusal issue arose over the fact that the union's lawyer was one Crompton Harris, who 24 years before had been Justice Black's law partner. Traditionally, each member of the Supreme Court decided for himself whether or not some conflict of interest justified disqualification from the particular case. However, in a conference on the case, Justice Jackson vehemently contended that Mr Harris' presence as counsel required Justice Black's disqualification. Justice Black 'stridently refused'.[2] Originally a majority had been prepared to uphold the interests of the employer and Chief Justice Stone had asked Justice Jackson to write the court's opinion. But then Justice Reid changed his views, leaving the entire case in Justice Black's hands. In the result, the new majority, in a judgment written by Justice Murphy, found broadly in favour of the miners.

The debate was further inflamed when Justice Jackson wrote an opinion for the four dissenters that quoted out of context statements Justice Black had made when he was in the Senate, during the debate over the Fair Labour Standards Bill. Justice Black was incensed. Relations between he and Justice Jackson became, in the time-honoured judicial phrase, 'difficult'.

Because of the connection between Justice Black and Mr Harris, Jewell Ridge petitioned the Supreme Court for a rehearing. The court refused to entertain the petition, but for the remainder of his life Justice Jackson remained convinced that Justice Black had acted improperly.

Still the case did not go away quietly. Congress enacted legislation that overturned the Supreme Court's decision. This vindicated Justice Jackson and other dissenters.

The rehearing petition by Jewell Ridge engendered significant public debate at the time. The level of tension within the court seems to have remained high, but was at least kept confidential until after Chief Justice Stone died in 1946. Fred Vincent, who was a friend of President Harry Truman, was nominated as Chief Justice. By that time, Justice Jackson was serving (on leave) as Chief Prosecutor at the Nuremberg war crimes trials, where his difficulties were even more intense.[3]

[2] T Freyer, 'The Jackson-Black Feud', above n 1, 514.

[3] Justice Jackson's involvement with the International Military Tribunal (IMT) is of great interest. It was he who had a large hand in selecting Nuremberg as the place of the trials. It was he as Chief Prosecutor who oversaw one of the main objectives of the IMT: that of establishing a detailed record of the Nazi government's reprehensible history. However, to some extent there was documentary 'overkill' and in the view of some commentators what really made all the difference was one of the early uses of film in a major prosecution. The infamous one-hour film called 'Nazi Concentration Camps' apparently had a stunning effect on the IMT. That in its turn raised a whole series of evidential problems. The film was generic and film was relatively new to the rules of evidence. The difficulty was to drive the general wrongdoings home to individuals. Jackson also came under considerable fire for his desire to prosecute Gustav Krupp. Jackson wanted to prosecute munitions manufacturers. However Krupp senior fell ill and Jackson wanted to substitute a 'lesser' Krupp, Alfried. Sir Hartly Shawcross, the British Attorney-General who was head of the British prosecution team said, 'This is a court

In any event, Justice Black took over as Chief Justice during Fred Vincent's nomination period. But Justice Jackson chose to publicise his feud with Justice Black. Freyer records that when these events became headline news in the United States, President Truman said angrily, 'The Supreme Court has really made a mess of itself'. Freyer goes on to suggest that 'the Jackson-Black feud suggested, however, the degree to which personal tensions shaped the court's resolution of vital issues. It indicated, too, that the public image of impartiality upon which that role rested was often tenuous'.[4] Quite apart from being illustrative of what is at stake, as a matter of doctrine, Justice Black had stood on the 'principle' (if such it is) that each member of the court decides for himself whether or not some conflict of interest justified disqualification from the particular case, and his colleagues had not interfered in that respect.

In a more recent High Court of Australia case, *Kartinyeri v Commonwealth of Australia*,[5] the technical issue was whether the Hindmarsh Island Bridge Act 1997 (Cth) or any part of it was invalid for inconsistency with the Australian Constitution. The Act had restricted the operation of an earlier Act—the Aboriginal and Torres Strait Islander Heritage Protection Act 1984 (Cth)—so that no step could be taken under that Act towards the protection and preservation of an area of land that would itself either prohibit or restrict the construction of a bridge in the Hindmarsh Island geographical area.

Justice Callinan was a member of the High Court. The plaintiffs sought to have him disqualified on the ground that, when he was at the Bar, Justice Callinan had been party to a joint opinion advising the Minister for Aboriginal Affairs that the Act was valid. It was then in the form of a Bill. The Minister was not a party to the proceedings, but the Commonwealth of Australia was the defendant.

The plaintiffs' contention was that the judge should disqualify himself for apprehended bias. The earlier giving of an opinion to a party to the proceedings was said to be prejudgment on the very question which was reserved for the consideration of the court. There was also an argument of 'association' in that Justice Callinan had given advice to Mr Ian McLachlan,

of justice, and not a game in which you can play a substitute, if one member of a team falls sick.' The other judges on the panel were shocked and appalled by Jackson's arguments in this respect. But in fairness, all present were laudatory of Jackson's opening address to the IMT, which is said to have been 'amongst the most moving, persuasive, and candid legal arguments his listeners had ever heard'. See S Landsman, *Crimes of the Holocaust: The Law Confronts Hard Cases* (Pennsylvania, University of Pennsylvania Press, 2005) ch 1.

[4] T Freyer, 'The Jackson-Black Feud', above n 1, 515.

[5] *Kartinyeri v Commonwealth of Australia* (1998) 152 ALR 540. For commentary on *Kartinyeri*, see A Mason, 'Judicial Disqualification for Bias or Apprehended Bias and the Problem of Appellate Review' (1998) *Constitutional Law and Policy Review* 21, 22.

the Minister of Defence, in matters relating to the contentious construction of the bridge while Mr McLachlan was in Opposition.

In fairness to the judge, it should be said that he had himself volunteered information concerning that association prior to the hearing. Also in fairness to the judge, it must be noted that he took the admirable step of delivering a reasoned judgment as to why he had declined to accede to the application for recusal.[6]

According to Sir Anthony Mason, Justice Callinan's recollection was that he had furnished an opinion as to the validity of the legislation which was in the form of a submission to the Senate Legal and Constitutional Affairs Committee. That committee was examining the legislation, with a view to reporting to the Senate. Mason says that, after reciting the appropriate test—namely, whether all of the circumstances gave rise to a reasonable apprehension that he might not bring an impartial and unprejudiced mind to the resolution of the question to be argued in the Full Court—Justice Callinan said that there were no issues of fact or credibility involved in any advice given, that the issues for decision were exclusively legal issues, and that His Honour played no part in drafting, advocating or implementing the legislation under challenge. His Honour had also thought it highly relevant that it was desirable that all of the judges of the High Court should sit on a constitutional case.[7]

After Justice Callinan delivered this 'decision', the plaintiffs sought a review of it by the High Court of Australia. This application was made in the exercise of its original, rather than appellate, jurisdiction. Indeed the Notice of Motion named the seven Justices of the High Court of Australia as defendants. In fact, as Mason further notes, the motion was filed after the hearing of the question at issue had been concluded and the High Court had already reserved its judgment. It would have been highly desirable if the application for review had been made prior to argument on the merits in the High Court.[8]

The application was made to the High Court which had been constituted to hear the substantive argument. However, the then Chief Justice of Australia (Brennan CJ) announced that Justice Callinan would not sit on the application for review. Given the traditional practice that an individual justice determines the issue for himself or herself, on what basis was argument to be addressed to the Full Court of the High Court, absent Justice Callinan?

The plaintiffs relied on two aspects of the original jurisdiction of the High Court, rather than its appellate jurisdiction: first, its inherent jurisdiction to

[6] *Kartinyeri v Commonwealth of Australia*, judgment of Callinan J, 5 February 1998 (unreported).

[7] A Mason, above n 5, 22.

[8] ibid 22.

ensure that proceedings before it are conducted in accordance with the rules of natural justice, including the bias rule; and secondly, the implication to be found in Chapter III of the Constitution that the traditional judicial process, including the rules of natural justice, must be applied by the High Court.

This argument would of course have raised a major jurisdictional issue. But if there was jurisdiction on this basis, the plaintiffs indicated that they intended to argue that the Full Court was in as good a position to decide the question of apprehended bias as was Justice Callinan. In the alternative, it would be for the plaintiffs to establish an error in the exercise of a judicial discretion by Justice Callinan.

The outcome of the application was awaited with considerable interest in legal circles in Australasia, and for that matter there was much public comment about the issue. But in the event, the review application was never heard. Justice Callinan decided to withdraw from the case, or more accurately the determination of it, given that he had participated in the course of the hearing to date. This was a 'prudential' decision by the judge, using the terminology adopted earlier in this work.[9]

These sorts of issues in appellate courts have great potential to damage the integrity, or the perceived integrity, of those important public institutions. As Sir Anthony Mason has said, 'there is much to be said for the view that, instead of leaving the question to the decision of the target judge, it should be left to his colleagues or, if not, to the court as constituted to hear the case'.[10] The difficult question of endeavouring to 'review' the decision by that judge, after the event as it were, would then simply not arise.

The arguments in favour of Mason's proposition seem utterly compelling.[11] It must surely be for the court itself to be satisfied that it is constituted in such a way that it will exercise its judicial functions both impartially and with the appearance of impartiality. One might helpfully have recourse to notions of prudence, but more formally this is surely an area which is squarely within the ECHR and Bill of Rights type provisions to which reference has already been made.[12] It must be a matter for a Court to see that it properly discharges its functions. And if that is so, then 'pre-emption' of the determination by an individual judge is no longer appropriate. It will be recalled that the same sort of suggestion was made by Lord Irvine after the *Pinochet (No 2)* case.

[9] See ch 8 above. Given the thrust of the decision in *Davidson v Scottish Ministers (No 2)* [2004] UKHL 34, the judge was probably wise to withdraw.

[10] A Mason, above n 5, 26.

[11] See, to like effect, E Campbell and HP Lee, *The Australian Judiciary* (Cambridge, CUP, 2001) 149.

[12] See ch 5 above.

One final point needs to be made. The general rule is that when the final court of appeal has given a decision, that is the end of the case. Everybody is entitled to rely on the finality principle and if anything more is to be done, it is a matter for Parliament or the legislature in a given jurisdiction. However, something may come to light subsequent to the final decision—as in *Pinochet (No 2)*—which gives cause to revisit the matter where there is an issue of 'fundamental justice' at stake. In that case, the House of Lords was quite untroubled by any jurisdictional issue, and held that it had an inherent jurisdiction to see that natural justice is done.[13]

[13] *R v Bow Street Metropolitan Stipendiary Magistrate and Ors, ex p Pinochet Ugarte (No 2)* [2000] 1 AC 119, 132. See also *Mafart v Television New Zealand Ltd* [2006] 3 NZLR 18 (SC): 'except to the extent modified by statute and rules, the Court continues to have inherent jurisdiction and powers to determine its own procedure ... [w]here rules do not apply, the inherent jurisdiction can be invoked by a judge to regulate or adjust the procedure of the Court to give effect to the interests of justice' (at [16]–[17]).

Part D
Some Specific Problem Areas

15

Judicial Misconduct in Court: Judges Who Go Too Far

WE HERE ADDRESS the troublesome issue of judicial 'misconduct' in court. The issue is whether such conduct may amount to bias on a 'stand alone' basis, or whether it is better treated as an objection that a party has not had a fair trial. This may not raise any real difference in respect of the legal tests to be applied, but of course the point at which one can mount a complaint and the procedures to be followed thereafter may well differ depending on how a court sees this issue.

An appropriate place to begin is to consider what is generally expected of a judge conducting a hearing. As long ago as 1660, Chief Justice Hale composed certain principles for his own guidance. Principles 4–7 read as follows:[1]

> That in the execution of justice I carefully lay aside my own passions, and not give way to them however provoked.
>
> That I be wholly intent upon the business I am about, remitting all other cares and thoughts as unseasonable and interruptions.
>
> That I suffer not myself to be prepossessed with any judgment at all, till the whole business and both parties be heard.
>
> That I never engage myself in the beginning of any cause, but reserve myself unprejudiced till the whole be heard.

Every common law jurisdiction has examples of some truly appalling judicial behaviour. Some episodes of what could be termed 'misconduct' in court are relatively isolated and case-specific, where the particular incidents have arisen out of the fraught nature of a civil or criminal trial. Moreover, it has to be recognised that court hearings are no place for the faint hearted. They are after all a contest, often with the most acute consequences, and they are fought out in public where a 'loss' is distinctly less palatable. Court cases are therefore (appropriately) hard fought.

[1] These are reproduced in JB Thomas, *Judicial Ethics in Australia* (Sydney, Law Book Co, 1988) 203.

Regrettably however, in most jurisdictions, the bar and judiciary will be able to recall judges who, on a *systematic* basis, are less palatable occupants of the bench than others. Lord Justice MacKinnon has remarked:[2]

> Mr Justice JC Lawrance was a stupid man, a very ill-equipped lawyer and a bad judge. He was not the worst judge I have appeared before: that distinction I would assign to Mr Justice Ridley. Ridley had much better brains than Lawrance, but he had *a perverse instinct for unfairness* that Lawrance could never approach.

On the same occasion, Lord Bingham recounted how Norman Birkett, who later became a distinguished English judge, appeared as a young man for a plaintiff.[3] Birkett thought he had clearly won. After his opponent's closing speech he said, 'I don't know if your Lordship wishes to hear me?' 'No', said the judge. Birkett sat down. But he had to listen with horror as the judge delivered judgment against his client. At the end of that exercise, Birkett rose and protested: 'But your Lordship said you didn't wish to hear me.' 'I didn't', replied the judge, 'and I still don't.' Perhaps that could be regarded as partisanship, but today it would surely be dealt with as a fair trial issue.[4]

The problem is that there is a difference in real life between distinct partisanship and things merely getting out of hand somewhat. As to the first, somewhat ironically, given his famous statement in the *Sussex Justices* case,[5] Lord Hewart was said to be an extraordinarily partisan judge.[6] But what of a criminal case where a Chairman of Quarter Sessions on several occasions during a defendant's case observed in a loud voice, 'Oh God', laid his head across his arm, and made distinct groaning and sighing noises.[7] Again this suggests difficult lines between true bias, in the shape of partisanship, or something which goes to fair trial issues, or merely poor judicial behaviour (which might today be subject to disciplinary proceedings).

In any event, how are we to deal, as a matter of principle, with these in court incidents which are said to amount to recusable bias? The law on this is decidedly different in the British Commonwealth and the United States of America.

[2] See TH Bingham, 'Judicial Ethics' in *The Business of Judging: Selected Essays and Speeches* (Oxford, OUP, 2000) 69, 80 (emphasis added).

[3] ibid 80.

[4] For dozens of extraordinary instances of judicial misdemeanours, see D Pannick, *I Have to Move my Car: Tales of Unpersuasive Advocates and Injudicious Judges* (Oxford, Hart Publishing, 2008).

[5] *R v Sussex Justices, ex p McCarthy* [1924] 1 QB 256, 259 where Lord Hewart CJ stated that a reasonable suspicion of bias was sufficient to quash a determination.

[6] CP Harvey, *The Advocate's Devil* (London, Stevens, 1958) 32.

[7] That instance was held to be unobjectionable on appeal: *R v Hircock, Farmer, Leggett* [1970] 1 QB 67.

THE BRITISH COMMONWEALTH

It is convenient to begin with two relatively recent Australian decisions and to then consider three recent English Court of Appeal decisions, all of a somewhat lurid variety, which have attracted their fair share of press. These cases show that judicial horror stories are not just a thing of the past, and are still too frequent today. They show that contemporary Commonwealth appellate courts are prepared to treat some instances under the head of bias. But again a caveat has to be entered that appellate courts have been less concerned about the niceties of classification than they have been about behaviour which in their view ought to be impugned, under whatever head.

The first Australian decision is *Antoun v R*.[8] In that case, the appellants were said to have 'stood over' the proprietor of a night club in Sydney. They were charged with a single count of demanding money with menaces, in contravention of the Crimes Act 1900 (NSW). Their defence was that they had an honest claim of right for the money demanded. There was a trial in the District Court of New South Wales by a judge sitting without a jury. Plainly the appellants and their counsel did not consider that they were getting a 'fair crack of the whip'. During the course of the trial, three separate applications were made by counsel for the appellants to the trial judge that he disqualify himself for apprehended bias because of his in-court conduct.

The first of these applications was made after counsel for one of the accused foreshadowed that he would make an application for a directed verdict of acquittal at the close of the Crown case on the familiar basis that there was 'no case to answer'. The judge summarily said that application would be refused before hearing submissions. The following morning, another application was made to the trial judge to disqualify himself. This was rejected on the basis that 'an application for a no case cannot succeed in this particular trial', again before hearing any submissions. Counsel thereafter persisted and asked that the trial judge disqualify himself. This third application was also rejected.

Antoun gave evidence in his own defence. The trial judge, who seems by then to have been thoroughly provoked, said he had formed 'a very strong preliminary view in this case, very, very strong, to a stage where I am considering, indeed have almost made up my mind of my own motion, to revoke bail.' The trial judge later revoked bail and the appellants were convicted and imprisoned. Their appeal was dismissed by the New South Wales Court of Appeal.

[8] *Antoun v R* (2006) 224 ALR 51 (HCA).

The High Court of Australia unanimously allowed the appeal, holding that the trial judge's conduct presented an appearance of prejudgement. The strength of the respondent's case, and the weakness of the appellants' defence, could not be used as a justification or excuse for the trial judge's expressions of a determination to reject submissions foreshadowed but not yet made and developed. In the view of Gleeson CJ (for himself and three colleagues), it did not matter that the 'no case to answer' submissions were entirely without merit. That did not alter the consequence that flowed from the manner in which the trial judge dealt with it. Gleeson CJ said:[9]

> The terms of the written opening handed up by counsel for the first appellant suggests that, from the beginning, the trial judge would have been anticipating a no case to answer submissions. He would have been thinking about the argument foreshadowed in the opening. If he had surmised that it would be very difficult to sustain, he would have been correct. Nevertheless, his peremptory announcement, as soon as the application was mentioned, that he would dismiss it, was a departure from the standards of fairness and detachment required of a trial judge.
>
> Judges do not have to devote unlimited time to listening to unmeritorious arguments. Sometimes, a brief hearing will suffice. Judges may anticipate events at trial, and foresee lines of argument that may be developed. Here, the appellants made it clear from the outset that they hoped to be able to secure acquittal without giving evidence themselves. Perhaps the judge felt indignant about the conduct disclosed by the evidence, or about the tactics adopted by the appellants. Indignation is a natural reaction to some facts that are disclosed, or some events that occur, at a criminal trial or, for that matter, on an appeal. It should never be permitted to compromise the appearance of impartiality that is required of judges.

The case was not viewed under the rubric of 'fair trial' or 'due process' considerations notwithstanding that an individual's right to a trial, conducted according to law, is fundamental, despite the cost, efficiency and (in criminal proceedings) crime control and prevention considerations present in each case.[10] Had *Antoun* occurred in England, Canada or New Zealand, the relevant human rights statutory provisions there would surely have had to be considered.

The second recent Australian case is *Concrete Pty Ltd v Parramatta Design & Developments Pty Ltd.*[11] That case involved a copyright dispute of some complexity. The issue of present concern was whether there was a reasonable apprehension of bias arising out of an exchange between bench and counsel and the questioning of a witness by the judge.

[9] ibid [21]–[22]. For comment, see F Strachan, 'Keeping Up Appearances: Apprehended Bias in *Antoun v The Queen*' (2007) 29 *Sydney Law Review* 175.

[10] See also G Hammond, 'The New Miscarriages of Justice' (2006) 14 *Waikato Law Review* 1.

[11] *Concrete Pty Ltd v Parramatta Design & Developments Pty Ltd* (2006) 229 CLR 576.

The respondent's application for disqualification of the trial judge was based on certain comments which he made during the opening stages of the trial and during the cross-examination of a particular witness. The judge said that there was something 'enigmatic' about the claims being advanced by Parramatta Design. During the cross-examination of the witness, the judge commented on the paucity of documentary records and indicated that he thought that was unusual. He went on to say that he thought it was fair that he should indicate this concern that he had to both parties.

The High Court repeated what it had said in *Ebner*[12] to the effect that sometimes judicial interventions and observations can exceed what is a proper and reasonable expression of tentative views. Whether that is so is necessarily a matter of judgment. The High Court again affirmed that the expression of tentative views during the course of argument as to matters on which the parties are permitted to make full submissions does not generally amount to partiality or bias, and did not do so in this case.

In light of the assistance that it had previously endeavoured to give to trial court judges, the English Court of Appeal could legitimately have felt some real concern at three matters which came before it within a space of months in 2007.

The first was *Amjad v Steadman-Byrne.*[13] This was a routine personal injury action arising out of a motor vehicle collision. Three people were seeking relatively smallish sums for minor injuries. The central dispute was over how many claimants—two or three—had been in the motor vehicles at the relevant time. The defendant was concerned that a 'third man' had intruded himself into the case as a spurious plaintiff.

The claimants gave their evidence. They were cross-examined in accordance with the defendant's case. But then the judge invited counsel for the parties into his chambers. Counsel settled a note as to what then transpired, which was as follows:[14]

> (1) Having heard the claimants give evidence, [the judge] believed them. (2) He had considered the manner in which they gave their evidence and in particular the quickness with which they responded to questions. (3) He had warned each one of them of the consequences of his deciding that they were pursuing a fraudulent claim and had seen their reply. He did not consider the men to be dishonest. (4) He accepted that he had not yet heard the defendant give evidence, but in view of his decision that the claimants were honest he could not see how the defendant could win. (5) He wanted to give both counsel an indication of his thoughts. (6) It was 'flavour of the month' for insurers to prosecute claimants with 'Asian sounding names'. (7) He would, if necessary, say something about that in his judgment. (8) Insurance companies were trying to send out a message

[12] *Ebner v Official Trustee in Bankruptcy* (2001) 205 CLR 337.
[13] *Amjad v Steadman-Byrne* [2007] 1WLR 2484 (CA).
[14] ibid [4].

> about fraudulent claims to the Asian community, if there was such a thing. (9) There were some discrepancies in the evidence given by the claimants but not such as to make him think that this was a fraudulent claim. (10) He noted that the defendant worked for the police. (11) Someone with a police background 'always thinks that they are right' (or 'never thinks that they are wrong') and 'find it difficult to accept that they might be mistaken'. (12) The defendant might or might not have been mistaken, but he believed that he saw two people in the car and might have concluded that the claimants were 'at it'. (13) He would continue to hear the case, but the defendants' counsel might wish to take instructions over the lunch break.

Counsel for the defendant said that the judge, by saying what he had said, went well beyond giving counsel an indication of his thinking, and had expressed firm views adverse to a defendant whose evidence he had not yet heard. When he found against the defendant in his judgment the next day, a reasonable observer knowing what had been recounted would infer that he might well have done so because of a prior prejudice in favour of the claimants or against the defendant.[15]

Permission to appeal against the judge's declinature to recuse was granted. The judge was invited to respond, and did so by a letter which he wrote to the Head of Civil Appeals.

Lord Justice Sedley, for the court, held that what was being advanced here as to bias had to mean 'the premature formation of a concluded view adverse to one party'.[16] His Lordship said that a judge may legitimately give assistance to the parties by telling them what is presently in the judge's mind. However, 'what is not acceptable is for the judge to form, or to give the impression of having formed, a firm view in favour of one sides credibility when the other side has not yet called evidence which is intended to impugn it.'[17] One of the things that troubled the Court of Appeal was that whilst it may have been open to the judge to say to the defendant's counsel that he had not, from his perspective, succeeded in discrediting the claimant's evidence, the judge went further and said that he did not see how the defendant could win, 'by expressing the view that his insistence that there were only two people in the car was, in paraphrase, rigid thinking typical of members of the police service.'[18]

Sedley LJ said:[19]

> Both the common law and the Convention for the Protection of Human Rights and Fundamental Freedoms recognise the fundamentality of every litigant's right to a tribunal free of both bias and of the objective appearance of bias. The

[15] ibid [5].
[16] ibid [10].
[17] ibid [10].
[18] ibid [14].
[19] ibid [16].

> appearance of bias includes a clear indication of a prematurely closed mind. In our respectful view the district judge, albeit acting out of the best of motives, gave the parties an inescapable impression that he had formed a view not only favourable to the claimants but such that the defendant was not going to be believed if he contradicted them.

The second English case is *Howell v Millais*.[20] The context was that certain trustees had applied to the court for directions with regard to the operation of a trust. This is commonly called a 'Beddoe' application in the British Commonwealth, after an early case in this area.

One of the applicants was Mr Howell, who was a partner in Addleshaw Goddard ('AG'), a large solicitors firm of some 178 partners and 400 fee earners. The difficulty was that there had been, in the recent past, some exchanges between members of AG and Peter Smith J, the trial judge allocated to this application, albeit in his personal capacity. Those exchanges related to the fact that between November 2006 and May 2007, there had been quite lengthy exchanges between AG and the judge about the possibility of the judge leaving the bench and joining that firm. It is apparent that this was a 'dead serious' set of negotiations.

On 21 May 2007, Peter Smith J had emailed one of the partners in the firm expressing concern over the length of time this consideration was taking. He received a reply which concluded by saying:[21]

> Regrettably, although there was agreement that this was an innovative and good idea, we concluded that the level of investment required cannot be supported in the context of the overall priorities for our business. Our Banking and Corporate practices are our immediate priorities as we seek to build the firm to deliver on our strategy.

The judge was greatly disappointed. He replied, saying that he did not think the senior management of the firm had given 'a fair appraisal to [his] proposal'.[22] He said the firm had got it wrong in treating the proposal as one of partnership, when in fact it was not.

More emails were exchanged, and things became rather testy. Towards the end of these exchanges, one response from the judge was:[23]

> I found your first email insulting and your second one condescending. I do not think the response should have been from you by such emails. You really should have had the courtesy to speak to me.

The judge then complained that his time had been wasted.

[20] *Howell v Millais* [2007] EWCA Civ 720. See L Flannery, 'Judges in the dock' (3 August 2007) *New Law Journal* 1097.

[21] ibid [10].

[22] ibid [11].

[23] ibid [12].

As soon as the identity of the judge to hear the application was known, senior counsel for the trustees invited the judge to recuse himself. He referred to the matters which had transpired. He indicated to counsel for the other parties that he had written to the judge asking him to recuse himself, for reasons which he was not at liberty to impart. The judge responded to this by saying that he did not think he would have had to recuse simply because '[AG] is on the record'.[24] He also contended that the shortness of time should not make any difference to the recusal decision.

Things got no better at the hearing. The judge gave counsel for the applicants who had made the recusal application a distinctly hard time of it. Counsel had finally been driven to say that he did not think 'your Lordship [is] actually going to pay attention to anything further I say on this subject'.[25] This produced further contributions from the trial judge which the Court of Appeal later described as 'intemperate'.[26]

Sir Anthony Clarke MR, for the court, said: 'I am bound to say that [the various] exchanges seem to me to be somewhat extraordinary. In my judgment, [counsel] was entirely justified in saying that the judge was in the process of giving evidence. The judge's approach was quite wrong. It is one thing to test counsel's submissions as a judge. It is quite another for a judge to give evidence of fact.'[27]

The Court of Appeal concluded that 'in all the circumstances, a fair-minded and informed observer would conclude that the judge was biased against [AG] and its partners, including Mr Howell'.[28] The Court of Appeal held therefore that the judge should have recused.[29]

As if that incident was not colourful enough the third one, *El-Farargy v El-Farargy*,[30] attracted national notoriety. It was described by Ward LJ in the Court of Appeal as a 'singularly unsatisfactory, unfortunate and embarrassing matter.'[31]

The context of the case was a bitterly contested ancillary relief application for matrimonial support, in the Family Division of the High Court, involving substantial and complicated assets. The Sheikh, the third respondent in the current proceedings, was not the most willing of participants in the litigation. There was all sorts of interlocutory skirmishing of a character which is depressingly familiar in that jurisdiction. The Court of Appeal

[24] ibid [15].
[25] ibid [24].
[26] ibid [25].
[27] ibid [22].
[28] ibid [30].
[29] In July 2007, the then Lord Chief Justice, Lord Phillips, announced that Peter Smith J's behaviour had been referred to the Independent Office for Judicial Complaints. In April 2008, the Office found that misconduct had been established against the judge. The Lord Chief Justice then issued a reprimand to the judge.
[30] *El-Farargy v El-Farargy* [2007] EWCA Civ 1149.
[31] ibid [1].

was in no doubt what the Sheikh was up to: '[h]e had shown himself to be contemptuous of his wife and equally contemptuous of the court, as, on a number of occasions, the court has found'.[32] On any view of the matter, Singer J was seized of a most difficult case.

In March 2007, the Sheikh applied for an order that the judge recuse himself and that the application be heard before another judge of the Family Division. The basis of the application was with respect to 17 comments said to have been made by the judge in prior applications and proceedings in the cause. It was said on the appeal that those statements would cause a fair-minded and informed observer to conclude that there was a real possibility that the judge was (whether or not consciously) mocking the Sheikh for his status as such and/or his Saudi nationality and/or his Arab ethnic origins and/or his Muslim faith.[33]

The British press did not hesitate to report in lurid detail the remarks the judge had made about the Sheikh. When commenting on the husband's alleged delaying and prevarication, the judge memorably observed, in what will presumably roll down the years at the English bar:[34] '[W]hat good would that do [the wife] ... if [the Sheikh] chose to depart on his flying carpet?' Commenting on the husband's affidavit, which Singer J obviously viewed as being evasive, the judge asked his counsel: 'A bit gelatinous is it? ... A bit like Turkish Delight?' Probably what turned out to be fatal in the end is that the judge somewhat prophetically observed that: 'I have formed a view about this case, not dissimilar from that which Lord Justice Thorpe formed [in an earlier interlocutory appeal], and maybe I should not ultimately take the final hearing.'[35]

The Court of Appeal would have none of this, and allowed the appeal:[36]

> Making every allowance for the jocularity of the judge's comments, one cannot in this day and age and in these troubled times allow remarks like that to go unchallenged. They were not only regrettable ... they were also quite unacceptable. They were likely to cause offence and result in a perception of unfairness. They gave an appearance to the fair minded and informed observer that there was a real possibility that the judge would carry into his judgment the scorn and contempt the words convey. Singer J may talk too much; yet he is a good judge. Unfortunately for him and for all of us, on this occasion he crossed the line between the tolerable and the impermissible.

[32] ibid [15].
[33] ibid [16].
[34] ibid [17].
[35] ibid [17].
[36] ibid [31].

It is worth repeating in full something that was said by Ward LJ, as a postscript:[37]

> It is an embarrassment to our administration of justice that recusal applications, once almost unheard of, are now so frequently coming to this Court in ways that do none of us any good. It is, however, right that they should. The procedure for doing so is, however, concerning. It is invidious for a judge to sit in judgment on his own conduct on a case like this but in many cases there will be no option but that the trial judge deal with it himself or herself. If circumstances permit it, I would urge that first an informal approach be made to the judge, for example by letter, making the complaint and inviting recusal. Whilst judges must heed the exhortation in *Locabail* not to yield to a tenuous or frivolous objections, one can with honour totally deny the complaint but still pass the case to a colleague. If a judge does not feel able to do so, then it may be preferable, if it is possible to arrange it, to have another judge take the decision, hard though it is to sit in judgment of one's colleague, for where the appearance of justice is at stake, it is better that justice be done independently by another rather than require the judge to sit in judgment on his own behaviour.

These general comments may be made about this awful parcel of recent cases. First, it may of course be a statistical aberration, but it does not reflect well on the English justice system that three different trial courts sitting in different contexts seem to have made most ill-advised decisions within a short space of each other. Secondly, the cases as a whole show the spectacular difficulties of a judge sitting in judgment on his or her own comments. Thirdly, the cases reflect the acute pressure on trial judges to get through 'difficult' cases, and the practical effects that can have. Fourthly, the English Court of Appeal appears to have little sympathy for any niceties between stand-alone bias rules, 'fair trial' requirements, or even whether there was a curial order to be appealed.

AMERICAN FEDERAL JURISPRUDENCE

In stark contrast to the way the matter is approached in the British Commonwealth, United States federal law has long held that '[t]he alleged bias and prejudice to be disqualifying [under § 144] must stem from an extrajudicial source and result in an opinion on the merits on some basis other than what the judge learned from his participation in the case.'[38]

In only the second case to reach the United States Supreme Court on this issue, *Liteky v US*,[39] Justice Scalia said of the first case—*Grinnell*—that it 'clearly meant by 'extrajudicial source' a source outside the judicial

[37] ibid [32].
[38] See *US v Grinnell Corp* (1966) 384 US 563, 583 (Justice Douglas).
[39] *Liteky v US* (1994) 510 US 540.

proceeding at hand, which would include as extrajudicial sources earlier judicial proceedings conducted by the same judge.'[40]

The essential idea is to separate off, as not being subject to the bias rule, things that the judge has heard, learned, made observations on or so forth in the course of the hearing itself. Justice Scalia put it this way:[41]

> The judge who presides at a trial may, upon completion of the evidence, be exceedingly ill-disposed towards the defendant, who has been shown to be a thoroughly reprehensible person. But the judge is not thereby recusable for bias or prejudice, since his knowledge and the opinion it produced were properly and necessarily acquired in the course of the proceedings, and are indeed sometimes (as in a bench trial) necessary to completion of the judge's task. ... Also not subject to deprecatory characterisation as 'bias' or 'prejudice' are opinions held by judges as a result of what they learned in earlier proceedings. It has long been regarded as normal and proper for a judge to sit in the same case upon its remand, and to sit in successive trials involving the same defendant.

After *Liteky*, recusal debates relating to in-court misconduct have been dominated by this distinction between intra- and extrajudicial sources, although there is at least one federal circuit which has never adopted that approach.[42]

It follows that in American federal jurisprudence, judicial rulings and comments alone can rarely ever be a valid basis for a bias motion, though they may amount to proper grounds for appeal. However, judicial remarks during the course of a trial that are critical or even hostile to counsel, the parties or their causes may be impugnable if they reveal an opinion that derives from an extrajudicial source. But even so, they will do so only if they 'display a deep-seated favoritism or antagonism that would make fair judgment impossible.'[43]

The majority in *Liteky* expressly regarded *Berger v US*[44] as an example of a case which, on the record, revealed such a high degree of antagonism as to make fair judgment impossible. Given that the challenged matters in that case related to pre-trial proceedings, the United States Supreme Court unsurprisingly found there was no claim to impugnable bias in that instance.

[40] ibid 545.

[41] ibid 550–51.

[42] SP Flaherty, "*Liteky v United States*: The Entrenchment of an Extrajudicial Source Factor in the Recusal of Federal Judges under 28 USC § 455(a)' (1995) 15 *North Illinois University Law Review* 411, 418. It is the First Circuit that holds the outlier stance: *US v Chantal* (1990) 902 F 2d 1018, 1022. There are a minority of United States Supreme Court judges who think *Liteky* is simply wrong. As Justice Kennedy said in *Liteky*, '[t]he doctrine crept into the jurisprudence more by accident than by design' (at 559).

[43] Above n 39.

[44] *Berger v US* (1921) 255 US 22.

Conceptually this approach largely takes courtroom matters and manners out of the bias arena and removes them to the 'fair trial' arena. This then has the important practical consequence of pushing those concerns 'downstream', so that the inquiry becomes one 'after the event' as to the fairness of the trial.

16

Prior Viewpoints

JUDGES SOMETIMES ENTER judicial life after decades of service in other public roles. Many have been public figures. Virtually all have occupied significant positions within the legal profession, government or the academy. The views of such persons will often be publicly known and have been strongly contended for and committed to print in the course of public life.

It is perhaps inevitable that litigants, and in particular litigants in person, will be wary of a presiding judge who has observably, for example, stood somewhere on the political spectrum, or who is in print with a view which may be diametrically opposed to the basic concern of that litigant. How should the law deal with this phenomenon?

POLITICAL CONNECTIONS

In 1975, the then Lord Chancellor, Lord Hailsham, made the following observations:[1]

> When I first went to the Bar something like half the Common Law Bench had at one time or another been in Parliament. A number of these, although a decreasing number, were, in the worst sense, political appointments. Since 1945 I do not know that any appointments to the High Court Bench have been criticised on this score. The great majority of judges who were former MPs became good common law judges, and some of them were among the best. This is because experience in politics and Parliament can broaden the mind and knock some of the angular corners off it. I regard it as a sad thing that I was unable to appoint a single High Court Judge from among members of the House of Commons, although I was able to maintain the principle of giving recorderships to members of the House of Commons. [His Lordship then gave reasons for his inability to do so.] It is a great mistake to suppose that the possession of definite political ideas or the experience of having contested elections constitutes a slur on a judge's impartiality. Indeed, it is arguable that the opposite may be the case. Simonds, Maughan, and Goddard were far to the right of most Conservative Members of Parliament, and unless I have misjudged him, Lord Gardiner is

[1] Lord Hailsham, *The Door Wherein I Went* (London, Collins, 1975) 256–57.

> politically far to the left of Roy Jenkins, Lord Elwyn Jones, or the late Mr Justice Donovan. Impartiality does not consist in having no controversial opinions or even prejudices. The Bench is not made up of political, religious, or social neuters. Impartiality consists in the capacity to be aware of one's subjective opinions and to place them on one side when one enters the professional field, and the ability to listen patiently to and to weigh evidence and argument and to withhold concluded judgement until the case is over.

One particularly serious problem is the vastly increased politicisation of the judicial role, in jurisdictions where judges are elected. In the United States, 39 states apparently use some form of election to select or retain their judges. According to a recent report, between 1994 and 1998, candidates for state supreme courts raised a total of \$73.5 million towards their respective elections, and 19 candidates broke the million-dollar threshold on their own. Things are getting worse: between 2000 and 2004, candidates raised a total of \$123 million, a 67 per cent increase over the previous period, with 37 of the candidates breaking the million dollar mark. Winning judicial candidates who did not accept public financing raised an average of more than \$650,000 in 2004.[2]

Even more significantly, the survey revealed that 56 per cent of state court judges believed that 'judges should be prohibited from presiding over and ruling in cases when one of the sides has given money to their campaign.'[3] That survey also recites empirical studies finding 'a remarkably close correlation' between outcomes in cases, and the source of campaign funds.[4]

Fortunately, British Commonwealth jurisdictions do not have to grapple with the judicial elections factor. It is not pursued further here, save to say that the literature regrettably demonstrates some degree of causal connection between political affiliation and the way in which judges actually decide things. The foolishness that can result was graphically illustrated by a criminal case in the Texas State Court which became very well known in the United States. The case concerned Representative Tom DeLay and involved illegal corporate campaign donations. A whole chain of recusals occurred, first for the judge being in the opposite political party from the defendant, and then for being in the same one. Ultimately this ludicrous dilemma was only resolved by the hand-picking of the judge who had given the least amount of money to any political party![5]

[2] J Sample, D Pozen and M Young, *Fair Courts: Setting Recusal Standards* (New York, Brennan Center for Justice, 2008) 10, citing D Goldberg, *The New Politics of Judicial Elections 2004* <http://www.brennancenter.org/content/resource/the_new_politics_of_judicial_elections_2004/> accessed 18 April 2009. See app F for recent developments.

[3] ibid 11.

[4] S Banner, 'Disqualifying Elected Judges from Cases Involving Campaign Contributors' (1988) 40 *Stanford Law Review* 449.

[5] See R Blumenthal, 'DeLay Case Turns Spotlight on Texas Judicial System' *New York Times* (New York 8 November 2005).

When the past political affiliations of a judge have been dragged into a recusal scrap, the result, as we have seen in the *Jewell Ridge* case,[6] is that those past political affiliations have almost inevitably resulted in something of a messy *cause célèbre*.

Generally speaking, courts have not ordered recusal merely because a judge was involved in promulgating a procedure or the drafting of a statute or the making of legislative submissions with respect to a measure that later comes before that judge. The reason appears to be partly based in pragmatism and partly in the belief that somebody with appropriate professional training will be able to see the matter in a judicial light.

As to pragmatism, in *Buell v Mitchell*, it was said that '[e]stablishing a rule that a judge must recuse himself in cases involving legislation that had been enacted when a judge served as a legislator would force recusal in an inordinate amount of cases.'[7]

It is however possible to point to cases in which judges have recused or been required to recuse on a principled basis because of a political backdrop.[8] Such a case was *Davidson v Scottish Ministers (No 2)*.[9] There, the House of Lords ruled that there was a risk of apparent bias where a judge had been called upon to rule judicially on the effect of legislation that he had drafted or promoted during the Parliamentary process. This was because the fair-minded and informed observer would conclude that there was a real possibility that the judge would subconsciously strive to avoid reaching a conclusion which would undermine the very clear assurances he had given to Parliament.[10]

What should the principle be here? One line of argument is to say that where the issue is in any way factual, or involves significant factual elements, the judge should not sit. But if it is strictly speaking a question of law then it is less objectionable for the judge to sit: the judge will have to give reasons which, in all but a final court, would be further reviewable by an appellate court.

Another approach could be termed a 'separation of powers' principle.[11] It is certainly intellectually plausible, and defensible in constitutional theory, to say that a judge simply should not participate in a case in an area in which he or she had helped to 'create' the law, and perhaps even distantly promoted it, as in *Davidson*. In a human rights or 'fair trial' context, the separation of powers argument may come to assume greater sway than the

[6] *Jewell Ridge Coal Corp v Local No 6167 United Mine Workers of America* (1945) 325 US 161.

[7] *Buell v Mitchell* (2001) 274 F 3d 337, 347 (6th Cir).

[8] In Australia, see *Kartinyeri v Commonwealth of Australia* (1998) 152 ALR 540.

[9] *Davidson v Scottish Ministers (No 2)* [2004] UKHL 34.

[10] ibid [17] (Lord Bingham of Cornhill).

[11] See generally D Williams, 'Bias, the Judges and the Separation of Powers' [2000] *Public Law* 45.

older proposition that the case depends on whether the issue was one of fact or law.

EXTRA-JUDICIAL DISCOURSE

This area also raises some challenging problems. For analytical purposes, it may be useful to separate three situations.

The first is that prior to taking judicial office, many judges will have held positions in public life, or in the legal academy, in which they have had to write reports of one kind or another. They may have been Law Commissioners or served on other law reform bodies, such as the American Law Institute. They may have written books, articles or chapters in which they have tackled the very issue which later comes before them in the course of argument on the bench.

The conventional view is that judges may sit in such instances, both as a matter of professional ethics and in relation to recusal law. The point of view at issue will almost inevitably be a question of law, and counsel will likely be aware of whatever it is that the judge has had to say in a previous position. If they do not, it would seem to be good practice that the judge draw the publication to counsel's attention. Counsel can then consider for themselves whether the judge has 'got it wrong' and urge whatever they have to say about the case on the court. In many situations of this kind, the judge will be a member of a collegiate court where his or her view may not of course be shared by colleagues. It is not unknown for a judge who has espoused a particular point of view to have to watch that point of view turn to ashes in the hands of colleagues. That is a humbling thing, and the judge must accept that outcome with as much grace as he or she can muster.

The second situation, which is as much a question of judicial ethics as of recusal law, is participation in extra-judicial speech making and writing, after elevation to the bench. There appear to be two opposing points of view on this.

The first, now generally acknowledged to be outmoded, is that judges should retire from public life because of a perceived need to keep the judiciary insulated from the controversies of the day. That could reasonably be said to be a very high price to pay for the relatively limited objective which is being pursued.

The more modern view is that judges should continue to enjoy the fundamental freedoms of other citizens, and may be entitled to under Bill of Rights provisions. Formality aside, involvement in the community is thought to be a good thing. Certainly it has become the practice that judges engage in a variety of academic legal pursuits, whether they be extra-judicial articles and chapters in professional and academic journals; conference attendances; or even lecturing and teaching in the law. It might be pointed out that the undertaking of this particular monograph would not have been possible under an inflexible rule the other way!

As always, the concern is with extremes. It is possible to conceive of cases in which something could realistically give rise to a reasonable apprehension in the minds of the parties in subsequent litigation that a judge would not bring a totally unprejudiced mind to the resolution of a matter raised before him or her in their judicial capacity. For instance, if a judge takes a particularly strong line on a question of law, and extra-judicially 'rubbishes' several contending answers, perhaps even excoriating judges who have taken that view, there is genuine cause for concern.

A distinction which is sometimes made is that judges may properly comment on matters affecting the protection or improvement of the administration of justice, as distinct from matters of general policy. Judges generally do not comment on the latter, or, if they do, the convention has been that any such comment should be done through the regular channels of the particular courts. Normally this will involve comment moving upward through whatever structure is adopted, and on to the desk of the Chief Justice or his or her delegate. This is patently a separation of powers issue. It is the case that judges can sometimes offer useful comments which may bear on the formulation of policy, but of course considerable circumspection is required as to how those suggestions are advanced. Some areas which can give rise to considerable difficulties include the resourcing of the judicial system, or criminal sentencing policy. Those are institutional rather than personal matters.

These are difficult issues. The fact is that judges in specialist divisions like (say) a Family Court or an Employment Court will have considerable insights into how something is working or is not working. But on the whole, it is institutionally sounder if their views go through regular channels. For present purposes, this also has the very distinct advantage of avoiding the recusal problem because the view being advanced is then that of the collective institution rather than the individual judge.[12]

An instructive recent case in the United States, illustrative of the difficulties caused by extrajudicial comments and again involving Justice Scalia, is *Elk Grove Unified School District v Newdow*.[13] The context was that Mr Newdow had raised a constitutional challenge in a federal district court, on behalf of his daughter, against the recitation of the Pledge of Allegiance in public schools. The asserted ground was that the phrase 'under God' violates the First Amendment's Establishment Clause. The matter proceeded through the federal trial court and the United States Court of Appeals for

[12] See generally JB Thomas, *Judicial Ethics in Australia* (Sydney, Law Book Co, 1988).

[13] *Elk Grove Unified School District v Newdow* (2004) 542 US 1. See generally CL Roberts, 'The Fox Guarding the Henhouse?: Recusal and the Procedural Void in the Court of Last Resort' (2004) 57 *Rutgers Law Review* 107, 122–25.

the Ninth Circuit, with a majority in the latter eventually ruling that the recitation of the Pledge of Allegiance was unconstitutional.[14]

On 12 January 2003, Justice Scalia attended a religious event in Virginia. His speech included remarks on his general stance on religious freedoms and also a direct criticism of the 9th Circuit decision in *Newdow*.[15] Unsurprisingly, the school district applied for certiorari, and also for Justice Scalia to recuse himself. The application emphasised that Justice Scalia had 'already applied his Establishment Clause analysis to the case at bar and reached his conclusion before ever reading the briefs or hearing the arguments'.[16]

The Supreme Court granted certiorari. Justice Scalia then recused himself, without comment, from the case. Quite what would happen if another Pledge of Allegiance case came along has been the subject of some controversy in the United States.

The learning of this case is surely that there is still real force in the old adage that the less that is seen of a judge off the bench, the better. Judges are not celebrities. Unfortunately, however, judicial attitudes with respect to that proposition appear to be changing, at least in some quarters.

As long ago now as 1953, Judge Learned Hand spoke of 'this America of ours where the passion for publicity is a disease, and where swarms of foolish, tawdry moths dash with rapture into its consuming fire'.[17]

There can hardly be a better illustration of a moth foolishly getting too close to the flame than the extraordinary events which occurred in *US v Microsoft Corporation*.[18] This case concerned some consolidated civil actions filed against Microsoft Corporation in 1998 by the United States Department of Justice, along with 20 states. The essence of the allegation was that Microsoft had abused monopoly power in the way it handled its bundling of its flagship Internet Explorer web browser software together with its Microsoft Windows operating system. This bundling was said to have been responsible for Microsoft winning what was colloquially called the 'browser wars', because every Microsoft Windows user had a copy of Internet Explorer. This also placed what was said to be unfair restrictions in the way of competing web browsers such as Netscape Navigator, which was slow to download over a modem or which had to be purchased from a store. There were other aspects at issue including Microsoft's conduct in allegedly forming restrictive licensing agreements. On the other side, Microsoft had stated that merging Microsoft Windows and Internet Explorer was simply building a better mouse trap: it was the result of innovation and competition.

[14] (2003) 328 F 3rd 466 (9th Cir).

[15] JL Salmon, 'Scalia Defends Public Expression of Faith; Recent Rulings Have Gone Too Far, Justice says during Tribute to Va gathering' *The Washington Post*, 13 January 2003, B3.

[16] (2004) 124 S Ct 2301 (Suggestion for Recusal of Justice Scalia).

[17] Learned Hand, *The Spirit of Liberty: Papers and Addresses of Learned Hand*, 2nd edn (New York, Alfred A Knopf, 1953) 132–33.

[18] *US v Microsoft Corp* (2001) 253 F 3d 34.

It said the two were now really the same product, and inextricably linked together. Further, it was said consumers were getting a good deal as they were getting all the benefits of Internet Explorer for free.

The sternly contested trial started in 1998 before Judge Thomas Penfield Jackson. The stakes were very high indeed. Microsoft was after all not only one of the biggest and brightest stars in the United States industrial firmament, but its activities had also spread worldwide. As is not uncommon in a trial of that length and complexity in the United States, Judge Jackson broke the trial into various findings. In 1999, after a 76-day trial before him—sitting without a jury—he issued his 'Findings of Fact',[19] holding that Microsoft's dominance of the personal computer operating system did constitute a monopoly. He further held that Microsoft had taken actions to crush threats to the monopoly, the victims being Apple, Java, Netscape, Linux and others. After argument about the law, in April 2000, the judge issued a two-part 'law' ruling.[20] His thinking was that the remedy in the case must be that Microsoft should be broken into two separate units, one to produce the underlying operating system, and one to produce other software components. This left as the sole issue remaining for determination the exact form of the relief to be ordered under the Sherman Act antitrust statute in the United States. The judge required Microsoft to submit a proposed plan of divestiture, with the company to be split into an operating systems business and an applications business.[21]

Microsoft endeavoured to appeal directly to the United States Supreme Court because of the time delays and expense involved in the case, but that court declined to hear the appeal. The case accordingly then went to the United States Court of Appeals in the District of Columbia.

Before turning to what was done to endeavour to disqualify Judge Jackson, it is worth noting that the case aroused enormous interest and disputes in the business and technology sectors and across all spectrums of professional life. Economists were divided on the case. For instance, the late Nobel economist Milton Friedman thought the whole case set a dangerous and misguided precedent: technology develops fast, was relatively free of regulation, and progress in the industry would be impeded. On the other side of course were those who castigated Microsoft for alleged predatory behaviour, and opined that it was consumers who would ultimately suffer from what Microsoft had done.

Unfortunately it came to light that, before the critical judgments, the judge had been giving 'secret' interviews to some reporters, as early as September 1999. That was shortly after the evidence had closed, but before he had issued his Findings of Fact. The judge endeavoured to 'embargo'

19 (1999) 84 F Supp 2d 9 (DDC).
20 (2000) 87 F Supp 2d 30 (DDC).
21 (2000) 97 F Supp 2d 59 (DDC).

those interviews, insisting that reporters had to keep them secret until the court's final judgment. It appears that this had come about because the judge had become increasingly troubled about what he had seen and heard in the case. And as the Court of Appeals noted, citing a *New Yorker* article, the judge could not get out of his mind a picture he had seen of Bill Gates and Paul Allan with their 'shaggy-haired first employees at Microsoft'.[22] The appeal judgment also records that long before final judgment the judge had recited a 'North Carolina mule trainer' story to some reporters, indicating that restructuring the company was not something he personally wanted to do. The story which the judge related was:[23]

> [The trainer] had a trained mule who could do all kinds of wonderful tricks. One day somebody asked him: 'How do you do it? How do you train the mule to do all these amazing things?' 'Well', [the trainer] answered, 'I'll show you'. He took a piece of 2-by-4 [timber] and whopped upside the head. The mule was reeling and fell to his knees. and the trainer said: 'You just have to get his attention.' The judge then added, 'I hope I've got Microsoft's attention.'

The District Court of Appeals related a number of other startling interviews between the judge and reporters over a period of time before, and continuing after, the final judgment.

Unsurprisingly, the District Court of Appeals would have none of this. It may be significant that it was noted that this particular Microsoft case had not been an isolated problem, for the judgment lists a number of other cases in which judges had made comments to the media during their cases.[24]

The seven judges of the Court of Appeals who sat on this matter were unanimous and delivered a *per curiam* opinion. Having referred to the *Code of Conduct for United States Judges* and § 455, they found that Judge Jackson 'violated each of these ethical precepts by talking about the case with reporters. The violations were deliberate, repeated, egregious, and flagrant.'[25] The court noted that the United States did not attempt to 'defend' the judge on the appeal; rather, the only disqualification issue was what consequences should follow. The Court of Appeals did not spare the judge: it found he was 'posturing for posterity, trying to please the reporters with colorful analogies and observations bound to wind up in the stories they write.'[26]

The court was left with a dreadful remedial problem. Microsoft of course wanted the judge disqualified, the judgment vacated as to the Findings of

[22] Above n 18, 110.

[23] ibid 111. See also J Brinkley and S Lohr, *US v Microsoft: The Inside Story of the Landmark Case* (Ohio, McGraw Hill, 2000) 277–78.

[24] ibid 112, citing *Re Boston's Children First* (2001) 244 F 3d 164 (1st Cir); *Re IBM Corp* (1995) 45 F 3d 641 (2nd Cir); and *United States v Cooley* (1993) 1 F 3d 985 (10 Cir).

[25] ibid 107.

[26] ibid 115.

Fact, and the whole case remanded for a new trial before a new judge. The United States, as plaintiff, asked the court to do nothing given that there had been litigation for years about this case. The Court of Appeals was faced with a very difficult technical problem because the whole case had not finished and some time periods had not elapsed. Yet Judge Jackson had continued making statements in press interviews in which he called Bill Gates 'Napoleonic', and declared that Microsoft was 'untrustworthy'.[27]

In the result, having castigated the judge, the Court of Appeals came up with a compromise remedy. A disqualification order against the judge was entered as at the date of the order breaking up Microsoft, and the case was remanded for review by a different judge. The Court of Appeals reached its views on what could be termed a 'mixed' theory of judicial wrongdoing. First, it relied heavily on the *Code of Conduct for United States Judges* to which we have referred, and also an earlier decision from the United States Supreme Court in *Liljeberg v Health Services Acquisition Corporation*[28] which many commentators considered had made rather a better job of the issue of impartiality than later views in that court.

The case continued to go downhill. Not long after another judge commenced a review of it in September 2001 on remand from the appeals court, the Department of Justice announced that it was no longer seeking to break up Microsoft, and would instead seek a lesser antitrust penalty. In November 2001, an agreement was reached to settle the case, which required Microsoft to share its application programming interfaces with third party companies with the oversight of a 'compliance panel'. Further controversy raged over the desirability of that settlement. The net outcome however was that most of Judge Jackson's factual findings as to Microsoft's practices under the Sherman Act were upheld.

Judge Jackson continued to publicly deny that bias existed on his part, insisting that any perception of bias in the minds of observers was created by Microsoft.[29] Eventually the judge left the bench to return to private practice. Many thought that ultimately the real loser in the case, given the way it was resolved, was the judiciary.[30]

[27] See J Rowley, "Anti-trust judge Continues to Blast Microsoft" *The Seattle Times*, 15 March 2001, A3.

[28] *Liljeberg v Health Services Acquisition Corporation* (1988) 486 US 847.

[29] See A Broache and D McCullagh, "Former Judge Defends His Bid to Break Up Microsoft", 21 June 2005 <http://news.cnet.com> accessed 18 April 2009.

[30] See SE Margolis and S Liebowitz, *Winners, Losers & Microsoft: Competition and Antitrust in High Technology* (California, Independent Institute, 1999).

17

Unconscious Bias

IN RECENT YEARS, the term 'unconscious bias' has begun to creep into discussions of recusal law, and has received some judicial imprimaturs.[1] However, when the phrase is used in the context of the modern test for apparent bias—that of the informed external observer—what the court is normally saying is that the *possibility* of unconscious bias *cannot be discounted*. This is not the same thing as an affirmative, and free-standing argument, that the judge was *subject* to unconscious bias.

That judges may have unconscious biases of their own is not really in contention. The possibility was acknowledged at least as long ago as 1921 by Benjamin Cardozo in a lecture entitled 'The Subconscious Element in the Judicial Process':[2]

> I have spoken of the forces of which judges avowedly avail to shape the form and content of their judgments. Even these forces are seldom fully in consciousness. They lie so near the surface, however, that their existence and influence are not likely to be disclaimed. But the subject is not exhausted with the recognition of their power. Deep below consciousness are other forces, the likes and the dislikes, the predilections and the prejudices, the complex of instincts and emotions and habits and convictions, which make the man, whether he be litigant or judge. ... Never will these loyalties be utterly extinguished while human nature is what it is.

Some commentators have argued that far more ought to be done about the unconscious, yet pervasive, elements of bias. What could be prayed in aid here is the growing body of scholarship on the potential impact of recent psychological research into unconscious bias upon judicial recusal and disqualification.[3]

[1] See K Mason, 'Unconscious Judicial Prejudice' (2001) 75 *Australian Law Journal* 676.

[2] BN Cardozo, *The Nature of the Judicial Process* (New Haven, Yale University Press, 1921) 167, 176.

[3] See generally AG Amsterdam and J Bruner, *Minding the Law* (Cambridge, Harvard University Press, 2000) and C Guthrie, JJ Rachlinski and AJ Wistrich, 'Inside the Judicial Mind' (2001) 86 *Cornell Law Review* 777, 784–821. The latter presents a study of magistrate judges and claims that judges rely on the same cognitive decision-making processes as lay persons in other respects. This includes framing effects, egocentric biases, anchoring effects, errors caused by the representativeness heuristic, and hindsight bias—all concepts which are well known to psychologists. This can leave judges vulnerable to cognitive illusions that can produce poor

In fairness to judges, the professional view up until the 1980s was that attitudes, including prejudice and stereotypes, operate consciously.[4] Today, psychologists usually make a distinction between 'explicit' and 'implicit' indices. Explicit measures operate in a conscious frame and are traditionally dealt with by self-reporting. Implicit attitudes on the other hand do operate in an unconscious fashion and represent inadequately identified traces of past experience that 'mediate' favourable or unfavourable reactions, thoughts or actions towards social objects.[5] The problem this sets up is that judges can honestly and conscientiously say that they are not biased, but they may nonetheless harbour unconscious beliefs or stereotypes.

These sorts of propositions seem intuitively correct, and are increasingly verified by professional research in psychology. The great difficulty is that how one could translate the professional literature into something approaching a stand-alone ground of intervention with respect to recusal is not at all obvious. One would have thought that considerable investigation of the individual judge or an entire collegiate panel would be required![6]

In the present state of our knowledge, it would appear that the course presently taken by some senior courts—that of acknowledging that there may be unconscious biases which may come into play—is a factor to be weighed in the overall equation but it is neither dispositive nor a stand-alone base for a recusal application.

judgments. Another area of research has been inter-racial bias in jury selection. IFH Lopez, 'Institutional Racism: Judicial Conduct and a New Theory of Racial Discrimination' (2000) 109 *Yale Law Journal* 1717 looks closely into the near total exclusion of Mexican Americans from grand jury service in the 1960s while each of the judges surveyed was of the view that 'he [or she] harboured no intention to discriminate'.

[4] AG Greenwald and MR Banaji, 'Implicit Social Cognition: Attitudes, Self Esteem, and Stereotypes' (1995) 102 *Psychological Review* 4.

[5] See MR Banaji and AG Greenwald, 'Implicit Gender Stereotyping in Judgment Frames' (1995) 68 *Journal of Personality and Social Psychology* 181.

[6] Jerome Frank thought judges should undertake psychoanalysis, a view doubtless shared by many litigants. See 'Justice and Emotions' in *Courts on Trial: Myth and Reality in American Justice* (Princeton, Princeton University Press, 1949) 247–50.

Part E
The Future of Recusal Law

18

Possible Reforms

IT IS APPROPRIATE now to revisit the fundamental premises on which the current body of recusal law presently stands, to ask whether more effective foundations are available in light of our current understanding; to inquire if there are flaws in the present system; and to consider what practical measures are available to address the concerns that have emerged in this area of the law.

THE UNDERLYING PREMISES OF RECUSAL LAW

Legal thought on the subject of recusal seems to start from the proposition that a judge is lawfully appointed to sit on a particular case and is therefore obligated to do so. The discharge of that obligation is not on some subjective personal basis. The judge is required to deliver a decision which finds the facts, applies the law as understood to those facts and produces a decision according to law as an outcome. Implicit in such a theorem is the notion that the judge will consider only that which is relevant, and weigh all arguments that are put to him or her, and which can properly be taken into account by the judge.

The law goes about the enterprise this way. First, to achieve his or her task, in an instrumental sense, it says that the judge must be left 'unaffected'. The judge should have proper working conditions under which this task can be undertaken and be free from extraneous influences to a reasonable extent. But further, in an instrumental sense, there are things that can impact on the judge's impartiality and it is desirable that these be 'removed'.

Things which might well unduly impact on judges are financial interests, which, if not the root of all evil, certainly contribute their fair share of mischief. Associations can also warp judgement. Once pecuniary interests and overt associations are dispensed with, the law starts to slide from such 'high risk' impingers on impartiality towards a broad number of things which might raise a concern that Lady Justitia has lost her blindfold.[1] At that

[1] See generally JT Noonan Jr and KI Winston, 'The Impartiality of God' and 'The Mask of Impartiality' in JT Noonan Jr and KI Winston (eds), *The Responsible Judge: Readings in Judicial Ethics* (Westport, Praeger, 1993) 3–34.

point, public confidence in the Rule of Law, one of the foremost pillars of Western society, might be affected and the resulting tendency is to proscribe such characteristics on a prophylactic basis. Such an approach avoids direct criticism of judges because the particular judge may be asked to stand down while appellate courts nevertheless continue to affirm their confidence in the judge's impartiality.[2] In the result, as Leubsdorf has discerningly put it, 'judges must outlie a cloudy region in which someone is not actually partial, but where it is nevertheless reasonable to question her impartiality'.[3]

Secondly, notwithstanding the concern with the 'appearance' of justice, necessity is a trump. It is thought that it is better to have a decision in a final court of appeal, even a potentially biased one, than no decision at all.

Thirdly, and in practical terms perhaps most importantly of all, the processes used to address recusal issues are the same ones to be found elsewhere in the law, notwithstanding the manifestly different context of recusal decisions. In particular, there is the truly extraordinary principle that the very judge whose acts are called into question for actual or apparent bias decides whether there is an adequate case made out of bias. If we assume a visitation from an intergalactic jurist on a fact-finding mission around our galaxy, it is difficult to see how such a jurist would not feel bound to report this feature of recusal jurisprudence as being strange to the point of perversity.

To return to the first point—that there are some things which are bad for objective judgment, or rather look that way, and which should therefore be removed—it is appropriate to ask whether there is a better or sounder base for the law. This is a very difficult issue, raising philosophical issues of historical pedigree that remain distinctly contestable. For instance, Noonan has demonstrated that there have been debates about partiality in the judicial or quasi-judicial context going back to evidence in Egyptian tombs in 3000 BC, which continued on through the Greco-Roman classical world, and on into Western civilisation as we know it.[4] Philosophers have long debated what is meant by 'impartiality' and 'objectivity'. It is not an unkind or pejorative comment to say that unanimity has not been reached in that discipline.[5]

There is much to be said for the proposition that the term 'objectivity' is more appropriate than the term 'impartiality' in the legal context. Why is this so? This is because, unlike other areas of human activity, law speaks

[2] See *Dimes v Proprietors of Grand Junction Canal* (1852) 10 ER 301.

[3] J Leubsdorf, 'Theories of Judging and Judge Disqualification' (1987) 62 *New York University Law Review* 237, 243.

[4] See JT Noonan Jr and KI Winston, above n 1.

[5] For particularly useful readings, see B Leiter, 'Law and Objectivity' in J Coleman and S Shapiro (eds), *The Oxford Handbook of Jurisprudence and Philosophy of Law* (Oxford, OUP, 2002) 969–89; and GJ Postema, 'Objectivity Fit For Law' in B Leiter (ed), *Objectivity in Law and Morals* (Cambridge, CUP, 2001) 99–143. See also the entry for 'Impartiality' in *The Stanford Encyclopaedia of Philosophy* 25 March 2002 <http://plato.stanford.edu/entries/impartiality/> accessed 20 April 2009.

with a distinct and authoritative voice. It does so in a way which was well summarised by Gerald Postema as follows:[6]

> Law is a distinctive form of practical reasoning. Distinctive of this form is the fact that it anchors the public justification of decisions and actions of officials and citizens alike to past decisions and actions of the community. Moreover, the form and structure of legal reasoning are decisively shaped by the fact that it is, in principle, designed to be presented in a public forum in which it is assessed and open to critical challenge. Legal arguments typically take the form of reasons for extending or delimiting a rule used and established by a past decision. The reasons are developed through the exploration of analogies with competing lines of cases (and relevant hypothetical cases). Public matters, then, are decided, and disputes in the present are resolved, by arguments drawn from analogies to past decisions. It is a highly refined device for the exploration and exploitation of the guidance provided by these past decisions.

Objectivity as such is important in law because 'it make[s] a difference to the ends, methods, or progress of our forms of inquiry'.[7] Or, to adopt the words of Justice Brandeis, society looks to law to help it govern itself simply because society has decided that 'deliberative forces should prevail over the arbitrary'.[8] To put all this another way, society itself has decided that 'legitimacy' in law matters; it must follow, as night follows day, that objectivity matters in practice.

This all begs a terribly awkward question as to whether objectivity is possible of attainment. There are those who maintain that, in any absolutist sense, this just cannot be so. For instance, Professor Young rejects altogether any notion that complete impartiality, or perhaps she would say 'objectivity', is possible:[9]

> The ideal of impartiality is an idealist fiction. It is impossible to adopt an unsituated moral point of view, and if a point of view is situated, then it cannot stand apart from and understand all points of view. It is impossible to reason about substantive moral issues without social and historical context; and one has no motive for making moral judgements and resolving moral dilemmas unless the outcome matters, unless one has a particular and passionate interest in the outcome ... when class, race, ethnicity, gender, sexuality, and age define different social locations, one subject cannot fully empathise with another in a different social location, adopt her point of view. ...

[6] GJ Postema, above n 5, 124. In passing, this is why a strong tradition of dissent is an essential structural condition of law's legitimacy. See C Sunstein, *Why Societies Need Dissent* (Cambridge, Harvard University Press, 2003). For an attack on Postema's essentially professional viewpoint, see R Dworkin, *Justice in Robes* (Cambridge, Belknap Press, 2006).

[7] P Seabright, 'Objectivity, Disagreement, and Projectability' (1988) 31 *Inquiry* 25, 44.

[8] *Whitney v California* (1927) 274 US 357, 375.

[9] IM Young, 'Impartiality and the Civic Public: Some Implications of Feminist Critiques of Moral and Political Theory' in S Benhabib and D Cornell (eds), *Feminism as Critique* (Cambridge, The Polity Press, 1987). While Young was addressing the making of moral judgments, her observation would seem to be more universally applicable.

The same sort of concerns had been raised by Benjamin Cardozo in describing what necessarily emanates from him as a human being, while sitting as a judge:[10]

> More subtle are the forces so far beneath the surface that they cannot reasonably be classified as other than subconscious. It is often through the subconscious forces that judges are kept consistent with themselves, and inconsistent with one another. We are reminded by William James in a telling page of his lectures on Pragmatism that every one of us has in truth an underlying philosophy of life, even those of us to whom the names and the notions of philosophy are unknown or anathema. There is in each of us a stream of tendency, whether you choose to call it philosophy or not, which gives coherence and direction to thought and action. Judges cannot escape that current any more than other mortals. All their lives, forces which they do not recognise and cannot name, have been tugging at them—inherited instincts, traditional beliefs, acquired convictions; and the resultant is an outlook on life, a conception of social needs, a sense in James' phrase of 'the total push and pressure of the cosmos', which, when reasons are nicely balanced, must determine where choice shall fall. In this mental background every problem finds its setting. We may try to see things as objectively as we please. None the less, we can never see them with any eyes except our own. To that test they are all brought—a form of pleading or an act of parliament, the wrongs of paupers or the rights of princes, a village ordinance or a nation's charter.

To summarise, law puts itself forward as an essential pillar of society because it provides a forum, language and structure for the practice of practical reasoning in a public setting, which must be sensitive to the high degree of pluralism of modern political society.

This means that the stakes are very high indeed. Law cannot hope to sustain its internal and external legitimacy in the modern political society it serves without objectivity. Objectivity itself requires judicial independence, adequate room for critical appraisal as to the correctness or validity of judgments, and a respectable degree of invariance.

The law is not always at its best when it deals explicitly with large philosophical issues. They are always there of course, and in some sense law is always connected to larger societal issues. But lawyers have to keep their feet on the ground because, as Lord Radcliffe once said, 'The law's achievement consists in the accumulation of small particles for general use that cohere into a solid structure.'[11]

[10] BN Cardozo, *The Nature of the Judicial Process* (New Haven, Yale University Press, 1921) 11–13.

[11] Lord Radcliffe, *The Law & its Compass* (London, Faber, 1960) viii. See also S Sedley, 'Law and Plumbing' (2008) 28(4) *Legal Studies* 629: 'The ineluctable thing about any theory of law or justice—including the hermetic notion that law is a self-defining system of logic—is that it keeps bumping into reality'. R Dworkin recognises that lawyers 'decide particular issues at retail, one by one, in a ... limited and circumscribed way' by the 'homespun and reliable

The law cannot do everything. Nor is it perfect. Indeed a proper appreciation of the limits of law is essential to an adequate understanding of the legal enterprise. In the recusal context, the law simply cannot penetrate the inner mind of a judge. But there is no reason why it should not, and indeed every reason why it should, do the obvious and remove distinctive impediments to objectivity, in the manner of that practical reasoning which is essential to the lawyer's craft. In short, we should do what practically can be done to ensure objectivity.

PRACTICAL MEASURES

What then can be done in a relatively straightforward and implementable fashion to address the concerns which have been noted from time to time in this work?

Disclosure

It is now well recognised as an ethical obligation, and as a statutory obligation in the United States federal jurisdiction under 28 USC § 455, that a judge should be sufficiently well informed about his or her affairs and associations that he or she can appropriately make known to counsel and litigants anything which might give rise to concern in relation to a case on which he or she is to sit, so that they can consider their position.

The purpose of such a requirement is obvious. Prophylactic measures are always preferable to *ex post* ones in the conduct of litigation. It seems relatively obvious that if 'proper' disclosure is made, then difficulties in a case may be avoided altogether, or at least substantially lessened. Once the matter has been raised, a judge knows what is concerning the parties and is in a much better position to determine whether he or she should recuse.

Whether by judicial fiat, rules of court, or ethical codes of conduct relating to the judiciary, it seems inescapable that there should be full disclosure by the judge, timeous transmission of that full disclosure to litigants, and advice as to the consequences of not objecting, namely, that the doctrine of waiver may well obtain. It is hard to see why prudent counsel would not obtain written instructions on such a matter much as they do in a decision as to whether or not an accused will give evidence in a criminal trial. The matter is of that order of importance.

This is an issue which can be readily tidied up in one or more of the above ways in a given jurisdiction, and it should be.

methods of close textual analysis and analogy': *Justice in Robes* above n 16. The author rails against an anti-theoretical bias in lawyers and even the academy.

One Rule for Bias?

The issue here is whether the rules relating to actual bias are now redundant, at least with respect to judges. At least in the case of judges, as has been suggested, there is a respectable case for 'one rule'.

A matter of great structural importance is that if this approach is adopted for judges only, and not adopted in public law in general (due to differing contextual considerations), the law will have gone from two relatively well-established tests around the common law world to one rule for judges and one for some other decision makers. This raises difficult questions of policy for public law on which reasonable minds can differ. If the law is to go in different directions on the issue in various jurisdictions, there will of course be a loss of doctrinal cohesion, which some might find regrettable.

Personal Judicial Determination

The fact that, in the vast majority of common law jurisdictions, judges determine their own disqualification motions is quite indefensible in this day and age. The justifications offered for the rule are thin, the arguments against personal judicial determination are overwhelming, and lower level solutions—such as a 'convention' or requirement for at least collegial mention and discussion—are not sufficient.

There is a hopeless tension between the state-fostered guarantee of a neutral and objective arbiter of a case and the state's current process arrangements for disqualification decisions, whereby it is the challenged judge who decides. This disjuncture, and its bearings on a fair trial, are further revealed by the requirements of modern human rights instruments.

There is also a very human dimension to this issue. As has been suggested earlier in this work, counsel make more recusal applications today. At least some judges appear to be very sensitive on this score, and take such applications as a professional slur on their objectivity. The result is an unfortunate double whammy with both bar and bench being dissatisfied. Doing away with personal determination should have the consequence of reducing this unfortunate tension between bench and bar.

Further, personal judge determination can hardly be described as a 'rule' in the conventional legal sense; rather, it is a somewhat murky 'practice'. The lack of a 'formal' basis for the practice makes it difficult for a litigant to challenge it. Fortunately, as has been noted, the existence of modern human rights instruments may provide the 'tipping point'.

Just how alteration of the current practice is to be achieved should not be beyond the wit of contemporary court systems.

At the trial level, a recusal request should first go to the allocated trial judge. But if she declines to recuse, there must be clear review mechanisms within the trial court structure. This would mean the creation of a review mechanism independent of the decision-making ambit of the particular trial judge. This could take various forms. There is the statutory precedent in the United States of requests for reallocation of judges. Another alternative would be a standing review panel within the particular trial court, doubtless chaired by the chief judge, or a senior judge. Provision would inevitably have to be made for urgent situations, as well as some accommodation for objections during the course of the trial. These sort of structural amendments would not be insurmountable when set against many of the complex problems faced by contemporary civil and criminal justice regimes, and to which answers have had to be found.

As to collegiate courts, the problem is surely straightforward. The principle should be that the panel appointed to the case should consider whether the objection is well founded. In what might perhaps be seen as a concession to old practice, it is difficult to see why the impugned judge should not have input and perhaps even sit with his colleagues. But the outcome should be for the panel as a whole. This addresses the 'information' problem, but the really critical point is that if it is thought to be necessary, for example, on a five-judge panel, four judges could vote the impugned judge off. One would have thought this would likely survive the necessary human rights scrutiny.

Little experience of judicial life is required to know that there is a potential for some 'in-house tension' here. But it is difficult to see that it would be of a more debilitating kind than, say, a fraught debate about an important substantive law principle, as sometimes occurs today. At the end of the day, judges must judge, and they understand the importance of living with collegial decisions.

Of course, in intermediate appellate courts, where 'replacement' judges can be found without too much difficulty, the practise of prudence may well kick in at an early stage: there may be a consensus that it really is not wise for a particular judge to sit, and the problem is then taken care of administratively.

The place of final courts of appeal is difficult, particularly those with no institutional capacity for substitutions. One of the really fundamental problems for such a court is that it is rightly conceived of as a unitary 'whole'. It will be comprised of judges of the highest standing who have been appointed to the court, very often for different attributes and outlooks. In part, the legal theory of staffing a final court of appeal is precisely that there should be a variety of viewpoints. It is not a 'representative' court in the political sense, but the various qualities, viewpoints and experiences of the justices are in many ways supposed to support a particular outcome, or even to cancel each other out. The result can of course be a lowest common denominator judgment, or at least one of appalling 'blandness', just as the result might produce three or four differing viewpoints which are very strongly contended for amongst the members of the court, leading to very close four–three or five–four outcomes. But it has to be acknowledged that the argument for a 'complete' court is a strong one at the final court level. Nevertheless, a potential 'substitution' arrangement ought to be of great importance for final courts.

Having suggested that there are workable alternatives open to courts for dealing with the problem of the impugned judge determining the recusal application, it may be thought useful to reduce those alternatives to schematic form. This is set out in Appendix E.

Interlocutory Appeals

It has been suggested that presently there are three avenues open to an unsuccessful applicant at the trial court level, in a recusal proceeding. One is to attempt to fit within the provisions for an interlocutory appeal, if such can be had. The chief difficulty is the argument which may arise in some jurisdictions that there is no 'curial' order to be appealed, or that the particular statute will not allow such an appeal. The second alternative is to resort to the old prerogative writs of mandamus or prohibition, or a modern form of judicial review, if it can be had. A third alternative is, more or less resignedly, to go through the trial and raise the issue as a 'true' ground of appeal, after the event.

If the problem of personal determination by the impugned judge is not displaced, the issue of interlocutory appeals becomes absolutely critical. The least a legal system should do is provide a clean avenue of prompt appeal. It ought to be a relatively straightforward amendment, whether to the rules of court or through other statutory changes, to ensure that there is an effective *de novo* review by way of interlocutory appeal of a recusal decision. Other bad habits could be discouraged at the same time: if the recusal application is not made at the pre-trial stage, the complainant could be required to wait until after trial to appeal, which might go some distance towards discouraging 'sand bagging' by counsel. Again, this is not a matter which poses an insurmountable hurdle for the realignment of court processes.

Mechanisms for the Replacement of Disqualified Judges

As has been indicated, many intermediate appellate courts around the common law world already have internal mechanisms for the replacement of recused judges. If they did not, it is a fair assumption that we would be seeing even more recusal cases than the number which are coming before the courts.

As has further been suggested, the most significant concern here is for final courts of appeal, such as the United States Supreme Court, which do not have replacement mechanisms for recused judges. It is very easy to be critical of a judge who has not stood aside when it is perfectly apparent, as it often will be, what the outcome of a significant constitutional appeal is going to be without her or his presence. Indeed it is grossly unfair, to the point of being unjust, to have a justice put in that position in the first place. And it *is* desirable to have a full bench of the permanent court on an important constitutional case.

Some modern final courts of appeal—perhaps with the benefit of past experience elsewhere—have been able to address this problem. For instance, the recently created Supreme Court of New Zealand has statutory provisions to be able to call on retired members of that court (up to a set age) in the event that one of the other members of the court is disqualified.[12] To avoid any concerns about the Chief Justice having to 'pick' a retired justice, it is understood that there is a rotational policy where generally each retired justice takes their turn to sit, sequentially, as and when required.

It seems that the idea of having a 'replacement' procedure may have at least been raised in relation to the United States Supreme Court. But it has never been seriously advanced. Professor Koh, the Dean of the Yale Law School, has participated in a Supreme Court oral history project. Professor Roberts has noted that in an interview about 'unusual or funny incidents during the mid 1980s on the bench', the following exchange took place between the then retired Justice Blackmun and Professor Koh:[13]

> **Blackmun:** During that term—it might have been during the 86 term Justice Stevens suggested that Congress should be asked to legislate to provide for a retired Justice to sit in place in a vacancy that happened for a particular case. If a Justice was recused or ill or the court was reduced to eight for a period, the legislation would have enabled a retired Justice to fill the vacancy so that there were always nine on a case. The court did not support this. I am not sure I know the reasons why. In any event, Congress did not enact it. ...
>
> **Koh:** What was your own view about that idea?
>
> **Blackmun:** Oh, I was rather on dead centre. I would not have objected to it at all, although it creates a problem. Who shall select the retired Justice? Right at the present time I think there were four of us. Would the Chief Justice make the selection? If so, would those not selected have their noses out of joint? Or would he follow the rule of seniority? Problems create problems, and maybe it is just as well we didn't bother with it.

12 See Supreme Court Act 2003 s 23, concerning acting justices.

13 This discussion is set out in CL Roberts, 'The Fox Guarding the Henhouse?: Recusal and the Procedural Void in the Court of Last Resort' (2004) 57 *Rutgers Law Review* 107.

The essential solution for final courts, if there is to be change, comes down to the panel itself 'taking over' the recusal decision, after due consideration, and itself 'recusing' the impugned justice, and instituting effective replacement mechanisms. The problem with the former approach, particularly on a final court of appeal, is likely to be the formal one that the court of final resort may have no power to 'absent' one of its members. The replacement mechanism approach, if it can be effected, seems both more practicable, and sounder in principle. For it confirms the point that actual or apparent bias is not acceptable, and it does what common sense would seem to suggest: it finds a replacement judge.

19

Judges or Legislators?

If it is accepted that there are compelling arguments for the adoption of some or all of the measures described in the preceding chapter, how are they to be effected?

A contemporary public policy analyst would doubtless proceed immediately to a discussion of whether recusal law is amenable to increased legislative regulation or not. If there is a case for formal regulation, the key questions would concern how that regulation is to be effected, and what form legislation might take. Such an approach would be less than adequate in the area of judicial recusal, and, indeed would pose real dangers for the judiciary.

The first thing we need to be clear on is just what the public policy problem is. After all, there is an existing body of principle which is not, on its face, utterly indefensible and in many respects will continue to be positively supported.

The real difficulty today is that there have been far too many high profile cases which have done quite appalling damage to the virtue of Lady Justitia. The Breyer Committee in the United States quite correctly took the view that the damage wreaked by these causes célèbres cannot be tolerated. But that does not mean that it automatically follows that the whole area needs turning on its head, save in the fundamental area of being a judge in one's own cause.

In the contemporary judicial landscape, we cannot start from Blackstone's proposition that wrongdoing by judges will not be presumed. Yet it does not necessarily follow that we should turn our backs on the considerable value of judicial self-regulation. There must surely be a practical and publicly palatable balance between absolute autonomy for the judges and what Professor Downing has rightly termed 'annihilative accountability'.[1]

If, as a matter of public policy, it is preferable that judges undertake the task of proper self-regulation, the next question is whether they have the means to do so. Recusal jurisprudence as it stands is a body of law which does have some aspects that can conventionally be described as legal

[1] B Downing, 'Action, Accountability, and the Judiciary: United States Federal Judicial Recusal Reform in a New Century' (2002) *Michigan Journal of Political Science* 33, 34.

principles or rules, such as the 'rule' of necessity. There are some statutory impingements, notably in the United States federal jurisdiction. What needs to be borne in mind though is that there is always an extensive body of 'lawyers' law' and 'understandings' in any given common law jurisdiction which has an important existence outside the formal sources of law, such as statutes and reported cases. Indeed, most introductory legal method textbooks are badly remiss in failing to note this phenomenon of the existence of professional 'understandings'. As Professor JH Baker quite properly put it in his Clarendon Lectures:[2]

> [Reports and records of cases] should not blind us to the existence of another body of legal thought and practice, which is equally 'law' in that it influences lawyers and has real consequences, which is vital to understanding both the history and present working of the common law.

Professor Baker was speaking of early English legal history, but his perceptive observation is still true today. Recusal practice is vitally important, yet it is currently perched in something of a no-man's land between statutes and common law. Present 'understandings' have been created and fostered by common law judges themselves down the ages. There is, however, the danger that they may themselves become too 'doctrinaire' or ossified, and require revisiting from time to time. When they do, it is traditionally, and appropriately, the judges who should be the first port of call. In short, lawyers understandings have to be subject to change too. And there is certainly no question about the legal capacity of common law judges to effect such change.

The argument the other way is that a formal regulatory response is required because the judiciary is beyond self-redemption. However, the case for legislative regulation is far from made out. What we are surely looking for in respect of recusal law and practice is the need for judicial independence and autonomy on the one hand, and on the other the need for some mechanism to deal with cases where judges have gone well over the line, and yet will not stand down. However, there still appears to be widespread agreement that critically important constitutional values are supported by an emphasis on judicial autonomy. Hence, we should not be looking at a pure 'balancing' exercise.

It would follow that a very clear case indeed is needed for tilting the scale too far in the direction of external regulation. That is the danger with legislation, which must necessarily try to be complete and cover worst-case scenarios. And if the legislation is too draconian, judges may in any event attempt to read it down, whether appropriately or inappropriately.

[2] JH Baker, *The Law's Two Bodies: Some Evidential Problems in English Legal History* (Oxford, OUP, 2001) vi.

What this really brings one to is the perennial problem in any consideration of power and autonomy: the relative importance of character and institution. In his marvellous Reith Lectures in 1951, Lord Radcliffe argued that we tend to value our institutions too greatly and do not place sufficient weight on the value of character.[3] Given the current debacle over regulation of financial institutions in the Western world, Lord Radcliffe's observations half a century ago seem eerily prophetic. Moreover, 'character' must be of the greatest moment in relation to recusal.[4]

In law, as in life, the margin fades forever and ever as we move.[5] On the issue which is seemingly nearest and dearest to judicial hearts in recusal law and practice—that an impugned judge should decide for himself or herself—senior figures in the law have begun to say quite distinctly that change should be considered. These include Lord Irvine after *Pinochet (No 2)*; Sir Anthony Mason after *Kartinyeri*; and Lord Justice Ward after *El-Farargy*. Some academic commentators have the same concern. Informal practices within some courts are changing. Some American legislatures have acted against the undue strictures of the duty to sit proposition, and there are appropriate judge reallocation statutes. These things all provide encouraging indications that the tide in the affairs of judges on this issue is slowly on the turn, in the direction the law should be taking.

If what is suggested here—that the judiciary is not yet beyond self-redemption—is thought to have respectable weight, then the argument runs that reform had better come from within, rather than being imposed from without. And the judge of character will know that often one gets things done in the real world through compromise, and the adoption of sensible intermediate positions. The preface to the Book of Common Prayer put it rather well when it spoke of that happy mean between the two extremes, of too much stiffness in refusing, and too much easiness in admitting, any variation of things once advisedly established. If that sage advice were heeded in the recusal context, there are things the judiciary could cheerfully cede, such as an overt attachment to judges being judges in their own cause, and in so doing support the much deeper value of judicial independence.

[3] See Lord Radcliffe of Werneth, *The Problem of Power: The Reith Memorial Lectures 1951* (London, Secker and Warburg, 1952).

[4] Lord Radcliffe might well have approved of JN Roxburgh's famous statement that his objective, as Headmaster of Stowe School, was to produce young men who would be 'acceptable at a dance and invaluable in a shipwreck.' See N Annan, *The Headmaster: Roxburgh of Stowe and his Influence in English Education* (New York, Schocken Books, 1966). That line might sound Whigish or antiquated today, but far too many of the judicial recusal cases noted in this work have revealed judges without elementary courtesy whose endeavours have promoted, rather than avoided, the wrecking of a given case, and afforded precious little utility in the subsequent rescue attempts.

[5] With apologies to Tennyson's 'Ulysses'.

Appendix A

The Australasian Protocol

The Council of Chief Justices of Australia, *Guide to Judicial Conduct*, 2nd edn (Victoria, Australasian Institute of Judicial Administration Inc, 2007) 15–16.

3.5 Disqualification procedure—

(a) If a judge considers that disqualification is required, the judge should so decide. Prior consultation with judicial colleagues is permissible and may be helpful in reaching such a decision. The decision should be made at the earliest opportunity.

(b) In cases of uncertainty where the judge is aware of circumstances that may warrant disqualification, the judge should raise the matter at the earliest opportunity with:

(i) The head of the jurisdiction;
(ii) The person in charge of listing;
(iii) The parties or their legal advisers;

not necessarily personally, but using the court's usual methods of communication.

(c) Disqualification is for the judge to decide in the light of any objection, but trivial objections are to be discouraged.

(d) It will generally be appropriate in cases of uncertainty for the judge to hear submissions on behalf of the parties and that should be done in open court.

(e) The judge should be mindful of circumstances that might not be known to the parties but might require the judge not to sit, and of the possibility of the parties raising relevant matters of which the judge may not be aware. It is not appropriate for a judge to be questioned by parties or their advisers.

(f) If the judge decides to sit, the reasons for that decision should be recorded in open court. So should the disclosure of all relevant circumstances.

(g) Consent of the parties is relevant but not compelling in reaching a decision to sit. The judge should avoid putting the parties in a situation in which it might appear that their consent is sought to cure a ground of disqualification. Even where the parties would consent to the judge sitting, if the judge, on balance, considers that disqualification is the proper course, the judge should so act.

(h) Even if the judge considers no reasonable ground of disqualification exists, it is prudent to disclose any matter that might possibly be the subject of complaint, not to obtain consent to the judge sitting, but to ascertain whether, contrary to the judge's own view, there is any objection.

(i) The judge has a duty to try cases in the judge's list, and should recognise that disqualification places a burden on the judge's colleagues or may occasion delay to the parties if another judge is not available.

There may be cases in which other judges are also disqualified or are not available, and necessity may tilt the balance in favour of sitting even though there may be arguable grounds in favour of disqualification.

Appendix B

28 USC § 144

Whenever a party to any proceeding in a district court makes and files a timely and sufficient affidavit that the judge before whom the matter is pending has a personal bias or prejudice either against him or in favor of any adverse party, such judge shall proceed no further therein, but another judge shall be assigned to hear such proceeding.

The affidavit shall state the facts and the reasons for the belief that bias or prejudice exists, and shall be filed not less than ten days before the beginning of the term at which the proceeding is to be heard, or good cause shall be shown for failure to file it within such time. A party may file only one such affidavit in any case. It shall be accompanied by a certificate of counsel of record stating that it is made in good faith.

Appendix C

28 USC § 455

(a) Any justice, judge, or magistrate judge of the United States shall disqualify himself in any proceeding in which his impartiality might reasonably be questioned.

(b) He shall also disqualify himself in the following circumstances:

(1) Where he has a personal bias or prejudice concerning a party, or personal knowledge of disputed evidentiary facts concerning the proceeding;

(2) Where in private practice he served as lawyer in the matter in controversy, or a lawyer with whom he previously practiced law served during such association as a lawyer concerning the matter, or the judge or such lawyer has been a material witness concerning it;

(3) Where he has served in governmental employment and in such capacity participated as counsel, adviser or material witness concerning the proceeding or expressed an opinion concerning the merits of the particular case in controversy;

(4) He knows that he, individually or as a fiduciary, or his spouse or minor child residing in his household, has a financial interest in the subject matter in controversy or in a party to the proceeding, or any other interest that could be substantially affected by the outcome of the proceeding;

(5) He or his spouse, or a person within the third degree of relationship to either of them, or the spouse of such a person:

(i) Is a party to the proceeding, or an officer, director, or trustee of a party;

(ii) Is acting as a lawyer in the proceeding;

(iii) Is known by the judge to have an interest that could be substantially affected by the outcome of the proceeding;

(iv) Is to the judge's knowledge likely to be a material witness in the proceeding.

(c) A judge should inform himself about his personal and fiduciary financial interests, and make a reasonable effort to inform himself about the personal financial interests of his spouse and minor children residing in his household.

(d) For the purposes of this section the following words or phrases shall have the meaning indicated:
   (1) 'proceeding' includes pretrial, trial, appellate review, or other stages of litigation;
   (2) the degree of relationship is calculated according to the civil law system;
   (3) 'fiduciary' includes such relationships as executor, administrator, trustee, and guardian;
   (4) 'financial interest' means ownership of a legal or equitable interest, however small, or a relationship as director, adviser, or other active participant in the affairs of a party, except that:
      (i) Ownership in a mutual or common investment fund that holds securities is not a 'financial interest' in such securities unless the judge participates in the management of the fund;
      (ii) An office in an educational, religious, charitable, fraternal, or civic organization is not a 'financial interest' in securities held by the organization;
      (iii) The proprietary interest of a policyholder in a mutual insurance company, of a depositor in a mutual savings association, or a similar proprietary interest, is a 'financial interest' in the organization only if the outcome of the proceeding could substantially affect the value of the interest;
      (iv) Ownership of government securities is a 'financial interest' in the issuer only if the outcome of the proceeding could substantially affect the value of the securities.

(e) No justice, judge, or magistrate judge shall accept from the parties to the proceeding a waiver of any ground for disqualification enumerated in subsection (b). Where the ground for disqualification arises only under subsection (a), waiver may be accepted provided it is preceded by a full disclosure on the record of the basis for disqualification.

(f) Notwithstanding the preceding provisions of this section, if any justice, judge, magistrate judge, or bankruptcy judge to whom a matter has been assigned would be disqualified, after substantial judicial time has been devoted to the matter, because of the appearance or discovery, after the matter was assigned to him or her, that he or she individually or as a fiduciary, or his or her spouse or minor child residing in his or her household, has a financial interest in a party (other than an interest that could be substantially affected by the outcome), disqualification is not required if the justice, judge, magistrate judge, bankruptcy judge, spouse or minor child, as the case may be, divests himself or herself of the interest that provides the grounds for the disqualification.

Appendix D

Statement of Recusal Policy

114 SUPREME COURT REPORTER 52 (IN THE 'ORDERS' SECTION)

We have spouses, children or other relatives within the degree of relationship covered by 28 USC 455 who are or may become practicing attorneys. In connection with a case four terms ago, the Chief Justice announced his policy (with which we are all in accord) regarding recusal when a covered relative is 'an associate in the law firm representing one of the parties before this Court' but has 'not participated in the case before the Court or at previous stages of the litigation.' [The letter concluded that recusal was not required.] We think it desirable to set forth what our recusal policy will be in additional situations—specifically, when the covered lawyer HAS participated in the case at an earlier stage of the litigation, or when the covered lawyer is a *partner* in a firm appearing before us. Determining and announcing our policy in advance will make it evident that future decisions to recuse or not to recuse are unaffected by irrelevant circumstances of the particular case, and will provide needed guidance to our relatives and the firms to which they belong.

The provision of the recusal statute that deals specifically with a relative's involvement as a lawyer in the case requires recusal only when the covered relative '[I]s acting as a lawyer in the proceeding.' 28 USC 455(b)(5)(ii). It is well established that this provision requires personal participation in the representation, and not just membership in the representing firm, eg, *Potashnick v Port City Constru Co,* 609 F2d 1101, 1113 (CA 5), *cert denied*, 449 US 820 (1980). It is also apparent, from use of the present tense, that current participation as a lawyer, and not merely past involvement in earlier stages of the litigation, is required.

A relative's partnership status, or participation in earlier stages of the litigation, is relevant, therefore, only under one of two less specific provisions of 455, which require recusal when the judge knows that the relative has 'an interest that could be substantially affected by the outcome of the proceeding,' 455 (b)(5)(iii), or when for any reason the judge's 'impartiality might reasonably be questioned,' 455(a). We think that a relative's partnership in the firm appearing before us, or his or her previous work as a lawyer on a case that later comes before us, does not *automatically* trigger these provisions. If that were the intent of the law, the per se 'lawyer-related recusal' requirement of 455(b)(b)(ii) would have expressed it. Per se recusal for a relative's membership in the partnership appearing here, or for a relative's work on the case below, would render the limitation of 455(b)(ii) to *personal* work, and to *present* representation, meaningless.

We do not think it would serve the public interest to go beyond the requirements of the statute, and to recuse ourselves, out of an excess of caution, whenever a relative is a partner in the firm before us or acted as a lawyer at an earlier stage. Even an unnecessary recusal impairs the functioning of the Court. Given the size and number of today's national law firms, and the frequent appearance before us of many of them in a single case, recusal might become a common occurrence, and opportunities would be multiplied for 'strategizing' recusals, that is, selecting law firms with an eye to producing the recusal of particular Justices. In this Court, where the absence of one Justice cannot be made up by another, needless recusal deprives litigants of the nine Justices to which they are entitled, produces the possibility of an even division on the merits of the case, and has a distorting effect upon the certiorari process, requiring the petitioner to obtain (under our current practice) four votes out of eight instead of four out of nine.

Absent some special factor, therefore, we will not recuse ourselves by reason of a relative's participation as a lawyer in earlier stages of the case. One such special factor, perhaps the most common, would be the relative's functioning as lead counsel below, so that the litigation is in effect 'his' or 'her' case and its outcome even at a later stage might reasonably be thought capable of substantially enhancing or damaging his or her professional reputation. We shall recuse ourselves whenever, to our knowledge, a relative has been lead counsel below.

Another special factor, of course, would be the fact that the amount of the relative's compensation could be substantially affected by the outcome here. That would require our recusal even if the relative had not worked on the case, but was merely a partner in the firm that shared the profits. It seems to us that in virtually every case before us with retained counsel there exists a genuine possibility that success or failure will affect the amount of the fee, and hence a genuine possibility that the outcome will have a substantial effect upon each partner's compensation. Since it is impractical to assure ourselves of the absence of such consequences in each individual case, we shall recuse ourselves from all cases in which appearances on behalf of parties are made by firms in which our relatives are partners, unless we have received from the firm written assurance that income from Supreme Court litigation is, on a permanent basis, excluded from our relative's partnership shares.

Appendix E

Who Decides?

(a) A recusal application should always be delivered, in the first instance, to the judge whose recusal is sought.

(b) That judge may recuse, on the merits, or for prudential reasons, after considering such submissions as have been made at that point by counsel, and after such consultation as he/she considers appropriate with colleagues.

(c) In the event that the judge elects not to recuse, and there is still a contest:

  (i) In the case of trial courts that contested application should be determined, under whatever procedures are appropriate in the particular trial court, either (a) before another trial judge (appointed for that purpose by the head of court), or (b) a judge from a standing judicial recusal committee in the particular court.

  (ii) In the case of intermediate appellate courts, the contested application should be heard by the panel appointed to hear the appeal, with the impugned judge as a member of the panel.

  (iii) In the case of final appellate courts, the contested application should be heard by the appointed panel of judges, or the court as a whole, as appropriate. In the case of a court without the ability to 'substitute' a judge, consideration should be given to obtaining, if necessary by legislative measures, the ability to 'substitute' a judge, preferably by the secondment of a retired judge of the court. Such substitute judges would sit, age and health permitting, in rotational order of retirement seniority.

Appendix F

Recent Constitutional Issues

Perhaps the ultimate question for a legal system is how well it performs at times of constitutional crisis. In such a context, recusal issues can become very important because who decides whether a given action is constitutional can have distinct implications for the lawful existence of a given administration, or for that matter even the lawfulness of a court. There are some important cases relating to these kinds of issues presently being addressed in the common law world. But because the cases have not yet been finally determined, or in some cases because they are part of a larger context, these "situations" are noted here, in case interested observers should wish to follow the ultimate resolution of them.

(a) The United States of America: Elected Judges

This text has voiced some concern at the difficulties created, in a recusal context, by the existence of elected judges. See also PD Carrington and RC Cramton, "Judicial Independence in Excess: Reviving the Judicial Duty of the Supreme Court" (2009) 94 *Cornell Law Review* 587, 611 ("... the resemblance of a judicial campaign contribution to a bribe is a special horror").

In *Caperton v Massey Coal Company* (No. 08-22), on 3 March 2009, the United States Supreme Court heard oral argument on, and has reserved for consideration, issues of very distinct importance in that jurisdiction on this issue.

In *Caperton* a coal company executive spent more than $US3 million to help elect a State Supreme Court Justice, Judge Benjamin. Later that Judge was part of a 3-2 majority that overturned a verdict (which now totals $US82.7 million with interest) against the coal company. In brief terms, the losing party, Harman Mining Corp, and its president, Mr Hugh Caperton, have sought to have the United States Supreme Court rule that Judge Benjamin's refusal to step aside from the case violated their constitutional right to due process.

The argument is that several factors combined to create an "overwhelming probability" that Judge Benjamin would not be impartial, including the size of the campaign support and the fact that it represented more than half the money spent on his behalf. In addition, Judge Benjamin made the decision to remain on the case by himself, not subject to review by his fellow Justices. Further, Judge Benjamin has ruled against Massey at least four times, including in a unanimous refusal to hear the company's appeal of a $US260 million judgment won in another contract dispute.

Caperton will inevitably become a leading United States decision on the law relating to recusal of elected judges in that jurisdiction, and perhaps more broadly.

(b) Fiji: the Military Coup

After the 2006 military coup led by Commodore Bainimarama in Fiji, inevitably there were attempts made to advance litigation to the High Court and the Fiji Court of Appeal to establish that the overthrow of the then Fijian Government was unlawful. There were considerable difficulties in advancing those cases to hearing, and over who would hear them, if they did come to a hearing.

The particulars of these difficulties are not presently easy to obtain. But concern has been expressed by the Governments (IBA) of both New Zealand and Australia and the International Bar Association over the erosion of the rule of law in Fiji. On 3 March 2009, the IBA's Human Rights Institute (IBAHRI) released a report entitled *Dire Straits: A Report on the Rule of Law in Fiji* (available on the IBA web site <www.ibanet.org>).

One of the concerns expressed in this valuable 113-page report is as to "the conduct of judges who have been appointed or promoted following the December 2006 coup and who have heard cases that relate to the constitutionality of their own appointment. This breaches the law of recusal, which prohibits judges from presiding over a matter in which he or she holds an interest".

(c) South Africa

The run up to the recent election of Mr Jacob Zuma as President of South Africa produced its own share of litigation which has raised recusal issues in litigation in that jurisdiction. It is not possible, from a distance, and without much closer consideration, to follow all the ins and outs of those issues. The difficulties are apparent from, for instance, *National Director of Public Prosecutions v Zuma* (12 January 2009, Supreme Court of Appeal, Republic of South Africa). That Final Court of Appeal noted that the litigation between the NDPP and Mr Zuma "has a long and troubled history and the law reports are replete with judgments dealing with the matter".

The litigation appears, at least in the trial courts, to have spilled over into the political arena. This necessitated a firm censure from the Final Court of Appeal: "In the course of [his judgment the Judge] changed the rules of the game, took his eyes off the ball and red carded not only players but also spectators". The Final Court said that it would be "naïve to pretend that we are oblivious to the fact that [the judgment] has had far reaching political consequences and that there may be an attempt to employ [the] judgment to secure political points". The Final Court of Appeal has plainly had a difficult burden to ensure that matters are dealt with under the rule of law in that jurisdiction, and that courts are not unwisely dragged in the direction of the political arena, on recusal as well as other issues.

(d) A Brief Conclusion

A collective concern which arises in this sort of area must be as to the eternal vigilance which is required of courts of law in legal systems which supposedly enjoy the benefit of the rule of law to enforce that very requirement and to keep abuses of the rule of law itself for political purposes firmly at bay. Secondly, these sorts of crises surely support the argument, advanced throughout this work, that the objectivity of judges deciding such important issues is of the utmost importance to the very rule of law itself, and that judges should not be deciding their own recusal motions.

Bibliography

A BOOKS

HJ Abraham, *The Judicial Process: An Introductory Analysis of the Courts of the United States, England, and France*, 7th edn (Oxford, OUP, 1998)

GW Adams, *Mediating Justice: Legal Dispute Negotiations* (Ontario, CCH Canadian Ltd, 2003)

AG Amsterdam and J Bruner, *Minding the Law* (Cambridge, Mass, Harvard University Press, 2000)

N Annan, *The Headmaster: Roxburgh of Stowe and his Influence in English Education* (New York, Schocken Books, 1966)

JB Atlay, *The Victorian Chancellors: Volume 1* (London, Smith Elder, 1906)

JH Baker, *The Law's Two Bodies: Some Evidential Problems in English Legal History* (Oxford, OUP, 2001)

TH Bingham, 'Judicial Ethics' in *The Business of Judging: Selected Essays and Speeches* (Oxford, OUP, 2000)

O Black, *Conceptual Foundations of Antitrust* (New York, CUP, 2005)

W Blackstone, *Commentaries on the Laws of England (1768)* (Buffalo, William S. Hein & Co, 1992)

H de Bracton, Twiss (ed), *De Legibus et Consuetudinibus Angliae: Volume 6* (London, Longman & Co, 1883)

H de Bracton, Woodbine (ed), *Bracton on the Laws and Customs of England: Volume 3* (Massachusetts, Belknap Press of Harvard University Press, 1977)

J Brinkley and S Lohr, *US v Microsoft: The Inside Story of the Landmark Case* (Ohio, McGraw Hill, 2000)

E Burke, 'Thoughts on the Cause of the Present Discontents' in EJ Payne (ed), *Select Works* (New Jersey, Lawbook Exchange, 2005)

A Butler and P Butler, *The New Zealand Bill of Rights Act: A Commentary* (Wellington, LexisNexis, 2005)

E Campbell and HP Lee, *The Australian Judiciary* (Cambridge, CUP, 2001)

BN Cardozo, *The Nature of the Judicial Process* (New Haven, Yale University Press, 1921)

P Catley and L Claydon, 'Pinochet, Bias and the European Convention on Human Rights' in D Woodhouse (ed), *The Pinochet Case: A Legal and Constitutional Analysis* (Oxford, Hart Publishing, 2000)

H Charlesworth, 'The Australian Reluctance About Rights' in P Alston (ed), *Towards an Australian Bill of Rights* (Canberra, ANU Centre for International and Public Law, 1994)

TM Cooper (ed), *Regiam Majestatem and Quoniam Attachiamenta* (Edinburgh, Stair Society, 1947)

P Craig, *Administrative Law*, 6th edn (Sweet and Maxwell, United Kingdom, 2008)

P Devlin, *The Judge* (Oxford, OUP, 1981)
G Drewry, L Blom-Cooper and C Blake, *The Court of Appeal* (Oxford, Hart Publishing, 2007)
R Dworkin, *Justice in Robes* (Cambridge, Belknap Press, 2006)
RE Flamm, *Judicial Disqualification: Recusal and Disqualification of Judges*, 2nd edn (California, Banks and Jordan Law Publishing Company, 2007)
JP Frank, *Courts on Trial: Myth and Reality in American Justice* (Princeton, Princeton University Press, 1949)
T Freyer, 'The Jackson-Black Feud' in KL Hall (ed), *The Oxford Companion to the Supreme Court of the United States*, 2nd edn (New York, OUP, 2005)
——, *Hugo L Black and the Dilemma of American Liberalism*, 2nd edn (London, Prentice Hall, 2008)
R Glanvill, *De legibus et Consuetudinibus Regni Angliae*, Bk II, Chap 11, in R Pound and TFT Plucknett (eds), *Readings on the History and System of the Common Law*, 3rd edn (Rochester, Lawyers Co-Operative Publishing Company, 1927)
AM Gleeson, *The Rule of Law and the Constitution* (Sydney, ABC Books, 2000)
E Grant, '*Pinochet* 2: The Questions of Jurisdiction and Bias' in D Woodhouse (ed), *The Pinochet Case: A Legal and Constitutional Analysis* (Oxford, Hart Publishing, 2000)
M Groves, 'The Rule Against Bias' in M Groves and HP Lee (eds), *Australian Administrative Law: Fundamentals, Principles and Doctrines* (Cambridge, CUP, 2007)
Lord Hailsham, *The Door Wherein I Went* (London, Collins, 1975)
HM Hart and AM Sacks, *The Legal Process: Basic Problems in the Making and Application of Law* (Westbury, Foundation Press, 1994)
CP Harvey, *The Advocates Devil* (London, Stevens, 1958)
AP Herbert, *Misleading Cases in the Common Law* (London, Methuen, 1989)
G Huscroft, 'The Right to Justice' in P Rishworth, G Huscroft, S Optican and R Mahoney, *The New Zealand Bill of Rights* (Melbourne, OUP, 2003)
F James, GC Hazard Jnr and J Leubsdorf, *Civil Procedure*, 5th edn (Minnesota, West Publishing Company, 2001)
M Kirby, 'Implications of the Internationalisation of Human Rights Law' in P Alston (ed), *Towards an Australian Bill of Rights* (Canberra, ANU Centre for Public and International Law, 1994)
AT Kronman, 'Practical Wisdom and Professional Character' in J Coleman and EF Paul (eds), *Philosophy and Law* (London, Blackwell, 1987)
——, *The Lost Lawyer: Falling Ideals of the Legal Profession* (Harvard, Harvard University Press, 1993)
S Landsman, *Crimes of the Holocaust: The Law Confronts Hard Cases* (Pennsylvania, University of Pennsylvania Press, 2005)
D Langum, *William M Kunstler: The Most Hated Lawyer in America* (New York, New York University Press, 1999)
Learned Hand, *The Spirit of Liberty: Papers and Addresses of Learned Hand*, 2nd edn (New York, Alfred A Knopf, 1953)
B Leiter, 'Law and Objectivity' in J Coleman and S Shapiro (eds), *The Oxford Handbook of Jurisprudence and Philosophy of Law* (Oxford, OUP, 2002)

JP MacKenzie, *The Appearance of Justice* (New York, Scribner, 1974)
P Mahon, *Dear Sam …* (Auckland, William Collins Publishers, 1985)
FW Maitland, *Roman Canon Law in the Church of England: Six Essays* (London, Methuen & Co, 1898)
SE Margolis and S Liebowitz, *Winners, Losers & Microsoft: Competition and Antitrust in High Technology* (California, Independent Institute, 1999)
TB Marvell, *Appellate Courts and Lawyers: Information Gathering in the Adversary System* (Westport, Greenwood Press, 1978)
SFC Milsom, *Historical Foundations of the Common Law*, 2nd edn (London, Butterworths, 1981)
DJ Mullan, *Administrative Law: Cases, Text, and Materials*, 5th edn (Toronto, Emond Montgomery, 2003)
SS Nagel, *The Legal Process from a Behavioural Perspective* (Illinois, Dorsey Press, 1969)
JT Noonan Jr and KI Winston (eds), *The Responsible Judge: Readings in Judicial Ethics* (Praeger, Westport, 1993)
S Optican and P Rishworth, 'Minimum Standards of Criminal Procedure for Trial, Sentencing, and Appeals' in P Rishworth, G Huscroft, S Optican and R Mahoney (eds), *The New Zealand Bill of Rights* (Melbourne, OUP, 2003)
D Pannick, *I Have to Move my Car: Tales of Unpersuasive Advocates and Injudicious Judges* (Oxford, Hart Publishing, 2008)
F Pollock, *A First Book of Jurisprudence for Students of the Common Law* (London, Macmillan, 1896)
RA Posner, *Breaking the Deadlock: The 2000 Election, the Constitution, and the Courts* (Princeton, Princeton University Press, 2001)
GJ Postema, 'Objectivity Fit For Law' in B Leiter (ed), *Objectivity in Law and Morals* (Cambridge, CUP, 2001)
Lord Radcliffe of Werneth, *The Problem of Power: The Reith Memorial Lectures 1951* (London, Secker and Warburg, 1952)
Lord Radcliffe, *The Law & its Compass* (London, Faber, 1960)
D Robertson, 'The House of Lords as a Political and Constitutional Court: Lessons from the Pinochet Case' in D Woodhouse (ed), *The Pinochet Case: A Legal and Constitutional Analysis* (Oxford, Hart Publishing, 2000)
S Sherry, 'Judges of Character' in C Farrelly and LB Solum (eds), *Virtue Jurisprudence* (Palgrave Macmillan, Basingstoke, 2008)
C Sunstein, *Why Societies Need Dissent* (Cambridge, Mass, Harvard University Press, 2003)
NN Taleb, *The Black Swan* (London, Penguin Books, 2007)
J Thibaut and L Walker, *Procedural Justice* (Hillsdale, Lawrence Erlbaum Associates, 1975)
EW Thomas, *The Judicial Process: Realism, Pragmatism, Practical Reasoning and Principles* (Cambridge, CUP, 2005)
JB Thomas, *Judicial Ethics in Australia* (Sydney, Law Book Co, 1988)
SE Thorne (ed), *A Discourse Upon The Exposicion & Understandings of Statutes with Sir Thomas Egerton's Advantages* (San Marino, Huntington Library, 1942)
W Twining and D Miers, *How to Do Things with Rules*, 4th edn (Cambridge, CUP, 1999)

JH Wigmore, *Evidence in Trials at Common Law: Volume II*, 3rd edn (Boston, Little, Brown and Company, 1940)

D Woodhouse (ed), *The Pinochet Case: A Legal and Constitutional Analysis* (Oxford, Hart Publishing, 2000)

H Woolf, J Jowell and A Le Sueur, *De Smith's Judicial Review*, 6th edn (London, Sweet & Maxwell, 2007)

Lord Woolf, *The Pursuit of Justice* (Oxford, OUP, 2008)

AH Young, 'Feminism, Pluralism and Administrative Law' in M Taggart (ed), *The Province of Administrative Law* (Oxford, Hart Publishing, 1997)

IM Young, 'Impartiality and the Civic Public: Some Implications of Feminist Critiques of Moral and Political Theory' in S Benhabib and D Cornell (eds), *Feminism as Critique* (Cambridge, The Polity Press, 1987)

H Young, 'The compromising of Lord Hoffman' in *Supping With The Devils: Political Writing from Thatcher to Blair* (London, Atlantic Books, 2003)

J Zekoll, 'Comparative Civil Procedure' in M Reimann and R Zimmermann (eds), *The Oxford Handbook of Comparative Law* (Oxford, OUP, 2006)

A Zuckerman, *Zuckerman on Civil Procedure: Principles of Practice*, 2nd edn (London, Sweet & Maxwell, 2006)

B ARTICLES

LW Abramson, 'Appearance of Impropriety: Deciding when a Judge's Impartiality 'Might Reasonably be Questioned'' (2000) 14 *Georgetown Journal of Legal Ethics* 55

N Anderson, 'The Appearance of Justice' (2004) 12 *Waikato Law Review* 1

S Atrill, 'Who is the 'Fair-minded and informed Observer'? Bias after *Magill*' (2003) 62 *Cambridge Law Journal* 279

MR Banaji and AG Greenwald, 'Implicit Gender Stereotyping in Judgment Frames' (1995) 68 *Journal of Personality and Social Psychology* 181

S Banner, 'Disqualifiying Elected Judges from Cases Involving Campaign Contributors' (1988) 40 *Stanford Law Review* 449

JN Barr and TE Willging, 'Decentralised Self Regulation, Accountability and Judicial Independence Under the Federal Judicial Conduct and Disability Act of 1980' (1993) 142 *University of Pennsylvania Law Review* 35

DL Bassett, 'Judicial Disqualification in the Federal Appellate Courts' (2002) 87 *Iowa Law Review* 1213

——, 'Recusal and the Supreme Court' (2005) 56 *Hastings Law Journal* 657

P Bryden, 'Legal Principles Concerning the Disqualification of Judges' (2003) 82 *Canadian Bar Review* 555

P Butler, 'The Assignment of Cases to Judges' (2003) 1 *New Zealand Journal of Public and International Law* 83

PA Cain, 'Good and Bad Bias: A Comment on Feminist Theory and Judging' (1988) 61 *Southern California Law Review* 1945

E Campbell, 'Waiver of judicial disqualification for bias or apprehended bias—a constitutional issue' (1999) 2 *Constitutional Law and Policy Review* 41

EM Campbell, 'Review of Decisions on a Judge's Qualification to Sit' (1999) 15 *Queensland University of Technology Law Journal* 1

R Carnwath, 'Tribunal Justice—a New Start' (2009) *Public Law* 48

RF Devlin, 'We Can't Go On Together With Suspicious Minds; Judicial Bias and Racialized Perspective in R v RDS' (1995) 18 *Dalhousie Law Journal* 408

B Downing, 'Action, Accountability and the Judiciary: United States Federal Judicial Recusal Reform in a New Century' (2002) *Michigan Journal of Political Science* 33

RE Emery, SG Matthews and KM Kitzmann, 'Child Custody Mediation and Litigation: Parents Satisfaction and Functioning One Year After Settlement' (1994) 62 *Journal of Consulting and Clinical Psychology* 124

WN Eskridge Jnr and PP Frickey, 'The Making of *The Legal Process*' (1994) 107 *Harvard Law Review* 2031

OM Fiss, 'The Forms of Justice' (1979) 93 *Harvard Law Review* 1

SP Flaherty, '*Liteky v United States*: The Entrenchment of an Extrajudicial Source Factor in the Recusal of Federal Judges under 28 USC § 455(a)' (1995) 15 *North Illinois University Law Review* 411

L Flannery, 'Judges in the dock' (3 August 2007) *New Law Journal* 1097

LA Foertsch, 'Scalia's Duck Hunt Leads to Ruffled Feathers: How the US Supreme Court and other Federal Judiciaries Should Change Their Recusal Approach' (2006–2007) 43 *Houston Law Review* 457

JP Frank, 'Disqualification of Judges' (1947) 56 *Yale Law Journal* 605

——, 'Disqualification of Judges: In Support of the Bayh Bill' (1970) 35 *Law and Contemporary Problems* 43

I Freckelton, 'Querulent Paranoia and the Vexatious Complainant' (1988) 11 *International Journal of Law and Psychiatry* 127

MH Freedman, 'Duck-Blind Justice: Justice Scalia's Memorandum in the *Cheney* Case' (2004–2005) 18 *Georgetown Journal of Legal Ethics* 229

A Frost, 'Keeping up Appearances: A Process-Oriented Approach to Judicial Recusal' (2005) 53 *University of Kansas Law Review* 531

TJ Goodson, 'Duck, Duck, Goose: Hunting for Better Recusal Practices in the United States Supreme Court in light of *Cheney v United States District Court*' (2005–2006) 84 *North Carolina Law Review* 181

J Goudkamp, 'The Rule Against Bias and the Doctrine of Waiver' (2007) 26 *Civil Justice Quarterly* 310

JM Greacen, 'Social Science Research on 'Procedural Justice': What Are the Implications for Judges and Courts' (2008) 47 *Judges Journal* 4

AG Greenwald and MR Banaji, 'Implicit Social Cognition: Attitudes, Self Esteem, and Stereotypes' (1995) 102 *Psychological Review* 4

C Guthrie, JJ Rachlinski and AJ Wistrich, 'Inside the Judicial Mind' (2001) 86 *Cornell Law Review* 777

G Hammond, 'The New Miscarriages of Justice' (2006) 14 *Waikato Law Review* 1

MI Harrison, 'The 2007 ABA Model Code of Judicial Conduct: Blueprint for a Generation of Judges' (2007) 28 *Justice System Journal* 257

P Havers and O Thomas, 'Bias Post-*Pinochet* and Under the ECHR' [1999] 4 *Judicial Review* 111

AD Hellman, 'The Regulation of Judicial Ethics in the Federal System: A Peek Behind Closed Doors' (2007) 69 *University of Pittsburgh Law Review* 189

AD Hellman, 'Judges Judging Judges: The Federal Judicial Misconduct Statutes and the Breyer Committee Report' (2007) 28 *Justice System Journal* 426

——, 'When Judges are Accused: An Initial Look at the New Federal Judicial Misconduct Rules' (2008) 22 *Notre Dame Journal of Law, Ethics and Public Policy* 325

MS Horwitz, 'Judges and the Rule of Necessity: *Ignacio* and the Ninth Circuit's Judges' (2007) 28 *Justice System Journal* 241

SA Ifill, 'Do Appearances Matter: Judicial Impartiality and the Supreme Court in *Bush v Gore*' (2002) 61 *Maryland Law Review* 606

S Kenny, 'Maintaining Public Confidence in the Judiciary: A Precarious Equilibrium' (1999) 25 *Monash University Law Review* 209

M Kirby, 'Acting judges: a non-theoretical danger' (1998) 8 *Journal of Judicial Administration* 69

AT Kronman, 'Alexander Bickel's Philosophy of Prudence' (1985) 94 *Yale Law Journal* 1567

WR Lederman, 'The Independence of the Judiciary' (1956) 34 *Canadian Bar Review* 769

G Lester and S Smith, 'Inventor, Entrepeneur, Rascal, Crank or Querulent?: Australia's Vexatious Litigant Sanction 75 Years On' (2006) 13(1) *Psychiatry, Psychology and Law* 1

J Leubsdorf, 'Theories of Judging and Judge Disqualification' (1987) 62 *New York University Law Review* 237

PB Lewis, 'Systemic Due Process: Procedural Concepts and the Problem of Recusal' (1990) 38 *University of Kansas Law Review* 381

RJ Litteneker, 'Disqualification of Federal Judges for Bias or Prejudice' (1978–1979) 46 *University of Chicago Law Review* 236

IFH Lopez, 'Institutional Racism: Judicial Conduct and a New Theory of Racial Discrimination' (2000) 109 *Yale Law Journal* 1717

K Malleson, 'Judicial Bias and Disqualification after *Pinochet (No 2)*' (2000) 63 *Modern Law Review* 119

A Mason, 'Judicial Disqualification for Bias or Appehended Bias and the Problem of Appellate Review' (1998) *Constitutional Law and Policy Review* 21

K Mason, 'Unconscious Judicial Prejudice' (2001) 75 *Australian Law Journal* 676

T Mauro, 'Furor over Scalia-Cheney Trip Casts Light on Murky World of Recusals' (2004) 175 *New Jersey Law Journal* 732

R Megarry, 'The Judge' (1983) 13 *Manitoba Law Journal* 189

KH Nadelman, 'Disqualification of Constitutional Court Judges for Alleged Bias' (1968) 52 *Judicature* 27

RK Neumann Jr, 'Conflicts of Interest in *Bush v Gore*: Did Some Justices Vote Illegally?' (2002–2003) 16 *Georgetown Journal of Legal Ethics* 375

R Noble and D Schiff, 'The Right to Appeal and Workable Systems of Justice' (2002) 65 *Modern Law Review* 656

AA Olowofoyeku, 'The *Nemo Judex* Rule: The Case Against Automatic Disqualification' (2000) *Public Law* 456

LB Orfield, 'Recusation of Federal Judges' (1967) 17 *Buffalo Law Review* 799

G Pesce, 'Disqualification for Judges—The 'Reasonable Man' Test Renamed' (1996) 70 *Australian Law Journal* 484

TFT Plucknett, 'Bonham's case and Judicial Review' (1926) 40 *Harvard Law Review* 30

GL Priest, 'Reanalysing *Bush v Gore*: Democratic Accountability and Judicial Overreaching' (2001) 72 *University of Colorado Law Review* 953

DG Pruitt, RS Pearce, NB McGillicuddy, GL Welton and LM Castrianno, 'Long-Term Success in Mediation' (1993) 17 *Law and Human Behaviour* 313

H Putnam, 'Recusation' (1923) 9 *Cornell Law Quarterly* 1

B Rayment, 'Bias: Recent Developments' [2001] 6 *Judicial Review* 93

MH Redish and L Marshall, 'Adjudicatory Independence and the Values of Procedural Due Process' (1986) 95 *Yale Law Journal* 455

J Resnik, 'Failing Faith: Adjudicatory Procedure in Decline' (1986) 53 *University of Chicago Law Review* 494

——, 'On the Bias: Feminist Reconsiderations of the Aspirations for Our Judges' (1988) 61 *Southern California Law Review* 1877

CL Roberts, 'The Fox Guarding the Henhouse?: Recusal and the Procedural Void in the Court of Last Resort' (2004) 57 *Rutgers Law Review* 107

P Seabright, 'Objectivity, Disagreement, and Projectability' (1988) 31 *Inquiry* 25

S Sedley, 'Law and plumbing' (2008) 28(4) *Legal Studies* 629

FA Sharman, 'Feudal Copyholder and Industrial Shareholder: the *Dimes* Case' (1989) 10 *Journal of Legal History* 71

S Smith, 'Inventor, Entrepreneur, Rascal, Crank or Querulent?: Australia's Vexatious Litigant Sanction 75 Years On' (2006) 13(1) *Psychiatry, Psychology and Law* 1

F Strachan, 'Keeping Up Appearances: Apprehended Bias in *Antoun v The Queen*' (2007) 29 *Sydney Law Review* 175

SC Styles, 'Judicial Impartiality: Involvement, Opinion and the Judicial Oath' (2009) 13(2) *Edinburgh Law Review* 312

M Taggart, 'Acting Judges' and the Supreme Court of New Zealand' (2008) 14 *Canterbury Law Review* 217

O Thomas, 'Bias Post-*Pinochet* and Under the ECHR' [1999] 4 *Judicial Review* 111

SE Thorne, 'Dr Bonham's case' (1938) 54 *Law Quarterly Review* 543

PW Tone, 'The Substitution of Judges in Illinois Criminal Cases' (1978) *Illinois Law Forum* 519

B Toy-Cronin, 'Waiver of the Rule Against Bias' (2000–2003) *Auckland University Law Review* 850

RRS Tracey, 'Disqualified Adjudicators: The Doctrine of Necessity in Public Law' [1982] *Public Law* 628

T Tyler, 'What do they Expect/New Findings Confirm the Precepts of Procedural Fairness' (2006) *California Courts Review* 22

J Varuhas, 'Acting Judges' (2006) *New Zealand Law Journal* 172

D Williams, 'Bias, the Judges and the Separation of Powers' [2000] *Public Law* 45

C REPORTS

J Bowman, *Report to the Lord Chancellor by the Review of the Court of Appeal (Civil Division)*, Lord Chancellor's Division, 6 November 1997

K Burke and S Leben, 'Procedural Fairness: A Key Ingredient in Public Satisfaction' American Judges Association White Paper, 26 September 2007 <http://aja.ncsc.dni.us/htdocs/AJAWhitePaper9-26-07.pdf> accessed 20 April 2009

Canadian Judicial Council, *Ethical Principles for Judges* (Canadian Judicial Council, Ontario, 1998)

The Council of Chief Justices of Australia, *Guide to Judicial Conduct*, 2nd edn (Victoria, Australasian Institute of Judicial Administration Inc, 2007)

Federal Judicial Center, *Recusal: Analysis of Case Law Under 28 USC 455 & 144* (Federal Judicial Center, 2002)

D Goldberg, *The New Politics of Judicial Elections 2004* <http://www.brennancenter.org/content/resource/the_new_politics_of_judicial_elections_2004/> accessed 18 April 2009

Judicial Conduct and Disability Act Study Committee, *Implementation of the Judicial Conduct and Disability Act of 1980: A Report to the Chief Justice* (2006) 239 FRD 116

Judicial Conference of the United States, *Rules for Judicial-Conduct and Judicial-Disability Proceedings* (Adopted March 11 2008)

Nova Scotia Royal Commission, *Royal Commission on the Donald Marshall Jr Prosecution* (Halifax, The Commission, 1989)

MA Perry, *Disqualification of Judges: Practice and Procedure—Discussion Paper* (Victoria, Australian Institute of Judicial Administration Inc, 2001)

J Sample, D Pozen and M Young, *Fair Courts: Setting Recusal Standards* (New York, Brennan Center for Justice, 2008)

Lord Woolf MR, *Access to Justice: Final Report to the Lord Chancellor on the Civil Justice System in England and Wales* (1996)

D MISCELLANEOUS

R Blumenthal, 'DeLay Case Turns Spotlight on Texas Judicial System' *New York Times* (New York 8 November 2005)

A Broache and D McCullagh, "Former Judge Defends His Bid to Break Up Microsoft", 21 June 2005 <http://news.cnet.com> accessed 20 April 2009

S Cravens, 'Impartiality: Balancing Personal and Professional Integrity in Judicial Decisionmaking' <http://works.bepress.com/cgi/viewcontent.cgi?article=1001&context=sarah_cravens> accessed 18 April 2009

MC Dorf, 'Justice Scalia's Persuasive But Elitist Response to the Duck Hunting Controversy', *FindLaw's Writ*, 24 March 2004 <http://writ.news.findlaw.com/dorf/20040324.html> accessed 20 April 2009

F Gibb, 'The £60 million makeover: new building, new law lords, new postcode' *The Times* (London 20 November 2008)

——, 'Tribunal service reform to create 2,700 new judges' *The Times* (London 3 November 2008)

Gleeson CJ, 'Some Legal Scenery', Speech to the Judicial Conference of Australia, Sydney, 5 October 2007

EN Griswold and E Gellhorn, '200 cases in which justices recused themselves' *The Washington Post* (Washington DC 18 October 1988)

N Hager, 'Appeal Court judge faces a question of judgment' *Sunday Star-Times* (Auckland 24 August 2008)

J Hellmer, 'Querulanz' <http://www.economy-point.org/q/querulanz.html> accessed 15 April 2009

Lord Irvine, *The Guardian* (London 29 December 1998)

A Lewis, 'Abroad at Home; Question of Judgment' *New York Times* (New York 27 September 1987)

Lord Mackay, *The Times* (London 3 December 1987)

Baroness Prashar, 'Equality in Justice Day', Speech at the Royal Courts of Justice, London, 24 October 2008

J Rowley, 'Anti-trust judge Continues to Blast Microsoft' *The Seattle Times* (Seattle 15 March 2001)

JL Salmon, 'Scalia Defends Public Expression of Faith; Recent Rulings Have Gone Too Far, Justice says during Tribute to Va gathering' *The Washington Post* (Washington 13 January 2003)

Impartiality' in *The Stanford Encyclopaedia of Philosophy* 25 March 2002, <http://plato.stanford.edu/entries/impartiality> accessed 20 April 2009

Index

www.ingramcontent.com/pod-product-compliance
Lightning Source LLC
LaVergne TN
LVHW020413220926
848484LV00017B/2559/J